134° 48′ East. 12° 2′ North.
July 30, 1945, 0002 hours.

The captain of Japanese submarine
I-58 has fired a spread
of six torpedoes. Two hits will
be enough to sink the
U.S.S. Indianapolis within the
next twelve minutes.

Painting by Chris Mayger

DEATH OF THE
U.S.S. *INDIANAPOLIS*

How did it happen? What went wrong? What did the men experience during those sun-scorched days and desperate nights, following the sinking of the heavy cruiser *Indianapolis*? How did the Navy explain away this colossal blunder?

Here, now, is the tense minute-by-minute story of this incredible affair, the terrible loss of life, the laxity of the Navy, and the travesty of a trial which followed. Extracting in full measure the human drama on ship and adrift in the sea, *Abandon Ship!* stands as a heroic memorial to the men of the *Indianapolis*.

THE BANTAM WAR BOOK SERIES

This is a series of books about a world on fire.

These carefully chosen volumes cover the full dramatic sweep of World War II. Many are eyewitness accounts by the men who fought in this global conflict in which the future of the civilized world hung in balance. Fighter pilots, tank commanders and infantry commanders, among others, recount exploits of individual courage in the midst of the large-scale terrors of war. They present portraits of brave men and true stories of gallantry and cowardice in action, moving sagas of survival and tragedies of untimely death. Some of the stories are told from the enemy viewpoint to give the reader an immediate sense of the incredible life and death struggle of both sides of the battle.

Through these books we begin to discover what it was like to be there, a participant in an epic war for freedom.

Each of the books in the Bantam War Book series contains a dramatic color painting and illustrations specially commissioned for each title to give the reader a deeper understanding of the roles played by the men and machines of World War II.

ABANDON SHIP!

Richard F. Newcomb

ABANDON SHIP!

*A Bantam Book / published by arrangement with
Indiana University Press*

PRINTING HISTORY
Originally published by Holt, Rinehart & Winston
Indiana University Press edition published April 1976
2 printings through August 1977
Bantam edition / February 1980

Drawings by Greg Beecham and Robert Blanchard.

Map by Benjamin F. Klaessig.

*To those who lost loved ones
in the Indianapolis disaster,
may understanding bring peace.*

PREFACE TO THE NEW EDITION

Incredible as it seems to me, it is now twenty years since I began investigating the real story of the U.S.S. *Indianapolis* and what had happened to her in World War II. I was serving in the Navy in 1945, and, quite by chance, saw the *Indianapolis* sail from San Francisco on what turned out to be her last voyage. As the war ended, a few details of her tragic end came out; not the whole story, by far, but enough to whet my interest.

After the war, as life settled back, I found time to begin looking for the answer to the question: "What really happened to the U.S.S. *Indianapolis?*" The farther I went in my research, the clearer it became; I had come upon one of the great human dramas of our time. It was essentially a story with two parts: a story of human fallibility and of human reactions to that, and a story of a group of men—just ordinary Americans, of many ages and stations in life—and how they met the classic crisis of men against the sea.

As a writer, and as a human being, I was excited by the story. I still am. My book was first published in 1958 and has been in print somewhere ever since, in a variety of languages; it is still being brought out in translations for countries that seemingly could have little interest in such an "American" story.

The fact is, we seem to have here the elements of a legend. I did not really perceive that back in the 1950s; I was simply excited by a tale, and concerned that in telling it I should not get in the way of its extremely moving events. It is gratifying to me, as a writer and as another simple sailor, that I seem to have succeeded in those objectives.

It is increasingly apparent, also, that the story of the *Indianapolis* has taken on a life of its own, as legends are supposed to do. That has been proven to me by many events; let me cite just two. In the summer of 1975 more than one hundred survivors gathered in Indianapolis on the thirtieth anniversary of the sinking. That is as one might expect. But this reunion also attracted many persons who clearly had had no part in these events but had now attached themselves to the *legend* of the *Indianapolis*.

Some of this was due, no doubt, to a related phenomenon, the movie *Jaws*. The film introduced a new generation to the story of the *Indianapolis*, for in one unforgettable scene, crazy old Captain Quint tells why he is obsessed with killing sharks. "I was on the *Indianapolis* when she went down," he begins, and then he tells a part of the legend, those terrible days in the water.

The reunion, the movie, the letters that still come to me—there is no question in my mind that the story of the *Indianapolis* lives on, and will live on; not because of me, but because of the fascination we have, as people, with what happens to other people just like ourselves. We can all ask, "My God, what would I have done?"

Two new things now give me great pleasure: This fine new edition and the fact that a new U.S.S. *Indianapolis* is coming along. I am proud to be associated with Indiana University Press, and I am grateful that they see enduring qualities in this story and are thus preserving it.

I welcome the new U.S.S. *Indianapolis* (SSN-697), a nuclear-powered submarine to be launched in 1976, the Navy's bicentennial year. Captain David D. Heerwagen, USN, summed up my feelings when he said at the reunion banquet: "A generation has passed; life has come full circle. I would like to believe that as the keel of this submarine was being laid, the character and soul of the cruiser *Indianapolis* was being attached to that first metal structure, and that through this happening the indomitable spirit of the cruiser *Indianapolis* will be handed down to the next generation."

December 1975   RICHARD F. NEWCOMB

ABANDON SHIP!

1

Lieutenant Commander Mochitsura Hashimoto, IJN, was not a happy man. A war that had started out so gloriously—both for him and for the Empire—was turning out disastrously. Even the opportunity of dying for the Emperor had been denied him, and he felt a sense of unworthiness.

His personal affairs might be said to have gone very well. He had advanced steadily in the Imperial Japanese Navy, he was happily married, and his wife had given him three fine sons. At thirty-six he was in command of one of the newest and finest submarines in the navy—in fact, one of the few still operating. If only he could have a chance to serve. . . .

His chance was coming, very soon, and it would find him well prepared. Hashimoto was born in 1909 in the quiet and beautiful shrine city of Kyoto, ancient capital of Japan for nearly eleven centuries. He was the eighth child and the fifth and last son of a high Shinto priest.

Mochitsura did well in his studies, and while he was in the Third High School in Kyoto, one of the best in Japan, his father began to think of entering him for the Japanese Naval Academy. The family was not particularly naval-minded, but there was the question of money. The income of a chief priest of an important Shinto shrine, even with the government subsidy granted to priests of the State religion, was barely enough when nine children had to be provided for. And the military was a respected tradition, providing education at government expense and promising a good future for those who qualified.

Mochitsura was graduated from high school in 1927. He was eighteen, still something of a country boy, but self-possessed and respectful, though not servile. He seemed well fitted for the navy which, as in some other countries, considered itself just a little superior to the army. The Japanese Navy, though young, already had a tradition. The sea was Japan's life, and nobody in the crowded islands lived more than a hundred miles from it.

Leaving home for the first time, young Hashimoto entered the Naval Academy in 1927. His oldest brother had already graduated from the national military academy and was now on active duty with the Japanese Army. The Naval Academy was located on Eta Jima, an island in Hiroshima Bay a few miles west of the great naval base of Kure, on the Inland Sea. Here for the next four years Mochitsura got the rough edges knocked off. He studied the history of Japan and the navy, engineering, and naval tactics. He also spent much time in judo and other military-style athletics.

Hashimoto was graduated in 1931, at the opening of an era. It was the dawn of Japan's Greater Asia Co-Prosperity Sphere. There may have been a depression in America but there was work for every hand in Japan. The Japanese Army overran Manchuria, launched the war in China, and made plans for still greater conquests. Hashimoto had his first assignment in submarines in 1934, followed by duty in destroyers and subchasers in China waters. In 1937 two things happened: Hashimoto's oldest brother, a full colonel, was killed in the fighting in North China, and Hashimoto married Miss Nobuko Miki, daughter of a well-to-do Osaka businessman. The following year Hashimoto was chosen for Navy Torpedo School and, in 1939, for Submarine School. In 1940, a great event occurred in the Hashimoto household. His first child, a son, Michihiro, was born. Remembering his own happy childhood in a large family, Hashimoto hoped for more.

By early 1941, it was clear that a crisis with the United States was approaching. Hashimoto of course knew nothing of the grand strategy being planned, but he sensed that great things were coming, and he felt ready. At thirty-two he was sturdy and well-built, his muscles hard and his mind keen. Like any good submarine man, he looked forward to his own command some day, and with events obviously shaping up, the future looked bright.

Right now, he was assigned to the *I-24*, a new submarine, as torpedo officer. At Kure, the *I-24* was formed into a squadron with four other new boats, and during the summer and fall they practiced maneuvers with a group of midget subs. On November 18, under sealed orders, the squadron sailed from Kure, a midget sub clamped to the afterdeck of each vessel. The night before, Admiral Chiuchi Nagumo, Commander of the Pearl Harbor Striking Force, had quietly slipped out to sea in his flagship, the carrier *Aragi*, and headed for a rendezvous with powerful units in the Kuriles. Mighty things were brewing.

The *I-24* moved steadily eastward, and on Saturday night, December 6, boldly surfaced ten miles off Waikiki. The skipper, Lieutenant Commander Hiroshi Hanabusa, led the way to the deck and the excited crew could see the glare of neon lights on the horizon, as Waikiki enjoyed its last carefree moments. Down below, Hashimoto tuned in radio station KGMB and enjoyed the Hawaiian music. Sublieutenant Kazuo Sakamaki went through his final ritual, for he was to ride one of the midget submarines with Seaman First Class Kyoji Inagaki as his crewman. The ritual over, including a visit to the Shinto shrine on board, they were cast off at 5:30 A.M.

In the waters nearby there were twenty-seven other Japanese submarines, several of them, like the *I-24*, engaged in launching midgets. It was the last the *I-24* ever saw of Sakamaki, but not the last of Sakamaki. Two days later he was found, exhausted but alive, on the beach near Bellows Field. It was his great dishonor to be one of the first, and the few, Japanese prisoners ever taken. His midget was nearby, hung up on a reef, but Inagaki's body was never found.

The *I-24*, with the other mother submarines, waited two days at the rendezvous point. None of the five midgets ever returned. On December 9, Hanabusa gave the order and the *I-24* started the long trip home. All hands felt a great sense of unworthiness. The boat reached Kwajalein in time for a New Year's celebration there. With the special significance this day holds for the Japanese, Hashimoto vowed he would find in the dawning year his opportunity for special service to the Emperor. The *I-24* re-

Japanese Midget Submarine

turned to a Japan still thrilling to one of the great naval
victories of all time. Hashimoto was detached at Kure, and
was overjoyed to find his wife and son well. Smiling there
in her rich kimono, Nobuko did not have to tell him the
family would soon be blessed again. Later that year a second son, Nobutake, was born.

Hashimoto was delighted to be assigned to the ad-

vanced course at Submarine School (it could mean only
one thing), and when he was graduated in July he was
given his first command, the *RO-31*. This was a boat of
the coastal defense class; not one of the fleet Class *I* boats,
of course, but still a command. For the rest of the year,
Hashimoto skippered the *RO-31* in home waters, out of
Yokosuka, training crews, trying out new equipment, and
doing research for improvement of the undersea fleet. In
1943, he commanded the *I-158* and the *RO-44* in important but tiresome tasks.

Finally, in May, 1944, the big chance came. He was
ordered to fit out and take command of a new boat, a
big *I*-Class boat of latest design. Despite the strong pull
of family and the birth of his third son, Tomoyuki, Hashimoto declined a month's leave and hurried down to Sasebo, on the southern island of Kyushu. He was a quiet man
and he loved his family, but many things pulled him from
home. He was anxious to see his boat, the *I-58,* and keep
an eye on her construction. The triumphant days of 1941
and 1942 were gone now. One did not speak, or even
think, of defeat, but truthfully the war was not going well.
Hashimoto felt guilty that he had not done more.

The *I-58* was a good boat by any standard. She was
108.7 meters (about 355 feet) overall, with a beam of
9.3 meters (30 feet), and displaced 2,140 tons. This was
slightly bigger than American submarines of a comparable
class, and nearly twice the size of the average German
U-boat. Two diesel engines, producing 4,700 horsepower,
gave her a cruising speed of 14 knots and a maximum of
17 knots on the surface. Submerged, she cruised at three
knots, with a maximum of seven. She had a range of
15,000 miles and could stay out three months. The *I-58*
had six torpedo tubes, all forward, and carried 19 torpedoes.

In that department, the *I-58* was distinctly superior to
anything the United States had even at the end of the war,
for she was armed with the famed Type 95. Oxygen-
fueled and wakeless, these fish were capable of the incredible speed of 48 knots and had a range of 5,500
meters. At 42 knots, the range was over 9,000 meters
(nearly five miles). Twenty-four inches in diameter, the
torpedoes carried a 1,210-pound explosive charge and
could be equipped with magnetic or inertia warheads.
Soon after Hashimoto arrived in Sasebo, his officers and

crew began to assemble. He was pleased to find that most of them were seasoned submariners. The Japanese submarine service, like the American, was a select arm of the navy, and most of Hashimoto's men were volunteers and proud of their calling. Nearly all had had advanced training, many of them on top of intense battle service in other branches of the navy.

As summer wore on, Hashimoto began to tauten his ship. Two of the latest radar were installed, Type 2M2 for surface and Type 1M3 for aircraft, along with two sonar, one electronic and the other acoustic. As for armament, everything was stripped off topside except one 25 mm. machine gun, for reasons that soon became known to all. The *I-58* would carry "kaitens"—human suicide torpedoes! These were the underwater counterpart of the kamikaze, and everyone was proud and elated that the daring kaitens would be aboard.

To make room for the special weapons on deck, workmen removed the housing for the reconnaissance plane, its catapult, and the usual deck gun. Now there would be room for six kaiten torpedoes. Radio equipment included two transmitters, and the newest (for Japan) type antennas. The *I-58* was the first Japanese submarine to use the Yagi antenna, strange indeed since it had been invented by a Japanese, Dr. Hidetsugu Yagi, long before the war. But the Japanese had ignored it, and Dr. Yagi had sold it to American and British firms. When the war broke out, the Yagi antenna was in wide use in both navies, but the Japanese paid little attention to it until after they found some among captured Allied equipment in Manila and Singapore. Only now, in mid-1944, was it reaching the Japanese fleet.

The *I-58* was formally commissioned on September 13, 1944, and immediately commenced sea trials off Sasebo. At this time she carried 105 officers and men, not to mention a host of rats. There seemed no way of keeping them off the boat, where they annoyed the men, rattled pans in the galley, and gnawed holes in the rice sacks. As the autumn days rolled by, Lieutenant Commander Hashimoto worked at knitting his men into a tight crew. He was delighted that his officer cadre knew their jobs. Lieutenant (s.g.) Toshio Tanaka, a veteran at twenty-eight, was chief torpedo officer and a man whose cool skill with the fish would one night pay off. Lieutenant (s.g.) Hiroshi Kuwahata, the chief engineer, also twenty-eight, knew everything there was to know about coaxing the best out of his diesels and batteries. The three navigators, all twenty-five and all lieutenants, senior grade, were Koya Mayama, Shozo Itsuno, and Hiromu Tanaka (no relation to the torpedo officer). Lieutenant (s.g.) Tameo Hosoi, twenty-eight, was assistant engineer, and the youthful Lieutenant (j.g.) Junji Kuroda, only twenty-three, was carried aboard as chief gunnery officer, though in truth there were no guns left for him, except the lone machine gun on the bridge.

Though Hashimoto drove them steadily, the officers and enlisted men responded well to his quiet brand of authority. There were no leaves and very little time ashore, as the *I-58* spent day after day in torpedo practice, diving and surfacing, evasive maneuvers, and attack problems. The hour was too far gone for slack training, and they knew it. At thirty-six (soon to turn thirty-seven), Hashimoto felt almost like a father to some of the younger ones, and he thought often of his own boys at home. And at times, though he never spoke of it even to himself, he worried, for he heard many things at the officers' mess ashore. He knew the Americans were carving giant aerodromes out of the flat coral in the Marianas. Japanese still hidden in those islands faithfully radioed every development to Tokyo. Then one day late in October, General MacArthur returned to the Philippines, as he had said he would. Late in November, word seeped down from Tokyo that over a hundred giant bombers, flying from the Marianas, had bombed the city on the twenty-fourth, its first attack since the Doolittle raid of April, 1942. Damage was not great, but the meaning was plain.

Early in December, Hashimoto completed his training and the *I-58*, shaken down to fighting trim, threaded Shimonoseki Strait into the Inland Sea and the great Kure base. Fuel, torpedoes, and provisions were loaded and the boat moved down to Hirao, to load kaitens. This was a tiny seacoast village, fifty miles down the coast from Kure. Here the fanatical Japanese youths, who had fought for the privilege of dying for the Emperor, learned to pilot their one-man suicide craft. The fires of patriotism raged high at the school, and by the time the pilots sailed on their missions they were so imbued with dedication they seemed as though intoxicated.

"Kaiten" Japanese Human Torpedo

The word kaiten, from ancient Chinese meaning "revolving the heaven," had gradually come to mean "turning the tide." This was the weapon with which the Japanese would "turn the tide" of the war. The kaitens were about eight tons, and had explosive warheads. They could travel about 30 miles at low speed, or 12 miles at top speed—20 knots. They were not recoverable. Once the pilot squirmed through a narrow trunk from the mother vessel into his kaiten and was cast off, there was no returning. Either he exploded with his target or went down with his kaiten. Banzai!

Six of these were fastened to the deck of the *I-58*, and twelve kaiten pilots reported aboard, two crews for each one. Immediately the kaiten men became the idols of the *I-58* crew, exemplifying as they did the highest ideals of the nation, honorable death for the Emperor. Back at Kure, the *I-58* topped off her fuel and stores, and on December 29 sailed on her first war patrol. As she glided out, crowds of people in motorboats, chanting the names of the crewmen, followed along in dramatic farewell. Above the Rising Sun emblem on the conning tower was painted the flag of the Kikusui, and at the masthead fluttered a large banner reading "Hiriho Kenten." The Kikusui

was the famed battle standard of the medieval warrior
Masashige Kusunoki, who fought against overwhelming
odds, knowing he had no chance to survive—for the
Emperor. Every suicide warrior, land, sea, or air, carried
this emblem and hoped to emulate Masashige. The Hiriho
Kenten was his war banner, and the phrase meant something akin to "God's will."

The *I-58's* first war patrol was not a glittering success.
After the fervid send-off, the boat made straight for
Guam, arriving off the island on January 11, 1945. The
Marianas were roaring with activity at that time, with the
B-29 bases coming into operation and fleets of ships piling
the islands high with materiel for the Iwo Jima and Okinawa operations. Two B-29 runways were already in use
at Isley Field on Saipan, and the first, 8,500-foot runway
at North Field on Tinian had just been opened. Eventually,
five great airfields were built, two on Guam, two on
Tinian, and one on Saipan, and men and materials were
gushing forward from Hawaii or the mainland. In addition, Admiral Nimitz had decided to make Guam his advance headquarters and base for the Pacific Fleet. Giant
depots for fuel, ammunition, and stores were being set up,
as well as naval-base installations, harbor facilities, and
staging areas for ground troops.

Commander Hashimoto made a run in on Guam on
the night of January 11, and at 3:00 A.M. the next day
launched four kaitens. It was a moment of high excitement on board—the maiden mission of the boat, the first
strike, and the first use of kaitens. The four volunteers for
perdition felt great honor in being selected, quickly
squeezed into their loaded coffins and were cast off. After
a while, explosions were heard, and the *I-58* tentatively
claimed a tanker. Later, Hashimoto said he could not
honestly claim any kills for the kaitens because it was
virtually impossible to verify them.

As though running from the scene of a crime, the
I-58 went straight back to Kure, arriving on January 20,
and there she stayed until March. There were several possible reasons for this: Fuel and stores were getting short,
and it was a question of priority of mission. Also, the
Japanese still clung to an out moded tactic—attacking
only the enemy fleet in battle, instead of his communication lines. Until the bitter end of the war, the Japanese
failed to realize the value, psychological if nothing else, of

attacks deep behind the line, east of Hawaii. Except for a few scattered raids along the West Coast, they never emulated their brothers in arms, the U-boat skippers who marauded for months off the Atlantic Coast.

On March 1, with the Iwo Jima battle still in the balance, the *I-58* was ordered there with a fresh load of kaitens. But, with typical Japanese indecisiveness, Hashimoto had hardly arrived there when he was ordered to jettison the kaitens (minus pilots) and return to Japan. When he got back to Kure, disastrous news awaited. The U.S. Air Force had found that high-level daylight bombing of Japan by the B-29s was not achieving the results expected of it and had decided to switch to low-level, night-time bombing with incendiaries. The results of this decision were catastrophic for Japan.

Tokyo was the first target for the fire raids, and the date was the night of March 9/10. A total of 334 Superfortresses, carrying 2,000 tons of bombs, literally set the city afire in the greatest single blaze in the history of mankind. When the fires had burned out, over one million persons were homeless and over 83,000 were dead, a toll greater than the atom bomb at Hiroshima or Nagasaki. The Japanese were stunned.

Two nights later, Nagoya was the target, and then came Osaka, and on the sixteenth it was Kobe, the latter two cities only twenty-five miles from Hashimoto's home at Kyoto. He had moved his family to Kure for the war, but his wife's folks lived in Osaka and his in Kyoto. Reports sifting down to Kure told of fantastic carnage, and for once the truth was worse than the rumors.

On April 2, one day after the landings at Okinawa, the *I-58* was ordered out again, and this time it was lucky to make it. The baleful B-29s, when not burning cities to the ground, were out every night dropping mines in the waters around the coast. The campaign began only on March 27, with 105 Superforts hitting the vital Shimonoseki Strait, between Kyushu and Honshu. Each plane carried an assortment of 1,000- and 2,000-pound acoustic or magnetic mines, some 12,000 pounds to the plane. In a few short nights, Shimonoseki was closed, and so was Bungo Strait. That left only one entrance to the Inland Sea.

As far as Okinawa was concerned, the *I-58* might better have stayed home. In seven days at the battle scene, Hashimoto was attacked by planes fifty times, and his longest time on the surface was four hours, in the dead of night. He limped back into Kure on April 29, the only Japanese submarine to return from Okinawa. It seemed that the *I-58* was destined for nothing but failure.

By May, the B-29s had burned out nearly every major city in the islands and were starting to work on the secondary cities, of 200,000 population or less. The mine-sowing Superforts had closed all Japanese ports on the Pacific, many on the Sea of Japan, and were busy mining the port cities high up in Korea. Like a man cowering in a doorway during a typhoon, the *I-58* lay still in Kure, waiting for the storm to pass.

Finally, on July 16, the boat was ordered out again, on what many sensed would be her last patrol. After all, Japan had only four large submarines left. Her orders were to "harass the enemy's communications," there no longer being any point in even trying for the enemy's fleet. She sailed with a full load of six kaitens, and the dauntless Kure people were still able to raise some cheers and a few strains of martial music for the farewell.

By a bitter stroke of irony, another ship left another port that day. A certain United States cruiser, whose decks had known the footfalls of the famous, cleared San Francisco shortly after dawn, bound westward on a high-speed run with top-secret cargo. These two vessels were to meet and the outcome of their meeting would reverberate throughout the history of the United States Navy for decades to come.

Hashimoto threaded his boat through the Inland Sea, past the hulks of Japanese warships wrecked deep in home waters by U.S. Navy planes, through minefields laid by B-29s, and into open water. Again, he was lucky to make it. His orders read "to attack enemy ships off the east coast of the Philippines." Whoever wrote those orders showed almost prescience in sealing the fate of the U.S. cruiser. The *I-58* passed east of Okinawa and found no targets on the Marianas-Okinawa route. This was incredible, for that route was one of the busiest in the Pacific, with Okinawa being built up for the war's climactic blow— invasion of Japan.

Hashimoto cruised southward with falling hopes. The moon was waning, signaling the end of good night hunting, and there was no fresh food left except onions. The weather was hot and overcast. Hashimoto went to pray at the Shinto shrine aft. On Friday, July 27, the *I-58* arrived on the Guam-Leyte route, normally a well-traveled track, and cruised slowly west. At 5:30 A.M. on Saturday, they sighted a plane and crash dived. Luck changed that afternoon when they sighted a tanker, escorted by a destroyer. Hashimoto decided to launch kaitens; time was running out and no opportunity was to be missed. He granted Lieutenant (j.g.) Ban the honor of piloting No. 1, and, not to be unfair, allowed an enlisted man, Naval Aviation Pilot First Class Komori, to take No. 2. The suiciders squirmed into their torpedoes shouting, "Three cheers for the Emperor," and were cast off at 2:31 and 2:43 P.M., respectively. Every man on the *I-58* waited tensely, but nothing happened. Finally, explosions were heard at 3:21 and 3:31, but a rain squall had blotted out the target and Hashimoto never knew what happened. He reported in a dispatch later "assume enemy tanker sank," but no one really believed it at the time. Gloom settled over the crew as they prayed for the departed kaiten pilots, asking happiness for them in a future life.

Hoping to better his luck, Hashimoto set course on Sunday for "the crossroads," the intersection of straight lines connecting Guam-Leyte and Peleliu-Okinawa. His intuition couldn't have been sharper. Bearing down on him was a certain U.S. cruiser which had departed Guam the previous day, no longer carrying top-secret cargo, but bearing nearly 1,200 men.

Sunday was overcast and squally, but the sea was calm and the *I-58* spent most of the day on the surface. Toward evening, visibility dropped almost to zero, and Hashimoto decided to submerge and wait for moonrise at about 11:00 P.M. Early in the evening he went to his bunk for a nap, and the boat moved silently west at two knots, most of the crew dozing. They were scattered all over the vessel, many naked, some sprawled on top of the torpedoes, others on rice sacks, between shelves, anywhere. And the rats scampered about, making an awful racket.

The petty officer of the watch gently roused his skipper at 11:30 P.M., according to orders. Hashimoto rose quietly, donned his uniform and made his way to the shrine to say a prayer for good hunting. Afterward, he went to the conning tower and gave the order, "Night battle stations." The ship came to life and Chief Engineer Kuwahata brought the speed to three knots.

As she came to sixty feet, the night periscope was raised and Commander Hashimoto took a quick look around. Visibility was much better, and one could almost see the horizon. The moon was some twenty degrees high in the east, and there were a few clouds. Adjusting the periscope Hashimoto made three or four slow sweeps. Seeing nothing, he gave the order to surface.

Even before the vessel leveled out, Lieutenant Tanaka, the duty navigator, sprang to the open bridge. Within seconds he cried out: "Bearing red, nine zero degrees, possible enemy ship." Impassively Hashimoto joined him and placed his ten-power binoculars to his eyes.

A black spot was clearly visible, some 10,000 meters away (slightly over five miles), the moon behind it. In a firm voice, Hashimoto ordered, "Dive." At the same time he brought the boat around to port and moved north, to get out of the way in case the target was approaching.

Tension ran through the crew. Entirely dependent on the eyes of one man, they could only imagine what was going on. As the *I-58* leveled off beneath the surface, Commander Hashimoto spoke to them:

"Ship in sight, all tubes to the ready. Kaitens stand by."

The time was 11:35 P.M.

But no orders were necessary. Lieutenant Tanaka, the chief torpedo officer, and his men were readying the torpedoes—five magnetic warheads and one inertia.

Hashimoto bent to the periscope. The target was approaching steadily and the silhouette began to take shape. The top of the large, triangular black spot gradually resolved into two distinct portions, with a large mast forward. Even Hashimoto was stirred as he perceived that it was either a battleship, possibly *Idaho* class, or a large cruiser. There was no doubt that it was enemy. Japan had few large warships still afloat, and none would have been this deep in enemy territory.

The range fell steadily. With eyes to the periscope and the hydrophones on his head, Hashimoto watched in amazement. The target, outlined sharply in the moon's path, approached on straight, near-collision course. No changes in course or speed. Set out before him was a problem so simple no naval school would presume to teach it. Culminating nearly four years of lean hunting at sea, Hashimoto allowed himself to think: "We've got her."

At 4,000 meters (two miles) Hashimoto made his first decision. A hydrophone report gave the speed as moderately high, and he decided to fire at 2,000 meters. Gradually his boat swung to starboard, turning back south now as it became clear the target would pass at optimum range. Hashimoto thought he could make out two turrets aft and a large tower mast. It must be a battleship!

Silence fell over the boat. The crew strained forward. Even the rats were quiet. Only the kaiten pilots broke the stillness as they crowded around asking, "Where is the enemy? Why can't we be launched?"

The critical moment was approaching, and Hashimoto made his final calculations. He revised his first estimate of target speed of 20 knots down to 12 knots, and dropped the firing point from 2,000 to 1,500 meters. The fish were set for a depth of four meters, speed 48 knots.

The instant arrived, and in a loud, steady voice Hashimoto shouted: "Stand by—Fire!"

At three-second intervals, the torpedo-release switch tripped. In fifteen seconds the torpedo room reported "All tubes fired and correct." There was no undoing it now. Six torpedoes, launched with a spread of three degrees, were speeding fanwise toward the target. The time was two minutes after midnight, exactly twenty-seven minutes from sighting.

In the moments left to him, Hashimoto took a quick look around. Not another ship was in sight. Coming around to course parallel with the target, the *I-58* waited. It seemed an eternity. Hashimoto counted softly to himself, his eyes never leaving the periscope. At precisely the calculated time, he saw it—first a column of water rising at the forward turret, then another at the after turret, followed immediately by flashes of bright orange flame, then a third one, by No. 2 turret.

"A hit, a hit!" he shouted, as each torpedo struck home, and the crew danced for joy. With the target slowing in an empty sea, Commander Hashimoto raised the day periscope and gave the men in the conning tower a look. As they watched, heavy explosions seemed to rock the target, seemingly far greater than the torpedo hits. Three tremendous blasts, then six more. Excited crewmen cried, "Depth-charge attack! Depth-charge attack!" but the captain reassured them. It was only the target exploding, no other ship was in sight.

But the target showed no sign of sinking. Hashimoto stood by, thinking of a second salvo, and the kaiten pilots clamored, "If she won't sink, send us."

Hashimoto pondered. The ship was certainly an easy target for them now, but what if she should sink before they reached her? Once launched, they never returned. Hashimoto thought of his own sons at home: kaitens would not be launched. The captain had planned to maintain position, but suddenly his sound men informed him that the enemy was using his underwater detection apparatus. (This was an error, for the target had none of any kind.) Hashimoto ordered a deep dive for reloading, and the *I-58* quickly disappeared. As she went, the noise from the target ceased.

Hashimoto could not know it, but no one would ever see the target again. She was on the point of sinking. For more than an hour, Hashimoto's men worked smoothly in their cramped quarters, reloading the tubes. As soon as the job was done, the *I-58* came to periscope depth. There was nothing in sight.

There was no question that the target had sunk. A ship so damaged could not have made off at high speed. A great sense of professional pride welled up in Commander Hashimoto, for he knew he had made a big kill. Seeking proof, he surfaced and searched the area for flotsam, but in the darkness found nothing. This was disappointing, and also nearly incredible, for the sea was strewn for miles around with debris, large slicks of fuel oil, and nearly a thousand men. Anxious as he was for proof, Hashimoto must clearly have surfaced some distance away from where he thought the sinking had occurred.

The search continued for more than an hour, and then prudence told Hashimoto he had better clear out. The target almost certainly had air or surface escort—ships of that size rarely traveled alone—and in any event there had been plenty of time for her to send out distress calls. Around 2:30 A.M., Hashimoto gave the order and the *I-58* made off to the northeast, on the surface. As she went, Hashimoto sat down to compose his dispatch to his superiors. He took out all the pictures and drawings of

American warships he had aboard and studied them close-
ly, for nearly twenty minutes. None resembled exactly the
big, black ship he had seen in his periscope, but he finally
decided to call it a battleship of the *Idaho* class. He was
quite skeptical, however, because a battleship rarely moves
alone. On the other hand, fellow officers had told him of
having sunk cruisers in the Solomons with one torpedo,
and this target had absorbed three hits amidships and still
remained afloat for a time.

The dispatch was encoded and transmitted by short-
wave about 3:00 A.M. on Monday, July 30. Addressed to
Sixth Fleet Headquarters at Kure and to Combined Fleet
Headquarters at Sagamihara, south of Tokyo, the dispatch
reported the attack on the tanker and the loss of two
kaitens. Then, of the Sunday night attack, it said in part
". . . released six torpedoes and scored three at battleship
of *Idaho* class . . . definitely sank it." The code used was a
relatively simple one, and the emission was on a standard
frequency in use by the Japanese Navy. Anyone monitor-
ing that channel—and the Americans certainly would be
—could have heard the message all the way to the West
Coast. Hashimoto didn't care, he was well away. He ordered a victory dinner to be served on Monday—beans,
corned beef, and boiled eels.

The *I-58* cruised slowly northward for several days,
but the hunting was bad, and late on Thursday the radio
operator intercepted a message from the Owada radio detachment in the Tokyo suburbs. It said: "We monitor
many enemy messages in the mid-Pacific indicating the
enemy is now searching for some very important ship
sunk." Hashimoto paid no attention to the dispatch, not
connecting it with his kill. That would have been known
on Monday. Such a large fleet unit could not have been
missing for nearly four days without the U.S. Navy knowing about it. Or could it?

On August 7, the *I-58* picked up enemy news reports
of an "atom bomb" obliterating Hiroshima, but the men
were not unduly disturbed. Nearly every large city in
Japan had been burned out weeks or months ago in the
great fire raids. To the Japanese, at this time, the atom
bomb carried no special impact. The people who had
burned in piles at street corners and bridges as they fled
in panic from the holocaust of fire raids were just as dead
as those vaporized in one short instant at Hiroshima. The

Nagasaki bomb went down August 9, and still the *I-58* was hunting. The next day the *I-58* sighted a convoy, penetrated it, and launched kaitens. Hashimoto claimed a destroyer. On the 12th he again launched kaitens, and this time claimed a merchant ship. It had been a fat patrol—his fattest ever—but all kaitens had been expended and the boat headed home.

The *I-58* entered Bungo Strait on August 15, the crew jubilant at a good score and a safe return. That evening, the radioman came to Hashimoto with a secret dispatch, the announcement that Japan had surrendered. Thinking it might be a trick, Hashimoto told his officers but ordered them to say nothing to the crew. Submerging often, to avoid enemy attacks, the *I-58* proceeded up the Inland Sea and arrived at the kaiten base, Hirao, on the seventeenth. The patrol was over, and more too. Hashimoto saw a motorboat coming out to meet him, and sensed that the hour had struck. He ordered his crew out on the afterdeck and there, with tears in his eyes, read to them the Imperial Rescript.

Without another word he boarded the motorboat and went ashore to report to the senior officer at the kaiten base on the valiant deeds of those fortunate ones who had not had to face this. He still did not know that he had sunk the U.S.S. *Indianapolis*, flagship of the Fifth Fleet. To Hashimoto, the disaster of defeat had blotted out everything else, except the knowledge that his wife and children were alive.

He went to them now, and it struck him that his wife's kimono was no longer rich; it now looked poor and threadbare. The children appeared to be suffering from malnutrition, in particular the oldest boy. Jobless now, Hashimoto passed into obscurity, but for only a few months. A strange adventure awaited him. The *I-58*, which had seemed like a home to him, was taken to Sasebo and there the rats had the run of her until April 1, 1946. Then the U.S. Navy took her sixty miles out to sea and blew her up with TNT. She went down quickly, in 900 feet of water, cherry blossoms still lashed to her periscope.

2

Captain Charles Butler McVay 3d, United States Navy, stepped down the gangway and into a waiting car. He was off to the Embarcadero, to see what Admiral Purnell and Captain Parsons wanted.

"Cherub" they had called him at the Academy, and it was easy to see why. His rosy complexion and good-humored face, set off by black eyebrows and graying hair, produced a definitely cherubic appearance. He was handsome, of medium height and trim figure, and gave the impression of a man in the midstream of life, swimming strongly. That's the way he thought of himself, on the rare occasions when his thoughts turned inward.

At forty-six, almost forty-seven, he was satisfied with life. For the moment, his most recent ambition, command of a cruiser, had been achieved and he could see nothing ahead but good sailing. In twenty-six years' service he had run up a solid, if not spectacular, record of diversified command. He could not match the achievement of his father, it is true, but not all sons do. The old gentleman, now seventy-seven and long since retired, had commanded the *Saratoga*, the *New Jersey*, and the *Oklahoma* during the first war, been Commandant of the Washington Navy Yard, Chief of the Bureau of Ordnance, and finally Commander-in-Chief, U.S. Asiatic Fleet. In 1932, Charles Butler McVay, Jr., retired as a full admiral and settled in Washington.

The McVays had originally come from Pennsylvania, where the first Charles Butler McVay had been president

18

of the Pittsburgh Trust Company. After his son entered the Academy in 1886, the father took such an active role in securing support for the young school (it was founded in 1845) that he was made an honorary member of the Class of 1890, the year his son was graduated. He was given a class ring, which he wore until he died. Nearly sundered by the Civil War, the Academy was at last getting on its feet, thanks partly to the support of private citizens such as the elder McVay. While his son attended, the superintendent was Acting Captain William Thomas Sampson, who eight years later became a national hero and first established the United States as a naval power with the destruction of the Spanish fleet at Santiago, Cuba. His late pupil, Ensign McVay, was there as watch and division officer on the U.S.S. *Amphitrite*.

But now, on Sunday morning, July 15, 1945, Captain McVay was not thinking of his family's long and distinguished association with the United States Navy. He was thinking, rather, in a mildly curious way, of his forthcoming conference. As the car whisked him south from Mare Island Navy Yard, along the eastern shore of San Francisco Bay and into the city, he wondered what could be the secret and mysterious mission for which he had been chosen. Three days previously he had been told that his ship, the heavy cruiser U.S.S. *Indianapolis*, must be ready for sea within four days. This was considerably earlier than had been planned, and quite a surprise to McVay. He could think of no reason for it. The war in Europe was over, the war in the Pacific was in a lull pending the buildup for the final blow—invasion of the Japanese homeland. The earliest possible target date for that was November 1.

Why should the *Indianapolis*, a venerable vessel of prewar vintage, suddenly be on urgent call? She was the flagship of Admiral Raymond A. Spruance, Commander Fifth Fleet, to be sure, but he was in Guam planning an invasion still four months off. Obviously, he had no need for the vessel for some time to come. Nevertheless, upon receiving orders to prepare for sea, Captain McVay had acted swiftly. He instructed his executive officer, Commander Joseph A. Flynn, to order all men away at service schools back to the ship immediately; the navigator, Commander John Hopkins Janney, was ordered to bring his charts up to date without delay, and the engineering officer, Commander Glen F. DeGrave, to prepare the engine rooms for a sea voyage. These officers were all seasoned men, received their orders without question, and executed them promptly.

Among the crew, however, and some of the junior officers, there was considerable confusion. The ship had been in Mare Island since early April for repairs to battle damage, and they had made their plans for at least six weeks more of shore duty. Ensign Ross Rogers, Jr., reporting aboard on May 13, straight out of Midshipman's School at Annapolis, had wavered back and forth about getting married, finally did and in less than two weeks found himself at sea on a top-secret mission. Watertender Second Class Lindsey Z. Wilcox brought his wife up to Vallejo from Texas, and Fireman First Class Elwood E. Dale, a pretty fair hand with the brush, painted her picture.

Captain Edward L. Parke, commanding officer of the Marine detachment on the ship, quickly married a school teacher from Illinois. Parke was a six-foot, 200-pounder, tough as a top sergeant, which he had been, and some of the boys secretly hoped his marriage would soften him up a little. Mrs. Thomas D'Arcy Brophy, wife of a New York advertising executive, came out to be with her only son after he reported on May 14. Ensign Thomas D'Arcy Brophy, Jr., just twenty-one, was an honor man at graduation from Columbia University Midshipman's School in April, and received a sword from Admiral Monroe Kelly, Commandant of the Third Naval District. Young Brophy, a graduate of Deerfield Academy and secretary of the Princeton University Class of 1947, was to join Admiral Spruance's staff.

Dozens of men came pouring back aboard from service schools, their training in the latest techniques of gunnery, radar, and radio abruptly terminated. Parents, wives, sweethearts, and girl friends in a radius of a hundred miles suddenly found their plans changed. From a routine yard-repair period, everything had now been transformed into a top-secret mission requiring speed. Liberty was canceled and all hands turned to preparing the ship for sea. Reaching the yard in April after a brush with a kamikaze plane off Okinawa on March 31, the *Indianapolis* had a badly mauled port quarter from the explosion of the suicide plane's bomb. The plane had crashed on the main deck and toppled into the sea, causing little damage. But the bomb released by the kamikaze pilot had pierced the main deck, passed through a mess hall, a berthing compartment, and the fuel tanks, and exploded under the hull. Nine men were killed, and two gaping holes were blown in the hull. There was some flooding, and the ship listed to port, but the damage-control parties soon contained the flooding and the *Indianapolis* was saved. Looking back, it was a foretaste of worse to come.

The *Indianapolis* had shown well in those hot days around Okinawa. She had shot down six planes and bagged two more probables in seven days, besides delivering a steady, week-long bombardment on Okinawa from her 8-inch main batteries. As the invasion opened, she crawled away under her own power and cruised 8,000 miles to California, despite damage to fuel tanks, propeller shafts, and water-distillation equipment. At Mare Island, largest yard on the West Coast, skilled artisans quickly set to work to tear away the damaged area. With cutting torches they burned away the twisted steel and laid bare the port quarter from main deck to keel. The yard was busy around the clock, welders' torches glowed, rivet guns created their usual din, and by late June, the new *Indianapolis* was shaping up. Besides a new port quarter, she was getting the latest in radio equipment, radar, and fire-control mechanisms.

She was also getting a new "team" aboard. Captain McVay and some of his senior officers were still there, but over thirty new officers, nearly half the complement, reported aboard and more than two hundred and fifty enlisted men joined the crew as replacements. Most of the new officers were distinctly junior, including some twenty ensigns right out of midshipmen's schools or the Academy, and many of the enlisted men were straight from boot camp. It would take training to shake this complement into a new team, and Captain McVay had looked forward to the regular training period off the California coast. But now there was to be no training period.

Suddenly, within three days, yard crews had to clear the ship of hoses, tools, and debris, and the ship's crew loaded stores and equipment from trucks and freight cars alongside. In the mad scramble to make ready for sea, one thing worried Captain McVay—no life jackets had arrived. After inquiring in several quarters without results,

McVay took the matter directly to the office of the Commander, Western Sea Frontier. Action then was swift and fortuitous. Forty-eight hours before the ship sailed, not one but two consignments of life jackets arrived at shipside. Now there was a double order, some 2,500 in all, and no one could have conceived what a stroke of fortune that was. The deck gangs cursed the idiots who had sent 2,500 life jackets for 1,200 men. Where the hell could you stow them on a fighting ship already crowded with twice her peacetime complement.

And then the passengers! They began streaming aboard a week before sailing time, assigned there for transportation to Pearl Harbor by Navy personnel who had no idea the vessel would be on a special mission. Commander Flynn met the emergency by preparing a special memorandum, a copy of which was handed to each passenger as he came over the gangway.

In good-natured tone, he told them:

"This ship has twenty more officers than its complement calls for, and, on the other hand, only eighty-four per cent of the steward's mates allowed for its normal complement. It follows, then, that our messing and berthing facilities are taxed to the limit. With all hands cooperating and showing consideration for others, there is no reason why we cannot be comfortable—at least much more comfortable than many of our service mates on the beaches in the Forward Area." He told them the ship could have no training period before sailing and thus would have to train while under way. "You will assist greatly by remaining clear of the activities," he said, meaning frankly, "Eat when you can and stay the hell out of the way."

"We cannot do your laundry," he told them sadly, then added a bright note: "We have just purchased a large supply of games from our wardroom funds. You are welcome to use them in the wardroom. And, oh yes, lights go out in the wardroom at 10:00 P.M. Ain't war hell?"

But finally, on Saturday morning, July 14, the ship was able to put out for sea trials. The vessel was by no means shipshape, with men and gear piled everywhere, and she put to sea like a man leaving the hospital, anxious to get out but wary of his newly stitched-up interior. The pitch and roll of the vessel as she passed out of the Golden Gate felt good to the old-timers and pleasant to most of the new men. With yard experts and company technicians aboard, Captain McVay put the vessel through the usual paces—speed runs, emergency turns, full backdown, check compasses, radar, radio, and fire control. She responded well.

On Sunday morning she put back into Mare Island, and now Captain McVay was on his way to get his final orders. The car dropped him at naval headquarters, and soon Rear Admiral William R. Purnell and Captain William Sterling Parsons were outlining the mission: You will bring your vessel to Hunters Point Navy Yard in San Francisco today. Sometime tonight, a small but vital and top-secret cargo will be loaded aboard. You will sail tomorrow morning at high speed, drop your passengers at Pearl Harbor, and continue, still at speed, to Tinian, where your cargo will be taken off by others. You will not be told what the cargo is, but it is to be guarded even after the life of your vessel. If she goes down, save the cargo at all costs, in a lifeboat if necessary. And every day you save will cut the length of the war by just that much. The cargo will be accompanied en route by two Army officers, and will be guarded by your regular Marine detachment. No other persons must go near it. One small package must be kept as far from the crew as possible, preferably in officers' country, and the Army officers with it.

Captain McVay was mystified, but he asked only a few routine questions. He was beginning to have his own ideas as to what the cargo was, but he kept them to himself. He was wrong, anyway.

Admiral Purnell and Captain Parsons were privy to the biggest and best-kept secret of all time—the atom bomb. When it came time to enlist Captain McVay's aid, they asked themselves the question that governed the entire project—"Does he *have* to know?" The answer was clearly "No," so he was not told. This quiet Sunday conference was just another step—and a vital one—in a project whose magnitude would stagger the world when it became known in a few weeks.

Long before the bomb fell on Hiroshima, and even before the first test in New Mexico, preparations were under way on a dozen different segments of the problem of making and delivering it. Even while the *Indianapolis* was being repaired at San Francisco, special Air Force crews were completing training in modified B-29s only 500 miles away. The highly secret base at Wendover, Utah, on the Nevada border, opened in the fall of 1944, with Colonel Paul W. Tibbets, Jr., of Miami, Florida, at the head of what later became the famous 509th Composite Group, 313th Wing, 21st Bombing Command, 20th Air Force. With seventy-five picked pilots and nearly 2,000 officers and men to back them up, they practiced steadily to perfect their technique in pinpointing a target by visual bombing. None of them, including Tibbets, knew what they were training for, except that it was secret and important.

B-29 "Superfort"

By now, all but three of the B-29s had flown out to Tinian, to prepare for the final act. These three would leave after the *Indianapolis*, with the last remaining parts of the bomb.

Admiral Purnell and Major General Leslie R. Groves, head of the Manhattan Engineer District, code name for the atomic bomb project, had decided months ago that a cruiser should be used to transport the heart of the bomb —a subcritical mass of Uranium 235—to the Forward Area. Chance decided that it should be the *Indianapolis*. She was available. Something larger than a cruiser was ruled out for reasons of vulnerability, something smaller for lack of space. A cruiser was just right from the standpoint of speed and space.

When Captain McVay had absorbed his orders, he returned to Mare Island and that afternoon they brought the *Indianapolis* down to Hunters Point and tied up at a pier. Final details for sailing were attended to and that night the men watched a movie on the hangar deck. It was their last night in the States, although they did not know it. Among the officers, only the exec, the navigator, and the engineer knew they would sail the next morning, barring accidents. And it was not likely there would be any, with the intensity of planning that had gone into this operation.

Major Robert R. Furman, crew-cut Princeton engineering graduate of 1937, had been with Manhattan Engineer District since it was set up. After a stint in the European Theater, where he had worked under extreme security, listening for enemy intelligence on atomic matters, procuring strategic materials, gathering scientific knowledge, and recruiting scientific personnel, he returned home in the spring of 1945 for several weeks' leave. When he reported to Washington, Major General Groves called him in and quickly outlined his next assignment:

> You will have custody of a shipment of uranium metal from Los Alamos to Tinian. Security will be arranged by the Army, transportation by the ATC and the Navy. At Los Alamos you will be joined by Captain James F. Nolan, who is attached to the base hospital there and will be radiological officer of the shipment. During the trip you will pose as artillery officers and no unauthorized person is to know of your true mission. Delivery of the shipment is of the utmost importance, and it must not be lost by accident or theft.

Along with his travel orders, Furman was given this letter:

> To Whom it May Concern:
> This will introduce Major Robert R. Furman, C.E., ASN O-350657, who is on a special mission of the utmost importance to the Secretary of War. All assistance should be given this officer as may be necessary to complete his mission.
> By direction of the Chief of Staff.
>
> FRANK MCCARTHY
> Colonel, GSC
> Sec'y, General Staff

Here was cloak-and-dagger stuff enough even for a twenty-nine-year-old Princeton man. The ATC lifted him out of Washington on Tuesday night, July 10, and the next morning he was in the presence of Dr. J. Robert Oppenheimer in Santa Fe, New Mexico. Dr. Oppenheimer had opened Los Alamos, or "Site Y," in late 1942 and had gathered there some of the world's most brilliant scientists. Their job was to make a fission bomb, of either plutonium or uranium, or both. Now he was en route to Alamogordo, some two hundred miles to the south, where in a few days they would try the first test shot. The result would tell whether the labors of thousands of men and the spending of millions of dollars over the past three years was wasted, or signaled a new era.

Dr. Oppenheimer was aware of Major Furman's mission, of course, and impressed on him the utter irreplaceability of the material he would be convoying. The giant works at Oak Ridge and Hanford were only now coming into production. The test bomb at Alamogordo would be of plutonium, the one destined for Japan of uranium, because that was all they could spare of either metal. He wished Major Furman luck, and set out for Alamogordo. Major Furman made his way up thirty miles of winding mountain roads to Los Alamos, on the mesa, and that afternoon Captain Nolan invited him to cocktails at his home. As they talked over drinks, and Mrs. Nolan fluttered about with hors d'oeuvres, it developed that she was considerably worried about the trip. Captain Nolan, with permission, had told her about it and how he considered himself extremely fortunate to get the assignment. He had taken his M.D. at Washington University in St. Louis in 1938, followed by internships and residencies in surgery and gynecology, topped off with a fellowship at Memorial Hospital for Cancer and Allied Diseases in New York. Now as post surgeon at Los Alamos, he was encountering problems heretofore unknown to medicine, and finding it fascinating.

Actually, there would be no possibility of premature explosion on the way out, since the uranium they were transporting was too little (subcritical) to explode. Captain Nolan did not dwell on the rest of his assignment, which was to join the 509th Composite Group at Tinian as medical overseer during assembly of the bomb. But as the evening wore on, and the drinks kept coming, even Mrs.

Nolan joined in the spirit of the mission as the two officers plotted their tactics.

Next morning, Furman and Nolan drove down to Santa Fe, and at the PX in Bruns General Hospital bought a card of field artillery collar insignia and fastened them on, upside down. They checked final arrangements with Army, Navy, and ATC authorities, and on Friday, the thirteenth, made a dry run down the mountain from Los Alamos to Santa Fe, for timing. On Saturday morning, while the *Indianapolis* was out on sea trials, the atomic convoy left Los Alamos. It consisted of a closed black truck, containing a cylinder about eighteen inches in diameter and two feet high, weighing several hundred pounds. Inside was the uranium, shielded by lead. Four cars filled with security men, in civilian clothes, preceded the truck, and three more followed it. In the one behind the truck were Furman and Nolan, off on a high adventure.

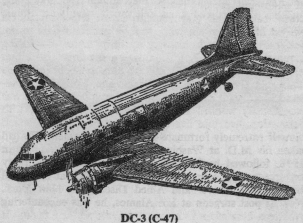

DC-3 (C-47)

Halfway down the mountain, a tire blew on their car, and the whole convoy jarred to a halt while it was changed. Resuming the journey, they passed through Santa Fe and on down to Albuquerque some sixty miles away, where three DC-3s were warming up at Kirtland Field. Furman and Nolan were given parachutes, and climbed in

the center plane along with the bomb, which had its own
chute. Security men climbed into the other two planes,
and they were off and winging. The instructions were
simple—if anything happens to the plane, to hell with the
men, save the uranium.

But the trip was without incident, and soon the
planes touched down at Hamilton Field, outside San Francisco, where another covey of security men swooped down
on them. They had made several dummy runs between
Hamilton Field and Hunters Point, checking traffic lights,
street corners, bridges, and railroad crossings—anything
that might interfere with a swift and safe trip. Two Navy
captains piled in the car with the Army officers and the
bomb, and by Saturday night it was reposing in the commandant's office at Hunters Point. Furman and Nolan
surrendered custody, temporarily, spent the rest of the
evening on liberty, and on Sunday checked in at Army
headquarters, the Presidio, for overseas shots, orders, and
their 45's. Nolan carefully stowed his pistol in one bag
and the shells in another, so they couldn't possibly come
together. He disliked guns, felt much safer with atomic
stuff.

U.S. Pistol, Cal. 45 (M1911A1)

Sunday night they were back at Hunters Point, and
lay down in the duty officer's quarters to catch some sleep.

About 3:00 A.M. Monday, July 16, the PA system on
the *Indianapolis* cleared its throat (you could always tell

something was coming by a sort of preliminary whistle through the speaker) and calmly announced:

"Now hear this. Now hear this. Heads of departments prepare to get under way. First Division work detail lay up to the hangar deck. Sea and anchor detail report to stations."

Curtains swished in officers' country as curiosity overcame dignity and officers bounded into the passageway to find out what was up. In the enlisted men's living compartments, where dignity was never a problem, men rolled out of their sacks with reactions varying from personal outrage through pained surprise to pleasant amazement. As usual, for anything short of a general catastrophe, an occasional man opened a cynical eye like a wise old hound dog and quickly shut it again. A few of the saltiest didn't move. The chiefs quickly took charge and what seemed like chaos was really disordered order.

On the bridge, Captain McVay advised his senior officers that the vessel would be at sea, before morning colors, at high speed for the Forward Area.

"I cannot tell you our mission," he said, "but every hour we save will shorten the war by that much."

Within an hour, he said, top-secret cargo would be brought aboard. Captain Parke would arrange for a Marine guard around the clock for a large crate to be stowed on the starboard hangar deck. Two Army officers would also come aboard and occupy the flag lieutenant's cabin. They would need the services of two shipfitters for a brief time, but were not to be disturbed otherwise. A few more instructions and the officers scattered to carry out their duties.

For once, the yard seemed quiet and deserted. It seemed almost as if the pierside had been cleared. It had. About 4:00 A.M. two Army trucks came alongside, one of them containing a large crate. The other seemed empty, except for a small metal cylinder. In the shadows, a close observer could have seen men in civilian clothes, lounging at the corners of buildings and street entrances. A huge gantry crane waddled down the pier out of the night. Louie DeBernardi, Boatswain's Mate, First Class, of Sacramento, California, leading petty officer of the Fourth Division, took a work party ashore and quickly threw straps around the big crate. The towering gantry easily lifted it aboard and deposited it gently on the hangar deck amidships. Shipfitters quickly secured it to the deck, and a Marine guard surrounded it.

In the excitement—for the crew knew instantly, somehow, that it was top-secret cargo—the men paid little attention to the small cylinder in the other truck. Two sailors slipped a crowbar through a ring on the cylinder, put the bar on their shoulders and carried it up the gangway and into officers' country. A couple of Army officers —more passengers—sauntered behind it. In the flag lieutenant's cabin, unoccupied since all the flag staff were with Spruance at Guam, the ship's first lieutenant, Lieutenant Commander Kyle C. (Casey) Moore, waited with a couple of shipfitters. Under his direction, they welded pad eyes to the deck in the center of the cabin and fitted them with steel straps on hinges. The strange cylinder was placed in the middle, the straps were closed over it. Major Furman secured them with a padlock and dropped the key into his pocket. Everybody left except Furman and Nolan.

Within an hour, of course, scuttlebutt was raging below decks. The big guessing contest opened with entries of everything from money to germs. The officers were not less curious, of course, but more dignified. Some frankly joined in the guessing, others pretended they weren't interested, and a few acted as though they knew.

According to instructions, Captain Nolan went to see Captain McVay as soon as the cargo had been secured. As Captain Parsons had suggested, Captain Nolan told the skipper that he was actually a medical officer, and that the cargo contained nothing dangerous to the ship or crew.

Captain McVay's only comment was: "I didn't think we were going to use B.W. (bacteriological warfare) in this war."

Captain Nolan said nothing.

By 5:30 A.M. there was a hint of dawn and if you had looked to the southeast you might have seen a flash in the heavens. It was gone in the winking of an eye, but it marked the opening of the Atomic Age. It was the Trinity shot at Alamogordo, vaporizing its steel tower and knocking men off their feet at five miles from ground zero. Captain Parsons saw it from a plane circling high over the New Mexico desert, and knew that the *Indianapolis'* trip would not be wasted. Furman and Nolan missed the flash, and there was no one to tell them whether the scientists had hatched a dud or a genie.

At exactly 8:00 A.M., the *Indianapolis* cast off and sailed, with the crew still at morning colors, and at 8:36 she passed under the Golden Gate Bridge, outward bound.

July 16 was an important date, not only for the world but for the *Indianapolis*. On the very day she sailed, another vessel put out to sea, a Japanese submarine, and they had a rendezvous, exactly two weeks hence.

3

As soon as the *Indianapolis* cleared the harbor, Captain McVay rang for full speed and by the time they reached the Farallon Islands, Commander DeGrave had the four screws turning for 29 knots, a very respectable speed for an old girl then nearly thirteen years of age. Coaxed by the engineer gang, the whine of the four geared turbines gradually rose in pitch, and by nightfall the vessel was making very nearly flank speed.

At the end of the day, Commander Janney figured they had made good twenty-eight knots despite a little rough weather, and Captain McVay was pleased.

"She's never been in better shape," he remarked to the navigator. "The men in the yard sure did a wonderful job on the baby."

Because of the hurried departure, the ship was still far from clean and trim, but there was little time for housekeeping now, with all hands standing four and four watches. She was crowded, too, making it difficult to hold the usual drills—antiaircraft firing, abandon ship, man overboard, fire and rescue, and the others. They would have to come later, when there was time for real training.

While the crate on the hangar deck took all other interest, Major Furman worried about his precious cylinder, and after talking with some of the ship's officers decided on several precautions. A life raft was carried up and fastened on the bulkhead in the passageway near Furman's cabin. In an emergency, the can could be lashed to the raft and cast overboard. In addition, they also tried a couple of dry runs on a plan to lug the cylinder to the main deck and lower it over the side into a boat. They couldn't actually lower it into a boat at twenty-eight knots, but that was the plan.

As a final preparation (no one was really serious about this one), they secured a thin line of tremendous length and fixed a buoy to one end, the idea being to attach it to the cylinder to mark the spot in case she sank. A glance at any Pacific chart showed how futile that one was.

On the second day, the weather moderated and the *Indianapolis* picked up speed to twenty-nine knots. Commander DeGrave was mad, and he directed all his ire into the engines. In his pocket were orders beaching him at Pearl Harbor as overage. He had had such orders before and always beat them, but this time they were definite, positive, and above all, final. He would have to get off at Pearl.

Despite the confusion on board, it was arranged to have target practice several times during the voyage. The gunnery officer, Commander Stanley W. Lipski, thought it only good manners to invite his opposite numbers from the Army to join in the fun. Anyway he was curious about Army artillery. So he asked Major Furman and Captain Nolan to be judges of a shooting match among the ship's batteries. Major Furman accepted, with misgivings, but Captain Nolan begged off on the ground that he didn't feel well. This was partly true, since he was a poor sailor, but actually he wouldn't have known a howitzer from a mortar. Nolan went back to his sack, with Furman's blessing, and the latter fast-talked his way through the contest somehow. He was thankful he didn't have to carry Nolan with him. He wanted no more scenes like the one the first day out, when a junior gunnery officer had asked Nolan what caliber guns he dealt with, and Nolan had said "Oh, about this big," and made a circle with his hands.

When the questioner looked puzzled and started to ask about range, muzzle velocity, etc., Furman cut in with "You don't look so hot today, Captain, why don't you go back to the sack?" Nolan was only too glad to, and they decided later the best place for him was in the cabin, sleeping or checking the instruments.

The doctor had brought with him several pocket-pencil ionization chambers, a portable Geiger-Muller counter, and a large ionmeter. The latter had been designed for the Normandy landings and thus was too heavy and bulky to withstand the shocks of combat or immersion. (The Army had anticipated that the Germans might strew the European beaches with harmful isotopes produced in their heavy-water plants.) With these tools, Captain Nolan took frequent readings on the cylinder to be sure that it was not going over-critical. In theory, of course, this was impossible, but this was, after all, a brand new science.

Tuesday was also the day of the fire. During the afternoon, a blaze broke out somewhere forward and great clouds of smoke billowed out of the engineering spaces. As the alarm rang, the bridge brought the *Indianapolis* to emergency back-down and damage-control parties raced below. They soon found the cause—suitcases and handbags stowed near the forward stack had begun to smoulder as the stack heated up under forced draft. A masked and helmeted fire party soon pulled them out and watered down the area with little damage except red faces. It was against standing regulations to bring suitcases aboard, much less stow them in fire-room spaces. But within a half hour the excitement was over and the *Indianapolis* began working back up to full speed.

Captain McVay, ever the gracious host, arranged an inspection tour for his Army guests on Wednesday, and everything went fine until they came to sick bay. The ship's medical officer, Lieutenant Commander Lewis L. Haynes, son of a doctor in Manistee, Michigan, was proud of his hospital and anxious to show it off. Major Furman showed a keen interest and asked many questions, but Captain Nolan hung back and said nothing. Dr. Haynes was nettled; he had had the feeling earlier that Captain Nolan was avoiding him in the wardroom.

"This guy is neither Army nor Artillery," Dr. Haynes thought, looking at the broken artillery clasp dangling on his left collar. "He's probably an FBI man." Back in the cabin later, Nolan told Furman: "I had to keep my mouth shut. I was scared to death I'd drop something technical, and if I'd pretended illness he'd have probably slapped me in his best bed."

That night, the last night out before Pearl, Radarman Third-Class Harold J. Schecterle, twenty-four, of Shelburne Falls, Massachusetts, finally turned himself in to sick bay. His stomach had hurt all day, and now it was getting worse. Within an hour they had him on the table and Dr. Haynes, aided by the assistant medical officer, Lieutenant (j.g.) Melvin W. Modisher, removed his appendix, using a local anesthetic. As he turned away from the table, Dr. Haynes said jokingly, "Okay, Schecterle, you can get up now."

Glancing back a moment later, he was amazed to see the patient swinging his legs over the side of the table. They quickly slapped him into a bed, but his surprising stamina was to be thoroughly tested within the next fortnight.

The next morning at dawn you could see the islands, and promptly at 8:00 A.M. they rounded Diamond Head. After some quick figuring, Commander Janney gave the word to the skipper, a new record of seventy-four and a half hours for the 2,091 miles between Farallon lightship and Diamond Head. The crew went wild when it was blared over the PA system. The mark still stands in the *World Almanac,* replacing the record of seventy-five hours set by the light cruiser *Omaha* in 1932.

But it was not in honor of this achievement that carriers, battleships, and other senior vessels stood aside while the *Indanapolis* steamed directly into the Pearl channel. The way had been cleared from above, and she made directly for Ten-Ten Dock, where fuel and stores were waiting. Passengers, up since 6:00 A.M., were debarked immediately, and Dr. Haynes prepared to send one of his corpsmen ashore for hospitalization. The exec changed that. None of the regular crew would leave the ship here, he said, except for men with orders, such as DeGrave. As for the latter, he didn't like it but he couldn't help it; he went down the gangway for the last time. He couldn't conceive, then, how lucky he was.

Into his spot on the *Indianapolis* went a twenty-seven-year-old reserve, Lieutenant (j.g.) Richard Banks Redmayne, a Yankee from Dedham, Massachusetts. He was an ex-merchant mariner and had considerable sea duty behind him, but here he was, after five months aboard as assistant, now engineering officer of the Fifth Fleet flagship. He was in the engine room at 5:00 P.M. when the bridge rang for steam and off went the *Indianapolis,* straight west for Tinian. The ship was less crowded now with only the regular crew aboard (except those two Army officers), so there was more time for drills.

"My God," thought Captain Nolan, as he put his pillow over his head, "must they fire night and day?"

At Pearl, Captain McVay had been advised that he was ahead of schedule and could reduce speed if he desired. He told Redmayne to make a steady twenty-four knots and the ship settled down to a tense routine, sky and surface watches extra alert, black gang solicitous of boilers, turbines, and shafts. Hour after hour, watch after watch, day after day, the *Indianapolis* plowed westward, her bow cleaving the water cleanly and the wake falling quickly behind. It was perhaps the old girl's finest hour as she sped westward with her vital cargo. The older PO's aboard wished they could see some of those wise guys on the new cruisers now, the ones who sneered and called her the "Swayback Maru." The cruel appellation was nonetheless descriptive, for the cut-away hull amidships (to allow for her catapults and hangars) did give her a definite swayback appearance. She looked like a dignified but aging lady, alongside the sleek lines of the modern flush-deck cruisers, with the big hook aft for recovery of planes.

She had known days of glory since she was commissioned on November 15, 1932, as the first of the *Indianapolis* class (only one other of this class, the *Portland*, was ever built) and the first major naval vessel authorized and completed after the London Treaty of 1929 limiting naval armament. In the innocent days of 1933 (how far away they seemed), she had taken President Roosevelt and a party of friends cruising in the Atlantic during the summer. Later that year Secretary of the Navy Claude A. Swanson was aboard for an "inspection tour of the Pacific," that went all the way to Hawaii, and the next year President Roosevelt reviewed the fleet off New York from her bridge.

Roosevelt was aboard for the last time in 1936, when he made a South American tour. When the war came, the *Indianapolis* was practicing bombardment off Johnston Island, 500 miles southwest of Pearl Harbor, and broke off to search, in vain, for the attacking Japanese fleet. During the war she had served in nearly every corner of the Pacific, bagging a Japanese ammunition ship in the Aleutians, three planes in widely separated actions at Tarawa, Woleai, and Iwo Jima, and six more off Okinawa. At one time or another she had bombarded nearly every enemy stronghold in the Pacific, including the Japanese coast several times. She suffered not a scratch in all that time, until the kamikaze at Okinawa, and now, rebuilt and modernized, she was singing along as good as new. Like most cruisers, she had never had, nor did she have now, any antisubmarine sound-detection gear. Cruisers relied on speed and escort, and while she had no escort now, no submarine could touch her at twenty-four knots.

As the vessel approached Tinian, Captain McVay spent more and more time on the bridge. He was available only to his top officers. Flamboyant or spectacular actions were alien to his personality, but McVay had a good Irish wit and usually appeared cheerful and quiet. Now he seemed almost grim. Men on topside watches could see him on the vessel's open bridge, at any hour and in any weather. From many yards away, old hands aboard could sense that this was not the McVay who went fishing with the enlisted men at Ulithi, or skeet shooting off the fantail in some backwater of the war. It was all business, and he set the tone of his ship.

Soon after daybreak on Thursday, July 26, just ten days and 5,000 miles out of San Francisco, the *Indianapolis* made landfall on Tinian and the dash was nearly over. It was going to be a warm, clear day and the vessel reduced speed as she neared the northeast corner of what was then, and may always stand as, the world's largest aerodrome. Two giant B-29 fields had been carved out on the island in one of the biggest construction jobs on record. Over 8,000,000 cubic yards of fill had been pushed around until the fields contained six main runways, each 8,500 feet long, together with taxiways, hardstands, service aprons, and maintenance buildings. The island, twelve miles long and six miles wide, somewhat resembled Manhattan Island, and the streets had been laid out and named in the same fashion, the avenues running north and south and the numbered streets east and west. From a tanker anchorage at the north end, a submarine pipeline led ashore to a huge tank farm, capable of storing 165,000 barrels of aviation gas, not to mention regular gas and diesel fuel, to keep the B-29 fleets flying.

Tinian had only a small harbor, but the sea was flat and the *Indianapolis* eased in toward shore and dropped the hook about a thousand yards out. This was the moment all hands had been waiting for, and as many as possible crowded topside to see what would happen. They still hoped the secret of the strange cargo might be divulged.

Within a short time, small craft of all kinds were buzzing around the *Indianapolis*, like flies swarming on a cow, and brass of all three services climbed aboard the cruiser. Colonels, commanders, generals, and admirals went aboard to watch the unloading. Not one in a hundred knew what the cargo was, but everyone sensed the excitement. An LCT, flat, low and ugly, waddled alongside, and again Big Nose DeBernardi, boss of the Fourth Division, presided over the deck gang. His buddy, Ed J. (Big Ed) Brown, Seaman First Class, handled the aviation crane and, as at 'Frisco, all eyes centered on the big crate on the hangar deck. Shipfitters cut away the deck fittings, and the crate was gently lowered over the side into the LCT. It was an anticlimax when the small cylinder, freed from its metal prison in the flag lieutenant's cabin, was lugged to the rail. Major Furman and Captain Nolan were right beside it, and the first thing they looked for were the reactions on certain key faces. Broad smiles in the right places told them what they wanted to know— the Alamogordo shot had not been a dud.

As the sailors lowered the bundle of uranium over the side, they got a rousing jeer from the assembled Army and Air Force brass and enlisted men—the wire on the winch was too short, and the cylinder swung at the end of it, a good six feet off the deck of the LCT. Furman and Nolan were doubly amused, thinking back to their elaborate plans of lowering the canister into a raft or boat in case the ship had threatened to go down.

A plane bearing Captain Parsons touched down on one of the air strips as the unloading was completed. He, among the very few who could really appreciate it, was happy to see the *Indianapolis* off shore as he landed. He had just come from Guam, where he had shown films of the Alamogordo shot to an awed and select audience, including Admiral Nimitz and Lieutenant General Curtis LeMay. Now that the momentous cargo was being ferried ashore, Captain Parsons's most important job awaited him. It was he who went along on the *Enola Gay,* with Colonel Tibbets at the controls, as "Bomb Commander and Weaponeer." Captain Parsons, to the honor of the Navy, assembled the bomb while the plane was en route from

Tinian to Hiroshima, and armed it before turning it over to the bombardier for the actual drop. The experts had decided against assembling the bomb before the B-29 took off, for fear it might crash at the end of the runway and blow Tinian right off the map. Captain Parsons's responsibility was a fearful one, absolutely new in the annals of military duty, but he executed it with coolness and efficiency. The Navy, incidentally, also armed the Nagasaki bomb, with Commander Frederick L. Ashworth performing the task this time.

By early afternoon, it was all over. The LCT departed toward shore with the precious cargo, and the military brass departed also, leaving the *Indianapolis* and her crew alone for the first time. For the ship, a small part in history was over, and every man on board felt it. Nobody knew exactly what their mission had been, but they all felt they had accomplished it efficiently. Two weeks later, those pitiful few still alive began to realize just what it was they had done, and it was to give them a good feeling deep inside for the rest of their lives.

As the tension disappeared with the strange cargo, Captain McVay at last looked forward to a chance to begin whipping his ship's company into that combination of efficiency and spirit so vital to a warship. In a few days or weeks, the Flag would come back aboard, and the ship simply was not ready for Admiral Spruance. An austere man, of impeccable taste, the admiral arranged for an hour of classical music to be played over the ship's PA system every afternoon when he was aboard, and not merely for his own enjoyment. His orderly soul would have suffered traumatic shock to see the vessel now—life jackets lying everywhere about the ship, hull and decks crying out for painting and chipping, and living spaces, rigging, and deck gear needing attention. But everyone understood that this would change as soon as real training could start.

And that would not be long, for hardly had the bomb parts been cleared from the ship than Captain McVay received his next assignment, by dispatch from CINCPAC on Guam. Being a warship, the *Indianapolis* did not take orders from local commands. Its movements were controlled, as were the movements of all other combatant ships, from the headquarters of Admiral Nimitz, who was CINCPAC (Commander-in-Chief, Pacific). In rare in-

stances, orders came direct from the Chief of Naval Operations in Washington. The new orders were simple—after
a stop at Guam, proceed to Leyte, on the east coast of the
Philippines, undergo training, and when ready report to
Vice Admiral Jesse B. Oldendorf, Commander Task Force
95 (CTF 95). The dispatch, directed to Captain McVay
for "action," also was addressed to Oldendorf and to Rear
Admiral Lynde D. McCormick, Commander Task Group
95.7 (CTG 95.7), for their "information." Admiral Mc-
Cormick, then in charge of Fifth Fleet training off Leyte,
was instructed to arrange 17 days' training for the *Indianapolis.*

4

And here, precisely, is where things began to go wrong for the *Indianapolis*. Admiral Oldendorf, then off Okinawa, received the dispatch, noted that it required no action from him and gave no dates for the vessel to report to him. Quite properly, the dispatch was received, noted, and filed. The dispatch was received by Admiral McCormick with the address garbled. It was never decoded, nor was a repeat requested, as would have been normal procedure. The dispatch was not addressed to any shore command in the Philippines, neither at Leyte nor at Manila. The first tiny link had been forged in a chain that would lead to the greatest disaster at sea in the history of the United States Navy.

The *Indianapolis* got under way on Thursday night, and arrived in Apra, the harbor of Guam, the following morning, having asked by dispatch that fuel, stores, and ammunition be ready for her. It was her first visit to Apra since she had taken part in the reconquest of the island a year ago. Captain McVay and a small party went ashore.

The captain went immediately to CINCPAC headquarters on a hill overlooking the harbor, and called at the office of Commodore James B. Carter, assistant chief of staff and operations officer. Captain McVay explained he had been out of the Forward Area for three months and inquired where he would get information on current conditions, his sailing orders, and departure date.

"First of all, you will not be routed by this office," he was told. "That is handled by the routing officer, Naval

41

Operating Base, Guam, and we are anxious to get you out to Leyte to have your refresher course, so that you will be ready to embark out Commander Fifth Fleet and his staff."

"Are conditions such that I should leave immediately, or may I sail tomorrow morning after I complete fueling?" Captain McVay asked.

The reply was that there was no particular rush, except to get the refresher training.

"That is handled at Leyte now, you know. We don't handle it here any longer," he was told.

The assignment seemed clear, and the conference was soon over. Captain McVay went over to the officers' mess and met Admiral Spruance and several of his aides for lunch. During the meal Spruance remarked that nothing big was in the wind. He told Captain McVay there was no immediate rush for the vessel, and indicated that after the training period at Leyte he might send the *Indianapolis* around to Manila. Part of the Flag staff might be there then, he said, and they could use the ship until he was ready to embark.

The admiral and his staff were busy on two projects —plans for the invasion of Kyushu, set for November, and plans for the Japanese surrender. Spruance, never a very sentimental man (many thought him cold and unapproachable), had picked the *Indianapolis* as his flagship for sound reasons—she had adequate quarters for his staff, she had speed enough to keep up with the fast carriers, and she was not too valuable to risk in amphibious operations. He was aware, of course, that she was a "tender" ship, or, as the engineers say, she had a small metacentric height. In plain language that meant it wouldn't take much water inside the hull to capsize her. But this, and the fact that she had no sound-detection gear were of small concern since she was always in company with other ships when the Flag was aboard.

As he was leaving the building after lunch, Captain McVay ran into an old buddy, Captain Edwin M. Crouch, Annapolis '21, now Director of the Maintenance Division, Bureau of Ordnance, Washington. While they talked, Captain Crouch remarked that he was flying over to Leyte in a few days for temporary duty.

"Fine, why don't you come along with me?" Captain

McVay asked. "We're leaving tomorrow and I'll have you there by Tuesday. And what's more, I'll give you my cabin."

"That suits me a damn sight better than flying, Charlie," Captain Crouch said. "I've got some notes I want to work up anyway. I'll be aboard by tonight." He was.

Captain McVay went down to the Naval Operating Base near the harbor and dropped in to see the convoy and routing officer, Lieutenant Joseph J. Waldron, USNR, who turned him over to a couple of aides, Lieutenant R. C. Northover and Ensign William I. Renoe. They quickly got down to business; Northover asked McVay when he would like to leave and what speed he would like to make.

"I'm a little surprised at the questions," McVay replied. "I haven't been in the Forward Area in over three months, and I don't know the conditions out here. The 16-knot speed limit is still on, isn't it?"

Northover said he didn't know. As a matter of fact, it was. As a fuel conservation measure (every barrel of oil had to be brought thousands of miles) no vesesel was allowed to make over 16 knots unless there was a good reason for it. Captain McVay said he would like to arrive off Homonhon Island, at the entrance to Leyte Gulf, early in the morning so the crew could get some gunnery practice on the way in. He would request tractor planes to come out to meet him towing sleeve targets.

Figuring backward, it was clear that a two-day trip would require 25 knots or better, while a three-day trip could be made at about 15.7 knots, average speed over all. There was little latitude for decision. To take care of the fleet order limiting speed to 16 knots and daylight arrival for gunnery practice, a three-day passage at 15.7 knots was arranged.

There was only one other question—escort, and that was quickly disposed of.

"I will ask for one for you, but I do not believe there is one available," Lieutenant Waldron said.

He rang up the office of Vice Admiral George Dominic Murray, Commander Marianas, and the answer was quick: "No escort necessary." Waldron was a little nettled, because he knew one was not "necessary"; what he had asked was whether one was "available." He had in mind, of course, if other vessels were going that way, it could be arranged for them to travel in company.

Waldron asked his question again, and this time the answer was made with a little more asperity: "You know very well an escort is not necessary." Waldron rang off, his question still unanswered. The *Indianapolis* would travel alone.

The escort question aroused some pretty bitter discussion later in civilian circles, but from a command standpoint in the Pacific the pattern was quite well established. The line behind which vessels might travel without escort was now far north of Guam. That is what Admiral Murray's office meant when Waldron was told an escort was "not necessary," using the expression in the sense of "required." But escort would not have been prohibited, either. The question was a local one, to be answered on the basis of escorts available and assignments required.

The Navy was heavily committed in support of the Air Force in the giant Superfort raids on Japan. Ships and men were strung out northward toward Japan, to rescue any cripples that splashed, and it was paying off. In the early days, nearly a hundred men a month were being lost; now in this month of July only forty-seven fly boys were lost for 6,536 sorties. In addition, men and supplies were being convoyed up to Okinawa for the invasion build-up. Down in the area where the *Indianapolis* would travel, merchant ships, baby carriers, tankers, and other vessels of that nature were often escorted. Cruisers? Sometimes.

There were still thousands of Japanese soldiers "withering on the vine" in the Marshalls, the Carolines, and the Philippines, but no Japanese warships or supply vessels were coming down anymore to attempt rescue or reinforcement. The homeland itself was in peril now.

Commander Janney arrived at the routing office shortly after Captain McVay had left and Lieutenant Waldron told him of the arrangements. Janney was told to use Course Peddie (all courses in this area were named after prep schools), the course in normal use at that time. It was virtually a straight line from Guam to Leyte. There were other, more devious routes, but they were rarely used in these late days of the war.

Routing instructions ordered the vessel to leave Apra Harbor at 9:00 A.M. on Saturday, proceed at 15.7 knots SOA and arrive in Leyte Gulf at 11:00 A.M. on Tuesday.

The trip was figured at 1,171 miles, and the vessel was "to zigzag at discretion of the Commanding Officer."

Janney also received the usual "Intelligence Report." This advised that Japanese forces were still holding the islands of Rota, Woleai, Sorol, Yap, and Babelthuap. Rota was north of Guam, and the others were far south in the Carolines and Palaus, and in any event the report said "no enemy activity from any of these bases has been reported in recent months. . . ."

The only entry of any import was the following:

"Enemy submarine contacts:

"22 July—Sub sighted surfaced at 10:34N-132:47E at 0015K. Hunter-killer ordered.

"25 July—Unknown ship reports sighting a possible periscope at 13:56N-136:56E at 0800K.

"25 July—Sound contact reported at 10:30N-136:25E. Indications at that time pointed to a doubtful submarine."

Certainly nothing there to worry a battle-tested warship. The July 22 report was now six days old, and by the time the *Indianapolis* reached the given location, over 700 miles from Guam, it would be eight days old. Even though the spot was only 72 miles south of Course Peddie, the fact that a hunter-killer group (destroyers or destroyer-escorts) had been ordered out was further grounds for reassurance. It should be noted that the alleged sighting was in the dead of night, fifteen minutes past midnight.

The "possible periscope" reported by an "unknown ship" on July 25 was about 500 miles from Guam and 95 miles north of the *Indianapolis'* route. The vagueness of the report, plus the fact that the *Indianapolis* would pass the spot four days later, in broad daylight, gave little cause for worry. The reported "sound contact" on the "doubtful submarine" of the third report was 105 miles south of Course Peddie. Again the *Indianapolis* would pass in daylight on Sunday. Commander Janney had already received this intelligence earlier by radio from Guam, and neither he nor Waldron attached any undue importance to it. Such reports, usually by alarmed merchant skippers, were as common as rain squalls and, experience had shown, about as important.

Janney returned to the ship, and when he met Captain McVay later, the skipper asked:

"Anything unusual in the intelligence report, Jack?"

"No, sir," Janney replied. "The three contacts they have we already know about, and they're just the usual kind."

Everybody on board felt pretty good that night. Fuel and stores were all aboard, there was a movie on the quarterdeck, and mail for nearly everyone. Mailman First Class John M. Potter, aboard the *Indianapolis* nearly five years, worked overtime getting out the mail, with the added chore of breaking in Mailman Third Class F. W. Peterson, who had just come aboard a month ago. As the letters were sorted, petty officers from each division were summoned to the mail room to pick them up for final distribution to outstretched hands.

Seaman Second Class Joseph E. J. Dronet from Cameron, Louisiana, hit the jackpot, with letters from his mother, his girl friend, and all four brothers in service, one on a can in the Pacific, the others in the Army in Italy, France, and England. Joe worried most about his mother, because he knew she was taking it kind of hard, with five boys overseas. But she sounded pretty cheerful.

The movie wasn't bad, and in fact had one outstanding virtue—most of the boys had never seen it before. And it was pleasant to watch it on the open deck for a change, in the cool of the evening. The inside of the ship was still like a hotbox from the summer sun, and even after the movie most of the men stayed topside, sleeping on cots or mattresses. Lying on your back you could watch a billion stars overhead, and think about the end of the war, or maybe liberty in Manila. Sweet dreams, sailor boy, you've only forty-eight hours more.

5

At 9:10 A.M. on Saturday, July 28, the *Indianapolis* dropped her moorings and steamed out of Apra harbor, bound for Leyte. There was none of the mystery or tension of the San Francisco sailing, and the aging vessel was soon making turns for a comfortable 16 knots. All hands turned to and began to put the vessel into condition to rejoin the fleet.

Soon after she cleared the harbor, the port director's office at Guam sent the following dispatch:

To: SCOMA/PD Tacloban/CTG 95.7

PMB-5 Mariner

Info: Com 5th Fleet/ComMarianas/CTF 95/ComPhilSeaFron/CINCPAC/ComWestCarolines

U.S.S. *Indianapolis* (CA 35) departed Guam 2300Z 27 July. SOA 15.7 knots. Route Peddie then Leyte. ETA position Peter George 2300Z 30 July. ETA Leyte 0200Z 31 July. Chop 30 July.

Translated, this meant the message was addressed, for "action," to the shipping control officer, Marianas Area, Port Director at Tacloban, Leyte, and Rear Admiral McCormick, Commander of Task Group 95.7, then off Leyte. The message was also addressed, for "information," to Admiral Spruance, Commander of the Fifth Fleet; Vice Admiral Murray, Commander of Marianas Area; Vice Admiral Oldendorf, Commander of Task Force 95, then off Okinawa; Commodore Norman C. Gillette, Acting Commander of the Philippine Sea Frontier, with headquarters at Tolosa, Leyte; Commander in Chief, Pacific; and the Commander of Western Carolines.

The message body would read:

"U.S.S. *Indianapolis* departed from Guam at 9:00 A.M. July 28. Speed over all 15.7 knots. Route Peddie then to Leyte. Expected time of arrival off Leyte Gulf 8:00 A.M. July 31. Expected time of arrival at Leyte 11:00 A.M. July 31. Will cross dividing line (chop line) between Marianas Area and Philippine Sea Frontier Area July 30." (The time specified was, of course, local to the area.)

In other words, the "action" addressees were the control area *from* which Captain McVay was going, the control area *to* which he was going, and the command to which he was to report (Admiral McCormick). A perfectly routine dispatch, and a simple, foolproof system— or so it would seem. Let's see.

Sunday broke overcast and there was a small chop on the sea, but the morning passed as usual on the *Indianapolis*—no work till after the noon meal, morning church service on the fantail, and no smoking about the ship until the services were over. Lieutenant T. M. Conway, a young parish priest from Buffalo, celebrated Mass first, then rang in Doc Haynes and a couple of other officers to help him with the hymns for the Protestant service. Later some said church attendance seemed better than usual that morning, but there is no reason to suppose it was. There was no feeling of foreboding about the ship. The war was far off to the north, and nothing of any consequence had occurred in these waters in months.

Around noon, the *Indianapolis* raised an LST waddling along to the north, and Lieutenant Commander Kenneth I. Stout, the communications officer, gave the order to call her on the TBS. The LST reported she was heading further north to get out of the ship lanes in order to do some antiaircraft firing. The conversation was squawky and short, and the LST rang off. She was the last friendly vessel ever to see the *Indianapolis*.

On Sunday afternoon, Drs. Haynes and Modisher set up shop in the after mess hall and began giving the crew their first round of cholera shots. The war was moving close to the China coast and there was always the possibility of a beachhead there. All the corpsmen worked through the afternoon, under the two Chief Pharmacist's Mates, Lloyd A. Watts and John A. Schmueck. They were none too happy, either, because they had wanted the afternoon to study for rating exams the next day. But the shots had to be given, and this lull might be the last opportunity, so the jabbing went on all afternoon, one division after another lining up for the inevitable.

During the afternoon the weather deteriorated, and by the time Lieutenant (j.g.) Charles B. McKissick took the watch on the bridge at 6:00 P.M. the sea was choppy to rough, and visibility only fair. McKissick, a young Texan, had been standing OOD watches only a few months, but there was certainly nothing unusual about this one. As per custom, he stopped off at CIC on the way to the bridge to see if there was anything he should know. There wasn't.

When he took the watch, the ship was zigzagging on course 262 True, or nearly directly west, riding easy with no strain. Half the boilers were on the line—Nos. 1 and 2 in the forward fire room, and Nos. 7 and 8 in the after fire room. The screws were making "staggering turns," in order to confuse enemy-listening devices. Under this procedure, the forward engine room was making about 167 turns per minute on the two outboard screws, while the after engine room made about 157 turns on the inboard shafts. This averaged out to 162 turns, the indicated rate for 15.7 knots, and produced a choppy pattern for anyone who might be eavesdropping on sound phones.

McKissick found on the bridge what later became

known as the *"Wild Hunter* message." The vessel of that
name, bound for Manila with Army cargo, had reported
the previous afternoon sighting a periscope at 10 degrees,
25 minutes North, 131 degrees, 45 minutes East. This position was some 75 miles south of the track the *Indianapolis*
would follow sometime on Monday. *Wild Hunter,* Captain Anton Wie commanding, sent two messages, the first
at 4:20 P.M. reporting the sighting, and a second 28 minutes later saying she had sighted the periscope "again and
fired on same." The sixty-year-old skipper, who had his
first command in 1914 and had been a master steadily for
the past eighteen years, put his stern to the scope to reduce
the target. The Armed Guard put a few shots toward
the sub, some 2,000 to 2,200 yards away, and it disappeared. All this was duly reported to Guam, and there re-
transmitted for all ships in the area. A routine reporting,
like dozens of others made daily. Not one in a thousand
led to anything more complicated.

Neither McKissick nor anyone else felt any alarm at
the report. In fact, that night at dinner in the wardroom
some of the officers were joking about it. Just a brief
laugh, soon over—but later it appeared as the words of a
prophecy.

"We're going to pass a Jap sub around midnight,"
said Commander Janney, the navigator.

And his favorite bridge partner cracked right back:
"Oh well, our destroyers will take care of that."

Not a huge joke, but relished for a moment in view of
the fact that there wasn't a destroyer within hundreds of
miles. Some of the old-timers were even a little proud of
the "Indy Maru," which had often traveled unescorted in
waters that were really dangerous.

After dining in his cabin with Captain Crouch, Captain McVay went to the bridge several times during the
evening. He was never very far from the bridge, and the
watch-standers knew it. They knew it not in fear, for he
was not a hard master. They knew he expected them to
stand an alert watch, but that he was available in case of
trouble. A captain is never out of command when he's
afloat. Captain McVay knew this so well he never even
thought of it. His philosophy was very simple—pick the
best officers you can, train them well, give them authority,
but never cast them adrift. There wasn't a junior officer

on board who feared McVay—he did not want it that
way. He wanted respect, and he got it, but the greenest
ensign aboard would not hesitate to ask his advice. That,
too, was as McVay desired it.

During one of his trips to the bridge, Captain McVay
remarked to McKissick, "You may secure from zigzagging
after twilight," and the OOD responded, "Aye, aye, sir."
It was as simple as that. A decision as routine as rising or
going to bed, yet had he not given it his whole life might
have been changed. It would not have changed the events
then impending in any manner, but within five months it
became Charge I, Specification I, in the only court-martial
in the history of the U.S. Navy of a commanding officer
for loss of his vessel in wartime.

"Aye, aye, sir," McKissick said, and he knew what
the order meant. It meant, "If it's a dark night, and it
appears that it will be, there is no need to zigzag. Naturally, if conditions change, I expect you to notify me, and I
know you will." That was the code of the ship. Orders
often had been modified to fit changing circumstances, and
the captain notified immediately. He slept only a few paces
off the bridge.

So when the time came, McKissick gave the order,
"Secure from zigzagging," and the vessel resumed straight
course at 262 degrees True. McKissick, off watch, went
below to catch the movie in the wardroom. The enlisted
men were watching movies on the hangar deck, for
that was one of the first orders McVay issued on taking
command—no movies for the officers unless the enlisted
men had them, too. This had not always been true, and the
men respected McVay for it.

The fleet orders on zigzagging were very simple—
zigzag during good visibility, day or night. In Captain
McVay's sailing orders, this had been reduced to the single
sentence, "Zigzag at discretion of the commanding officer."

Zigzagging is a tiresome business of questionable
value. Old salts like to argue the question far into the
night, with plenty of evidence on either side—ships sunk
because they were zigzagging, ships sunk because they
weren't. Japan's newest and largest aircraft carrier, the
Shinano, was outdistancing the U.S. submarine *Archerfish*
when suddenly she zigged, the wrong way—right toward

the sub. *Archerfish* promptly sank her on November 28, 1944, off the coast of Japan. But the zigzag order was on the books; the only subjective question was, what is "good visibility"? The court would decide that.

When McKissick turned over the watch, he left it in good hands. Commander Lipski, the gunnery officer, took over as supervisor of the watch. Everybody like Lipski, a thirty-four-year-old Annapolis man, because of his competence and good humor. He had been aboard over two years, and his shipmates knew he had put up a battle to get away from a desk. He was an expert in the Russian language, and before the war had been naval attaché in Helsinki, Finland. Naval Intelligence had wanted to keep him in Washington, but he finally escaped. On the bridge with him were Lieutenant Redmayne, the new engineering officer, and Lieutenant (j.g.) K. I. MacFarland, Lipski's Turret II officer. He was OOD and Redmayne was taking instruction as supervisor of the watch. Quartermaster Third Class Vincent J. Allard, aboard since 1942 and now serving under his fifth skipper, was quartermaster of the watch.

About 8:30, Commander Janney came out on the bridge with the night orders. They were the usual thing—course, speed, all submarines were to be considered enemy, any contacts, visual or radar, and any changes in weather or sea to be reported to the captain. The navigator had one other piece of information to impart.

"We have a report that a PBM and a DDE are searching for an enemy submarine ahead of us. We should pass the position at 8:00 A.M. tomorrow," Janney said.

No one on the bridge was any more concerned than had been those who heard Janney tell the same story at dinner. In fact, no one even worked up a feeble joke about it.

Visibility was poor during the early part of the watch, so bad that Allard could hardly make out his strikers, the boatswain's mate of the watch, or the messengers, unless he stood looking down their throats. The moon rose about 10:30, but it was not visible for another half hour or so, and then only intermittently. When Allard made his entries in the deck log, he noted there were alto-stratus clouds at medium altitude and cirro-stratus at high. He filled in nothing for "low," but where it said "total amount of sky covered, in tenths," he entered "six." Stars were dimly visible through the overcast.

As the watch wore on, visibility improved, and as the moon rose higher behind the ship, it was good in the moments when the clouds parted. It wasn't much of a moon, at that, being two days before the last quarter and just a little more than half of it illuminated. It was an easy watch, as shipboard watches go. Lipski and Redmayne were congenial, and MacFarland was quietly competent. There was the usual talk about the past and the future, very little about the present.

There was only one minor incident. Metalsmith Second Class John Anunti, on deck patrol from ten to midnight, made his first round and found everything secure—no lights showing, no gear adrift, all ports, doorways, and hatches secure. All those that should be, that is. On a ship that old and crowded (nearly twice her peacetime complement), you couldn't close all vents—the men below decks would have stifled. For example, all watertight doors on the second deck were open. Everybody knew that, right up to the Bureau of Ships, but there was nothing practical to be done about it.

As it was, hundreds of men lugged cots, mattresses, and blankets topside every night, preferring to sleep in wind or rain on the open deck rather than in the inferno below. In July, barely twelve degrees above the equator, the ship never cooled off, even at night. Anunti, on his second round, picked his way among the sleeping men, exchanged unprintables with dark figures standing lookout or gun watches, and eventually leaned over the rail amidships to watch the sea coursing by the hull. The phosphorus stirred up in the water made fascinating lights. Glancing forward, Anunti noticed light streaming from an open porthole, starboard side, far forward in officers' country.

He immediately reported it to Central, and made his way forward. It wasn't hard to find the source. Coming down the passageway he could hear laughter and loud banter from one of the aviator's rooms. Three fly boys were inside, with Sikes and Park doing most of the talking, and Malone most of the listening. Ensign D. A. Park, a tall, friendly lad, had been aboard for a year and this bull session was in the nature of a welcome back for T. A.

Sikes. Once an enlisted man aboard the "Indy," he had
qualified for pilot training, made the grade, and returned
to his ship only a month before, a brand new ensign.
Anunti knew them all, of course, and they took it in good
style when he told them, "You'd better secure that port
right away, the light's showing through. And you'd better
knock off the noise."

That's all there was to it, really. No harm done—or
was there? Was there, maybe, a Jap sub out there, lining
up torpedo tubes on that light?

Down below, in Damage Control, Ensign John Woolston had the duty. Here was a young man in a hurry. Entering MIT when he had just turned seventeen, he graduated three years later with a Bachelor of Science in Naval
Architecture and Marine Engineering. He went directly
into Midshipman's School at Cornell, was commissioned
in March, 1945, got married a month later, attended the
Navy's Salvage and Firefighting School, and reported
aboard the *Indianapolis* on May 2.

Woolston liked the ship from the start. He'd been
aboard her when he was a boy in Seattle and the *Indianapolis*, then young and new, had visited Bremerton. Now
on this night, two whole weeks of sea duty behind him
and his twenty-first birthday two weeks ahead, Woolston
had found the *Indianapolis* a taut ship and he was proud to
be aboard.

Damage Control was manned from dusk to dawn
with two men in Central and five repair parties scattered
about the ship—Repair 1 topside, Repair 2 and 3 below
decks, one fore and the other aft, and Repair 4 and 5 in
the engineering spaces. Woolston had the watch Sunday
night from dusk to midnight, and he was a bear for efficiency. Besides making regular rounds of the ship himself,
he had men reporting in to him by phone at intervals. As
he proved later, he knew every hatch, scuttle, and opening
on the ship, a remarkable feat in less than three months
aboard.

There's something kind of friendly about a big ship
at night. Darkened down inside, and relatively quiet after
the day's work, the ship takes on a warm hum from the
machinery, and the rolling motion of the water makes it
seem like a somnolent giant, plodding steadily forward.
Watch-standers going on or coming off slip silently through

the semidarkness, careful not to step on sleeping figures sprawled everywhere. Occasionally, in a blaze of light in some far corner, a quietly intense crap game or maybe a bull session goes on—while there is always the smell of coffee brewing behind the next door.

Woolston prowled the ship a good deal at night. He liked these sights and sounds and smells, and besides he had a lot to think about, including his pregnant bride at home. On trips along the open deck, he always looked up, for he was young and the tropic sky is a splendrous thing. This night there were only occasional stars to be seen through the overcast, but on his last round the moon flitted now and then from behind the clouds. The weather was definitely clearing.

As a naval architect, Ensign Woolston could not approve of the *Indianapolis*. She was a peacetime ship, and strongly built, but without the value of four years' experience in modern war. Everyone concerned knew her shortcomings, but there wasn't much to be done about it—short of scrapping or redesigning from her keel up. The only thing left was to make the best of it. For cruising, she used what was called Condition Yoke Modified. The "modified" meant it would be as near Yoke as practical. The entire main deck was open inside, all doors in the second deck were open, and in fact just about every door on the ship below decks was open, excepting dead spaces and storage. For those who like grisly thoughts, it was not hard to imagine that if water ever got inside the hull it could flow readily to the engineering spaces. If that happened, the ship would fill like a bucket and sink swiftly.

Lieutenant R. H. Hurst, the assistant damage control officer, was standing watch with Woolston that night. Hurst had come aboard three weeks after Woolston and was doing his best to familiarize himself with the ship. Woolston was eager to help him, and they got along well. As midnight neared, they were happy to see Boatswain S. A. Spencer show up to relieve them. Hurst went to his room, and Woolston went up to the wardroom for a cup of coffee before turning in.

After the speed run ended at Tinian, there was no longer any need to keep all four firerooms going, so No. 2 was secured. Watertender Wilcox, the twenty-year-old Texan, was glad of this because it threw him on the 8:00 P.M.

to midnight watch in No. 1, instead of the midnight to 4:00 A.M. At least you could get a little sleep on that watch. So at midnight, he picked up his sack, carried it to the port hangar, and turned in.

Ray Brooks took charge of the watch in No. 1 fireroom. Ulysses Ray Brooks, Chief Watertender, had been aboard this bucket since a week before Pearl Harbor, and it was home to him. Among the other five CWT's, Robert T. Makowski held the record. In just ten days he would celebrate five years aboard. Brooks found everything in order on setting the watch, and settled down with half-a-dozen ratings to keep steam on the line from the two boilers. Wilcox had a lot of friends on that watch, but this night he didn't stop to chew the fat. He headed straight topside for a breath of fresh air. Lucky Wilcox!

The watches started changing all over the ship from around 11:30 on. Some guys were always early to relieve, others had to be blasted from their sacks when they didn't show on time. Tonight was a bad night for the sack warmers.

On the bridge, the first reliefs were showing up by 11:40 P.M. McVay had turned in about eleven. Earlier he had dropped down to his regular cabin to talk with Captain Crouch, and left there a little after 9:00 P.M. to return to the bridge. From then on, he was on the bridge frequently, talking with Lipski and the other officers, watching the weather, checking to see if the lookouts were alert. The best of them tended to doze off at times, on this dullest of all routines.

Visibility was so poor the watch officers remarked on it. McVay was out on the bridge at 10:30, when the moon rose. It was not visible. Just before 11:00, Captain McVay looked over the night orders written out for him by Commander Janney. They were as usual—steaming on course 262 True, speed 16 knots, antiaircraft condition set, ship in material Condition Yoke Modified, engine plan split, steaming on boilers 1 and 2, 7 and 8, the captain to be notified of any change in weather or anything on the radarscope. At one point the orders read, "Call me in case of doubt." There was a voice tube at his ear in his bunk.

Captain McVay signed his orders and gave them to Commander Lipski. There was nothing specific in them about resuming zigzagging if the weather cleared, nor did

McVay mention this to Lipski. The question just did not arise in view of the clouded skies. McVay went to his emergency cabin behind the bridge and lay down in his favorite sleeping costume—nothing. With Lipski on watch and Casey Moore relieving him for the midwatch, the ship would be in good hands.

6

Lieutenant Commander Moore had been aboard three years. A newspaperman from Knoxville, Tennessee, he had taken to the sea like an old salt, and had been standing top watch for over a year. Counting the other officers, coxswain, quartermaster, helmsman, messengers, bugler and such, there were thirteen men on the bridge for that watch. Just three, all enlisted men, were to survive. Casey Moore had with him Lieutenant John I. Orr as OOD; Lieutenant (j.g.) P. I. Candalino, aide to Commander Flynn, as Junior OOD, and Ensign Paul T. Marple. Both Orr and Candalino had been aboard only since April, and Marple only a few weeks. But Jack Orr, at least, was a seasoned officer. He had been at sea three years, and just before coming to the *Indianapolis* had served on the destroyer U.S.S. *Cooper* (DD695), torpedoed and sunk in Ormoc Bay. He for one knew war was no game. Marple was on the bridge for experience and was, as they called him, "Gentleman officer of the Watch."

Sky Amidships was a sort of rumble-seat watch. Perched on the open deck behind the gently fuming after stack, one had a good view over the ship and the water. Just forward, were the archaic tripod mast (not many of them left in the Navy) supporting the radar antenna—revolving like a vertical bedspring—range and truck lights, radio and direction-finder antennas. At the base of the stack, on either side, were cranes for recovering the planes. There weren't many old-style cruisers left like this,

58

that carried their planes pocketed amidships like a kanga-
roo. The new-style flush-deck cruisers had a big hook aft
for recovery. In any event, the cruiser's old role of scout-
ing and spotting was being taken over increasingly by the
baby carriers. The cranes and hangars amidships were
passing from the fleet, but their appearance on the *Indianapolis* was partly responsible for her derisive nickname,
the "Swayback Maru."

Lieutenant (j.g.) L. J. Clinton had the 8:00 to 12:00
watch in Sky Amidships, along with Ensign Harlan M.
Twible, fresh out of the Academy and the last officer to
come aboard. When the relief did not show, Lieutenant
Clinton went below to check on them. Twible stayed
topside and was thus to escape injury. Clinton was never
seen again.

On the bridge, the watch began to settle down. Jack
Orr checked his course and speed, Casey Moore strolled
around the open navigation bridge and found all watch-
standers on duty. The moon was appearing more often
now, and was a little brighter, but at times it was difficult
to make out faces on the bridge and impossible to see far
out over the water. Just after midnight, the bugler of the
watch, Donald F. Mack, went into the chart house to see
the quartermaster, Jimmy French. French's striker, Seaman First Class William F. Emery, was also in there.

Suddenly, there was a tremendous blast forward, followed by a sheet of red-yellow flame and a giant column
of water rising higher than the bridge. The ship shuddered
and a few seconds later came a second blast, much nearer
the bridge, much more violent, louder and more terrifying.
For a split second after the second blast there was utter
silence, except for the swish of water and the hum of
turbines.

Nearly everyone on the bridge was thrown to the
deck by the first blast, then dashed again to the deck or
bulkhead by the second explosion. Within seconds, the ship
roused to life in a massive reflex action. For an instant
there was pandemonium, but no panic. There is always
something unbelievable about your ship taking a hit. As
in everyday life, things happen to the other fellow, not to
you. The first reaction is one of sheer surprise, tinged
with disbelief and perhaps resentment and the beginnings
of anger. But—and here is where training pays off—most

men snapped quickly to defense posture and began automatically to perform the tasks assigned for just such an emergency.

There was no panic on the bridge. Casey Moore raced to the splinter shield and peered forward in the murk. The bow seemed oddly down, and he could make out smoke and a few figures moving about on the deck. Orr steadied the helmsman, and the JV talker. Seaman First Class A. C. King, picked himself up from a maze of wires and put his phones back on his head. The bosun's mate of the watch, Coxswain Edward H. Keyes, went mechanically to the public-address box, whistled a test pipe down it and found it dead. The blue lamp on the control panel would never glow again. King raised nobody on his phones, and Keyes told Orr, "Everything is dead on the sound system, sir."

"Go below and pass the word 'All hands topside,'" Orr shouted, drawing both consciously and subconsciously on his recent experience with the sinking destroyer in Ormoc Bay. The fatal thud of torpedoes was familiar to him now.

After his first look around, Casey Moore reacted like any good damage-control officer. He sprinted to the ladder and went below to have a look.

Captain McVay's emergency cabin was port side at the back of the house built on the navigation deck, with the door facing aft. He awoke with a start at the first blast, and it flashed through his mind that a second kamikaze had found the target. The second blast threw him out of bed, and as he hit the deck it occurred to him that this was not kamikaze territory. Must be mines, or torpedoes, or internal explosion. Acrid white smoke was already seeping into his cabin, and as he went out on deck he noticed it there, too. Stark naked, he made his way around to the bridge.

"Do you have any reports?" he called to Orr.

"No, sir," the OOD replied. "I have lost all communications. I have tried to stop the engines. I don't know whether the order has ever gotten through to the engine room."

"I will send down word to get out a distress message," Captain McVay said. He was not alarmed. The ship had no list as yet, and this was not his first experience with battle damage. They had saved the ship before and they could do it again.

As he turned back to get his clothes, he told Orr, "See what information you can get."

McVay quickly picked up pants, shirt, and shoes and returned to the bridge, dressing as he went. As he reached the bridge, things began to happen pretty fast. For one thing, strange noises sounded from below, and strange noises on a ship usually mean trouble.

Casey Moore came back just then from his first quick look around, and reported the damage was severe.

"Most of the forward compartments are flooding fast," he said, "and there are no repair parties there. Do you want to abandon ship?"

"No," McVay replied, "our list is still slight. I think we can hold her. Go below and check again."

Moore left the bridge, but he never returned.

The whole ship was beginning to strain and groan in a way never intended.

"Have you any word from the radio room yet on whether they've gotten off a message?" the captain asked Orr.

"No, sir, no word yet."

The ship was definitely slowing down, and the bow was low and acting queerly. It seemed to plunge head on into the seas instead of rising with them. The list was only about three degrees to starboard.

Jack Janney appeared from his cabin, on the starboard side, exactly opposite McVay's. Captain McVay sent him to the radio shack, to get the distress message out.

"Send a message saying we have been hit, give our latitude and longitude, say we are sinking rapidly and need immediate assistance," Captain McVay told him. Janney went down the ladder, never to return.

No sooner had he left the bridge than Commander Flynn came up the ladder.

"We've been badly damaged, Charlie," he said. "We're taking water fast. The bow is down. I think we are finished. I recommend we abandon ship."

Captain McVay had been coming to the same conclusion himself. He could not see from the bridge, with flame and smoke pouring up from the foredeck, but there is a feel about a ship. She was acting most strangely, and she seemed to be almost totally without lights and power, a sure warning of mortal damage in the belly. All he needed was the opinion of a man of Joe Flynn's experience and judgment.

"Okay, pass the word to abandon ship," McVay said. Flynn left the bridge for the last time.

Not many skippers have to give the command "Abandon ship!" It is a fateful command, yet when it must be given there is no time for reflection. That time comes later, perhaps.

The captain's biggest worry was whether or not word had gotten out. Unescorted as they were, and 300 miles from the nearest land, it was vital that someone know of their plight. Not a single dispatch had been sent from the ship since she left Guam, nor had any been addressed to her, and it was another 36 hours before she was expected in Leyte. The potentialities for disaster were great, considering that the *Indianapolis* carried only two small boats.

Now that the command had been given, McVay wanted to be sure someone knew they were in trouble. None of his messengers had returned from the radio shack, so the captain decided to go himself. For all its benign look and air of tropical romance, it was not a friendly sea. Besides a probable enemy out there, who had been known to machine-gun helpless men, the ocean had its own perils. Shark, barracuda, and other strange and rapacious fish abounded, the sun and salt could be vicious enemies. Nor was there any hope of atolls or reefs, for the water here was some of the deepest in the world. It was imperative that someone know they were in serious trouble.

As McVay started for the ladder, Captain Crouch came up from below.

"Charlie, have you got a spare life preserver?" he asked.

"Yes, I have," the skipper replied, and stepped into his cabin to pick up a pneumatic type.

"Blow this up for Captain Crouch," he said, as he tossed it to an enlisted man, and he crossed over the bridge. That was the last time he saw Crouch. As McVay put his hand to the ladder leading down, the ship took a great lurch to starboard, going over to about sixty degrees. For a moment he clung to the ladder, then slid down to the signal bridge. The vessel paused for a moment in her roll, but it was obvious that McVay would never reach the radio room.

He looked to port and saw several men struggling to get to the lifelines.

"Don't go over the side unless you have a life jacket," he roared. "I think she may stay here a minute or two. Get the floater nets against the stack."

From above, Lieutenant Orr, still clinging to the splinter shield, cried, "That's the captain talking; get the floater nets."

But within thirty seconds the tired old ship rolled full ninety degrees to her starboard side. Now the bulkheads were horizontal and the decks vertical. McVay grabbed the communications deck lifelines, now above him, pulled himself up, walked across the bulkhead and pulled himself up another step to the side of the ship. There he stood for a moment, upright on her side, staring down at the vast expanse of red bottom.

He walked slowly aft, thinking she still might stay afloat. But he had gone only a few steps when the bow of the vessel began to sink. The water line advanced gently along the hull, and in a moment it washed him off. It was only twelve minutes since the first blast had ended his sleep.

Bugler First Class Donald F. Mack and the messenger of the watch were batting the breeze in the chart house when the blasts threw them in a heap. Mack scrambled up, retrieved his bugle, and started through the light-lock door to the bridge. The outer door was partly jammed, but Mack wormed his way out and found the quartermaster's desk had been thrown against it. A couple of men wrestled it back into place, and Mack turned to Lieutenant Orr.

"Bugler of the watch reporting, sir."

"Aye, aye," Orr acknowledged. "Stand by."

Orr turned to his JV talker and said, "Try the engine room again, and see if you can raise anybody." In the next breath, he ordered the messenger of the watch to go below to the after engine room and tell them to secure the engines.

"Still no answer from the engine room," the JV talker reported.

Mack took a turn around the after part of the bridge and returned in time to overhear Casey Moore's grim report to McVay on the flooding forward. For the second time, Mack asked Lieutenant Orr if there were any orders, and again it was, "Stand by."

20mm. Oerlikon

But McVay spotted him and asked him to check the list on the inclinometer in the chart house. Mack returned in a moment to report: "Eighteen degrees starboard list, sir," and McVay turned to speak to Coxswain Keyes, back from below.

"I passed the word aft, sir, but I couldn't get forward," Keyes said. "There's fire by sick bay and smoke in No. 1 mess hall—I couldn't go any farther. Everybody aft is already out or getting out."

Fire by sick bay? Most of the corpsmen were in there studying for rating exams. It was the only air-conditioned part of the ship.

"Mack, go behind the bridge and get us some life jackets," Orr shouted. The noise from crackling flame, furniture crashing in the quarters below, and equipment breaking loose topside was getting intense now. Mack was back quickly with a couple of life jackets and gave one to

Orr. Again no orders. Captain McVay was gone from the bridge. Mack waited quietly—the bow was down sharply now and the list was passing twenty-five degrees.

"Better go over the side, Mack," Orr finally said. Mack did, still clutching his unblown bugle.

Doc Haynes glanced into the warrant officers' mess as he passed and noticed a poker game. But it was nearly midnight, and he was tired. In his cabin he quickly undressed and stretched out on his bunk. He was already asleep when the impact of the first torpedo hurled him into the air and he landed on his desk. He had no sooner put his foot to the deck than the second one smacked home, directly under him. Flame swished down the passageway and singed him as he started out the door, a life jacket held in front of his face. Behind him, the room was now on fire, and forward the passageway was full of smoke and flame. The deck tilted crazily.

Haynes turned aft, hoping to get through the wardroom and onto the quarterdeck. Everywhere he turned there was fire, but he made it to the wardroom. Only a red haze illuminated it, and the heat was fierce. The doctor fell, and as his hands touched the deck they sizzled. He rose in shock and threw himself into an armchair. As he gasped for breath in this inferno, someone standing above him screamed "My God, I'm choking," and fell on him.

Haynes rose in fright, and across the wardroom someone yelled, "Open a porthole! Open a porthole!" The doctor struggled to the starboard side and reached for a port, only to find it had been blown open and was slapping against the hull. He hooked it up and leaned out, gulping in fresh air, and as he did so something kept slapping him in the face. It was a line, hanging from the deck above. Oblivious to the pain in his hands—a surgeon's hands—he grasped the line and yanked it. It held.

Scarcely knowing what he was doing, he eased himself through the porthole and pulled himself up to the main deck. The air was much better there, and he made his way across to the battle dressing station in the port hangar. He was still dressed as he had been in his bunk—pajama bottoms only. The ship was a shambles topside, and slowly Haynes' mind began developing the pictures his eyes had taken—papers and broken furniture in the water, fire-reddened decks and bulkheads, jagged metal,

and an awful hole beneath his escape port. He had no time
to draw conclusions yet, but in a mechanical daze turned
to the scene before him in the hangar. Wounded men lay
everywhere, singly and in bunches, limbs twisted, faces
contorted. Some were quiet and alive, others just quiet.
Chief Pharmacist's Mate Schmueck was already adminis-
tering morphine in no set pattern, just to those closest and
in the most violent agony.

Haynes pitched in, not as an officer but as a doctor,
responding automatically to years of training. Once he
collapsed across a man he was helping, and revived as the
man pushed him away. For the first time he noted that
his patients were beginning to slide away to starboard,
and with this realization the whole picture fell into place
—the gaping hole, the fire, the debris, the list, and down
below those now-ominous sounds—the death rattle of a
ship.

"Get some life jackets, John, we've got to get these
men ready," he told Schmueck. There was no question
about it, the ship would soon sink.

Schmueck and another sailor returned with armloads
of life jackets, but time was getting short. The starboard
rail was already under water. They struggled as best they
could, but some men shrieked and writhed in pain as they
tried to get jackets around them.

"Don't touch me, don't touch me," screamed one horribly burned man, who somehow had escaped from the
hell below. Escaped? He had only transferred the place of
his death.

Those still able to move were given a choice. As
the ship rolled on her beam, they could either drop into
the water on the starboard side or scramble up to the high
side. Doc Haynes and some others crawled up to port and
walked out on the hull. Soon they were walking on red
bottom paint, and then it was just water and thick black
fuel oil in great waving blankets.

When Ensign Woolston arrived in the wardroom a
few minutes after midnight for a cup of coffee after his
watch, he had barely sat down at the mess table when
flames from the first blast roared up the passageway and
through the wardroom doors. A few seconds later, when
the second fish cracked home just beneath him, the whole
room burst into flame like the inside of a firecracker.

Woolston instinctively rolled under the table, out the other side, and through the window into the pantry in one smooth continuous movement. As the flash flame died away, he picked himself up and returned to the wardroom. The steward's mate of the watch appeared and they began searching for a dog wrench in the reddening darkness, coughing and spitting from the smoke. Woolston felt himself slipping, growing faint from lack of air.

He shook himself and muttered out loud, "Wait a minute, Woolston, this is not the way to go."

His hand fell on the wrench, and he undogged two ports and thrust his head out into the blessed, cool air. The water was rising, even on the high side, indicating the vessel was both settling in the water and canting to starboard.

"I think I'll rest a minute," the steward's mate said, as Woolston slithered through the porthole. He may have gotten out of the wardroom later, but not one of the thirty-two stewards, stewards' mates, or officers' cooks survived.

Woolston climbed to the communications deck to get a life jacket and stumbled across a crack in the deck. Glancing forward, it looked to him as if the bow was under water, at least on the starboard side, but it appeared to be still holding. Splintered wood and steel were thrown up from the main deck in several places, and flames licked up from below. As a damage-control officer, he realized that the ship was in a bad way, with fire below and the sea probably cascading into the hull from at least two holes. As he ranged back and forth on the port side, trying to find somewhere to help, he heard the word from above, "Abandon ship! Abandon ship!"

By the time Woolston reached the well deck, the list was increasing rapidly. Hands reached down to him from above, and a human chain pulled him up onto the port side of the hull. The men slithered into the water, and Woolston found another life jacket floating by him. He passed it to a steward's mate, who had none.

When Redmayne left the bridge around midnight, he made directly for the head. He had barely entered when the blast struck. The lights went out, the ship shuddered, and almost immediately he could hear fire crackling nearby.

"This is going to get worse before it gets better," he

thought, and plunged out of the head with arms over his face. It seemed to get steadily cooler as he went aft. He threaded his way through the starboard hangar, found it clogged with cots, crossed to the port hangar and started down to the after engine room, his battle station.

Redmayne found the after engine room almost normal, with lights on and the turbines humming to spin the two inboard screws, Nos. 2 and 3. The officer of the watch told him he couldn't raise the forward fire room or engine room, and it appeared they had lost all steam and power. This would mean Nos. 1 and 4 engines had stopped. No. 2 seemed to be losing pressure, too, and Redmayne ordered it stopped. That left only No. 3 working.

"Make as many turns as you can on No. 3," Redmayne ordered. He noted the inclinometer by his desk was steady at twelve to fifteen degrees starboard, but the fire main pressure was down to about ten pounds, though the pumps were going full blast. That could mean only one thing—ruptured mains forward.

Then a miracle happened: A machinist's mate from the watch in the forward engine room appeared. How he got out of that hades even he didn't know.

"I got out because we had no lights, no steam, and it was hot as hell," he stammered. "Do you want me to go back?"

"No," said Redmayne, who began to realize the situation was far more serious forward than aft.

The oil king asked if he should pump oil from the starboard tanks to the port tanks, to help correct the list.

"Give it a try," Redmayne said.

The watch officer reported every phone out except the sound-powered system to No. 4 fire room and Repair Party 5, and they didn't know any more than he did.

"That settles it. I'll go up to the bridge and see what they want done," Redmayne said.

He made it to No. 2 mess hall, and as he was going up the ladder to the main deck, the vessel took another big roll. As she went, so did he, and pitched right out through the hatch, across the deck and into the water. Behind him down the ladder, the lights still burned in the after engine room.

Private First Class Giles G. McCoy, USMC, was sleepy and grumpy. Here it was atfer midnight and he had to stay awake to guard a couple of prisoners who were sound asleep. What could they do anyway, locked in a cell on a ship five hundred miles from nowhere? Swim ashore, maybe? Brig sentry was about the worst duty a guy could draw, stuck in the fantail in the dead of night while two bums snored behind the bars.

At the first blast the light went out, and the second one blew McCoy from one end of the compartment to the other. His head struck the side of the brig and he was stunned. He shook his head to clear it, and suddenly two prisoners were banging the cell door, yelling to get out. McCoy remembered his duty well. In the pitch black he fumbled with his keys, found the right one, and the door swung open. Grasping hands, the three men scrambled over sacks, lockers, and debris which had been hurled around by the blasts, and groped toward the ladder. Up they went and wriggled through the scuttle onto the main deck.

There stood First Lieutenant Edward H. Stauffer, junior officer of the 39-man Marine Corps detachment aboard the *Indianapolis*. Stauffer (a Phi Beta Kappa in psychology from Iowa State, 1942) was mustering the Marines on the fantail.

"Get a couple of life jackets for your prisoners up on the boat deck," he told McCoy, "and if you see any other Marines bring them back."

McCoy started up the ladder, but with so many men streaming down, it was like trying to go the wrong way on an escalator. He scrambled up the bulkhead and through the lifelines, found one life jacket and started back with it. But the ship was rolling now, and he heard someone shout, "Let's abandon ship!" In the circumstances, there was nothing else he could do, so he pulled himself up to the port rail and out on the hull. They were not his prisoners any more; they belonged to the sea now.

7

Little Johnny Reid, Lieutenant, Supply Corps, USNR, heard the explosions and recognized them instantly. He had been through this before and he knew all the signs. During the Battle of the Philippine Sea, when he was supply officer of the cruiser *Birmingham*, the heroic carrier *Princeton* had blown up alongside. The blast had cut down men on the *Birmingham*'s deck like a scythe, and Reid was blown clear through a passageway from one side of the ship to the other. He had dragged himself to his quarters and lain there several days in a haze of morphia, but after hospitalization at Mare Island he was back at sea in seven months, at his own request.

When he bounded from his sack on the *Indianapolis*, he grabbed two essentials for survival at sea—his bathrobe and a bottle of Scotch. Of course you can't have liquor on Navy vessels, but no law says you can't take it overboard if it happens to be there. It was quickly clear that it would be impossible to get down to the supply office to get the ship's pay records and some $50,000 in cash reposing in the safe. Even if he could, who needs money at a time like this? Besides, the disbursing officer, Lieutenant (j.g.) T. H. Backus, had the combination.

With unashamed single purpose, Reid made his way straight to the fantail. This was his abandon-ship station, not his battle station. That was in the wardroom, as a member of the coding board, but the wardroom was a ball of fire and any sensible man would be interested in getting out of it, not into it. Lieutenant Reid, schooled in Switzerland, France, and Amherst, was a sensible man.

He found the fantail crawling with men in great confusion, but no panic. There was no fire nor smoke there, but cut off from the forward part of the ship there was no one to tell them what to do. In any event, within a very brief time no orders were necessary. As the deck tilted to starboard and the stern began to rise, there was little choice. Reid climbed out through the lifelines and grasped one of the great bronze screws, now mercifully still. When the vessel plunged, he pressed the CO_2 capsule on his rubber life belt and bobbed to the surface like a cork. Little Johnny Reid, five-feet-five, had beaten the rap again.

A couple of Michigan boys, J. Ray Sinclair and Clarke W. Seabert, just out of boot camp at Great Lakes, went to the dark-adapter room shortly before midnight. When their eyes became adjusted to darkness, they went out on the bridge and took the lookout chairs side by side on the starboard wing. It was their job to watch the sea and sky in the arc from bow to starboard beam, from horizon to ninety degrees vertical.

"Pretty nice night, no?" Seabert said, as he looked at the glow of the moon from astern. "It's not too cold and not too hot."

"Yeah," Sinclair agreed, and they began using their binoculars toward the horizon. Sinclair could see it clearly, and he began moving his glasses along it in five-degree bites. It wasn't exactly a clear night. A little thing like a periscope would be awfully hard to see, at 1,500 meters, even if it was right in front of you. And torpedoes, coming right at you at 48 knots, twelve feet below the surface and leaving no wake—well, that would be impossible.

The first one knocked them right out of their chairs, and the second, directly beneath them, bounced them from deck to bulkhead like basketballs. They unscrambled themselves, and Sinclair found his phones and put them back on his head. He called into them, but the only answer he got was from the other side of the bridge. All the other circuits were dead. They ran around to the other side of the bridge where officers and men were coming and going, but no one said anything to them. Sinclair heard someone give an order to cut loose the life rafts, but he heard no order to abandon ship. He just stayed there, and as the vessel rolled he walked right up the side of Captain McVay's cabin and into the water.

William G. Quealy, Parachute Rigger Second Class, was coming up the port ladder to the quarterdeck, a little late for his watch on the 40-mm. guns near the hangar deck. The second blast slammed him against the bulkhead, and when he came to, the ship was already over about five degrees. On the second try, he made it to the quarterdeck and found some three hundred others already there. The men were quiet, as this part of the ship showed little damage and no fire.

Within a few minutes, Commander Flynn came out of the port passageway.

"Go over the side, men," he said, and they did.

Seaman Second Class Joseph A. Jacquemot was way up forward on the forecastle deck, lounging against the 20-mm. gun shield. It was nice up there, with a good breeze, and he could hear the bow singing through the water. Wham! and there was no bow in front of him. The whole first forty feet of the ship was gone, and along with it anchors, capstans, hawse pipes, windlass room, anchor chains, and two decks of storerooms and paint lockers. Even if nothing else happened that night, the *Indianapolis* was already in bad trouble. With the bow torn off in a ragged cross section and the ship plunging head on into the swells at 15 knots or better, the transverse bulkheads could not hold for long.

Jacquemot jumped to his feet and grabbed the gun shield just before the second blast nearly pitched him overboard. He tried his phone circuits and there wasn't a peep on them. Smoke was coming up through the deck now, and officers and enlisted men began pouring up through the hatches and scuttles from the cabins, offices, and sleeping compartments below.

Captain Parke charged out like a bull into the arena.

"Test your circuit," he roared.

"I already did, it's dead as a doornail," Jacquemot replied.

Parke ran aft, and Jacquemot helped some other fellows carry a wounded officer up to the communications deck. For no particular reason Jacquemot kept right on go-

ing until he was way up in sky control, where Lieutenant
R. T. Whitman, the watch officer, stopped him.

"This ship isn't going to sink," he said. "Now go back
to your station."

Jacquemot started down to rig No. 2 lifeboat, but it
was too late. Neither of the twenty-six-foot motor whaleboats would get away that night.

The Moran family of Johnstown, Pennsylvania, was
a real Navy family. Joseph D. Moran had enlisted in Naval
Aviation in 1917 and served 16 months. Now his two sons
were in the Navy. The older boy, Joseph John, enlisted in
March, 1941, at nineteen, and was now Radioman First
Class, USN, aboard the *Indianapolis*. He didn't have the
watch Sunday night, but he never could get very far from
the radio shack. He was batting the breeze with his buddies
in Radio I and heard all about the sub report. It came in as
a high-precedence message and was broken immediately.
The watch officer said it was "Just another merchant ship
report, a sub fired two torpedoes at her, about 300 miles
ahead, and south of us." Nobody worried about reports
like that any more; they were a dime a dozen.

About 11:00 P.M. Joe went down to the Flag coding
room, where he was bunking with three other men, and
turned in. It was like that on a flagship; when the Flag
wasn't aboard, enlisted men from ship's company moved
into the offices and established "squatter's rights." There
was more room, more privacy, and more comfort. You
could roll your sack out on deck or on the counters that
ran around the bulkheads. It was almost like a semiprivate
room.

The Flag office was just behind the wardroom, on the
starboard side, and the second torpedo rammed home directly under it. The room shook violently and immediately
began to fill with heat and smoke. Moran ran to the door,
but the passageway fore and aft was dancing with flame.
He slammed the door, crossed the room, and hung his head
out a porthole. There were voices on the deck above, and
Moran climbed out the port and up to the forecastle deck.
An officer passed the word to go to general quarters, and
Moran made his way to Radio I.

It was a shambles. The second torpedo cut the light
and power instantly, and nearly every receiver along the
port side was blasted off its table and smashed. A fire

broke out in the aft corner, and smoke eddied up into the
room. The watch men, busy copying routine transmission
schedules from shore stations, were dashed from their
chairs into a confused mass of typewriters, desks, head-
sets, wiring, and broken electronic gear. A couple of men
ran through the communications office just behind the radio shack and onto the communications deck, but flames
there drove them back.

"Go out the forward door," shouted Lieutenant (j.g.)
Dave Driscoll, the watch officer.

As they wrestled the forward door open, there stood
Lieutenant Orr, down from the bridge on Captain McVay's
orders.

"Get out a distress message right away," Orr said.
"Captain's orders. Say we've been torpedoed and need
help immediately."

Driscoll grabbed the phone to Radio II, to order the
transmitters set up. It was dead.

At that moment, the radio officer, Lieutenant N. P.
Hill, came through from the communications office and
Driscoll told him the bad news.

"I can't get through to Radio II, and we can neither
send nor receive from here—no power."

Hill made out Elwyn L. Sturtevant, Radioman Second
Class, in the eerie glow of flame and battle lamps.

"Go back there and tell Woods to set up on 4235
and 500 kilocycles," Hill said. "Meantime, Moran, you and
Sebastian see if either of the transmitter keys is still working."

Sticking to the port side, Sturtevant made it to Radio
II, where the ship's only transmitters were housed. Chief
Radio Electrician L. T. Woods had already arrived from
far forward in officers' country. He was still coughing
from smoke in the fiery passageways, but here was a
haven of normality in a ship gone topsy-turvy. Lights,
power, and ventilation were all working normally and
Woods was in calm control. First thing on arriving he
found the room already crowded with radio technicians.
Most of them slept nearby, and on the first blast they came
tumbling into the shack like potatoes into a sack.

"Warm up the transmitters, boys, then put on your
life jackets and stand by," Woods ordered. He knew the
ship was in a bad way, and orders to send might soon reach

him. They did, as Sturtevant pushed his way into the room.

"We can't reach you from forward. Lieutenant Hill says set up 4235 and 500, we want to send distress signals."

"They're already warmed up," Woods replied. "Tell Mr. Hill we will pipe 4235 through to him on line 3, and look, bring back a copy of the distress message and we will key it from here on 500."

When Sturtevant got back to Radio I (and none too soon, as the list was increasing rapidly), Moran and C. H. Sebastian, Radioman Second Class, he found the transmitter key positions intact. That didn't mean much, but they sat down anyway and began pounding the brass, keying out the ship's encrypted code name and ". . . torpedoed twice. Lat. 12 N. Long. 135 E. Need immediate assistance."

"Woods wants a copy of the distress message and he'll send it out from back there," Sturtevant told Lieutenant Driscoll. The lieutenant quickly scribbled it on a pad and gave it to Fred J. Hart, Radio Technician Second Class.

"Take this back to Mr. Woods as fast as you can," he said. Hart left, but time was growing short by then. He never made it to Radio II, and only minutes after he left, Lieutenant Driscoll ordered everyone out of Radio I. It had to be. Heavy equipment was now breaking loose and crashing from the bulkheads. One man screamed horribly; he was crushed to death.

It had been a valiant try, but foredoomed. No lights and no power meant no signal was going to Radio II, even if the line between them was intact, which was highly doubtful. And since all receivers were smashed in Radio I, they couldn't have monitored their own signal to see if it was going out. Nearly everybody in Radio I got out alive, but none of them really believed they had gotten off a message.

It was different in Radio II. Woods was no man to sit around waiting for orders that might never reach him (and never did). As soon as Sturtevant left, Woods himself sat down at a transmitter position and began sending on 500 kilocycles, the international distress frequency. Herbert J. Miner, Radio Technician Second Class, peered over Woods's shoulder and watched the antenna meter fluctuate. Woods was keying the simple SOS—three dots, three dashes, three dots—followed by the ship's position. Miner noted that the SOS was definitely going out—when that meter fluctuated it proved there was power in the antenna.

No one knew how many times it went out, but Miner told his buddies later, as they waited for rescue, that it was at least three times. In any event, Woods stuck at his key until the ship went so far over he told his men, "Get out of here as fast as you can." The men cleared the shack in a rush, just as the ship laid out flat on her side.

Every ship and shore station round the world is supposed to guard 500 kc. There was just a possibility—

When Lieutenant McKissick got back to his cabin after the movie, he was pretty tired. He quickly undressed and got into his bunk. He noticed a little paper-bound booklet on his sheet, glanced at the title, and flipped it away. He turned out the light—too tired to read. The booklet? *Survival on Land and Sea,* the Navy's handy guide to life *in extremis.*

In the confusion a short time later, when the blasts knocked him from his bunk, McKissick grabbed a towel, wrapped it around his head, and ran into the smoke-filled corridor. The booklet was forgotten on the chair. It would only have been torture later to read how to keep your feet dry in a lifeboat, what fish to eat, and how to subsist on desert islands. There were no chapters covering the ordeal facing these men.

McKissick, in his turbaned head, made his way up to the main deck, glanced aft toward the wardroom and saw nothing but fire and milling men. He turned into an empty stateroom, hoping to get a porthole open for some air. But he couldn't undog any of them and stumbled back into the passageway and went forward. Just as he became desperate, someone shouted, "Anyone in here want to get out?"

It was an enlisted man, and he told McKissick, "Follow me." The man led him into a powder-storage room and they crawled through a hole meant for powder bags into the powder circle inside Turret I, climbed up a narrow ladder to the pointer's booth on the forward 8-inch turret and down the mount onto the forecastle deck. Coughing and vomiting, they gasped on the deck for a few moments. McKissick staggered to his feet and turned to help some men break out a fire hose, but when the valve was turned, no water came out.

He ran to the starboard side in time to help some men squeeze through a crazily jammed door. Many were badly burned, their flesh hanging in pouches, and their screams were piteous. As best they could, the well helped the injured toward the port side, for the starboard side was falling and all about there was an ominous feel. To McKissick, it was as though some great obstruction was holding the vessel back and slewing it to starboard. There were life jackets on the port side, and the lieutenant told the men, "It's no use trying to save her, boys. Get a life jacket and get ready to abandon ship."

Water was moving up the forecastle now, and it was apparent she couldn't last long. The men sensed it, and a couple wondered out loud if an SOS had gotten off.

"I'm sure it did," said the minister's son, and they all felt better, unaware that McKissick knew no more about it than they did. As he searched for more life jackets, he beamed a flashlight into dark corners of the superstructure. Where he had gotten the light he had no idea, but somebody shouted down from the bridge:

"For God's sake, put out that light. There's liable to be an enemy submarine around here."

McKissick doused the light, and at times it was so dark you couldn't recognize a man two feet from you. At other times, in flitting moonlight or burst of flame you could clearly see the mainmast, two hundred feet away. The lieutenant heard no order to abandon ship, but he and those around him needed none. They merely swam away when the list passed fifty degrees and the water came up on the "high" side of Turret I.

CIC (Combat Intelligence Center) was a pretty slow watch those days, with practically no Japanese navy or air force left, at least in that area. The three enlisted men switched around every half hour to relieve the monotony, alternately watching the radar screen, plotting or guarding the lookout circuit with the earphones.

George Massier, Seaman First Class, was on radar watch when the torpedoes hit, and Raymond S. Jerkiewicz, Seaman First Class, had the lookout phones on. Goss

was at the plotting board with Ensign Moore, officer of
the watch, and Ensign Marple, who was down from
the bridge for instruction. Massier saw nothing on his
screens, and the lookouts reported nothing to Jurkiewicz,
so CIC was helpless. You can't plot a strikeback unless you
have some information on the attacker.

As the warhead exploded beneath them, the men
were trapped in an exploding greenhouse. Glass flew everywhere from the shattered plotting tables and radar tubes.
The lights failed and lethal objects flew through the air.
Finally a couple of battle lanterns came on, and Jurkiewicz
collected himself enough to try his circuits. They were all
dead. Ensign Moore sent him out on the bridge to find out
what had happened. The signalman told Jurkiewicz the
ship had been hit, but Moore was unimpressed.

"Stick around a while and see what happens," the
ensign said. Smoke was coming from somewhere now, and
you could hear men running around outside and on the
navigation bridge overhead. Moore sent Jurkiewicz out a
second time, and this time the men were scrambling for life
jackets.

Ensign Moore was all for hanging on, but there was
really no use. CIC is the brain center of a fighting ship, but
it cannot function without communications, any more than
the human brain can without its contributory senses. CIC
was just a black dead hole now, and when Jurkiewicz
came back from a third trip he said word had been passed
to abandon ship. Moore finally gave in, and the five of
them left CIC in a rush. Jurkiewicz scooted up to the
bridge, brushed past Captain McVay and Commander
Flynn, and down to the port side of the comm deck.

He grabbed a life jacket and was going through the
port lifelines when Captain McVay shouted down to free
the floater nets in their baskets. Jurkiewicz and Signalman
Second Class Thomas E. Davis tried to loosen them, but
time ran out and they had to go over the side. But the nets
were designed to float out of the baskets if the ship went
down.

Private First Class Robert Frank Redd, USMC, was
glad they didn't put him ashore at Pearl Harbor. On the
way out from San Francisco, he had dropped a 40-mm.
ammunition can on his foot, breaking some small bones.
Doc Haynes put it in a walking cast, and when they

reached Pearl he suggested Redd go to the hospital. But Redd begged not to be sent off; once you lost your ship during the war you might never find it again, and to most men their ship was their home. Redd won; they let him stay aboard. When the ship listed sharply and the starboard rail went under, he held on as long as he could. Then he had to let go, and the heavy cast took him down like a stone, 1,600 fathoms or more. If death must come, there is something to be said for making it swift.

The signal bridge is a pretty dull place at night when steaming alone in quiet waters. Nobody to send signals to, no messages to receive. But it sprang to life this night. At least half a dozen signalmen bounced to their feet in no time, ready for orders or whatever might come. There were no orders; you couldn't show a light in the presence of the enemy, and there were certainly no friends to be summoned, even with the infra-red "black light" equipment.

Signalman First Class Robert P. Bunai, senior man present, took charge, and when it became apparent the ship was starting to roll he knew it was time to act. "Let's get this classified stuff in the sack," he called to striker Kenley M. Lanter.

Signalman Third Class Frank J. Centazzo came running around from the forward splinter shield shouting, "The bow's off, the bow's off, about sixty feet of it." Lanter grabbed the weighted bag and the three of them began stuffing it with code books and restricted documents. They were scattered all over the deck when the blast blew the signal desk down. Three or four other men pitched in, and they all heard parts of the fateful conversation between Captain McVay and his exec on the navigation bridge just above them.

The closing words came through clearly:

"Okay, pass the word to abandon ship," McVay told Flynn.

Within minutes, the old ship rolled over and all the signalmen were in the water. The weighted bag went on ahead.

Even as they splashed into the water, Bunai and Centazzo both heard the sound they would never forget. Men were screaming inside the hull.

Centazzo helped a buddy, Signalman Third Class

David Singerman, fasten on his life jacket, then they all
swam away.

About a dozen men were in Radar Aft, making regular sweeps with the SG search radar, first in close, up
to 1,500 yards, then full out to the forty-mile limit.
Not a pip on the screen. And back here, behind the after
stack and just under Radio II, the blasts felt pretty far
away.

Allen M. Altschuler, Seaman First Class, on phone
watch, tried his phones and got no answer. Then he tried
the voice circuits, connected directly to speakers on the
bridge, in CIC, Flag Plot, and other vital centers. No
replies. He was about to secure when, somehow, he heard
a voice over the headset. It sounded like Goss in CIC.

"There's smoke in here, and we're getting out," the
voice said.

Altschuler thought he had better not shout that out,
with men milling around scrambling for life jackets. But
he did turn and whisper it to Radarman Third Class Francis Rider, standing next to him. Together they herded the
last few men out of the shack, secured the gear, and followed. Altschuler was the last man out of the shack.

The explosions bracketed Gunner Horner's room on
the second deck forward of Turret I and brought the
bunks down on top of him. Extricating himself, he ran
into the dark passageway and fumbled forward toward the
sprinkler station to wet down the 8-inch powder magazines
beneath him. He bumped into Machinist H. F. Fuchs,
borrowed a flashlight from him, and went up to the next
deck—the main deck. It seemed to be pitching forward,
and Horner, thinking the forecastle must be under water,
moved aft and opened the hatch into the circle around
Turret II. First belched toward him, and he quickly
slammed the hatch and dogged it down.

Turning forward, he saw water pouring over the
coaming from the officers' washroom. With a couple of
other men there, he tried to close the door, but it was
twisted on its hinges and wouldn't seal. There was no use
trying to stem that flood. Horner darted up the ladder,
skirted a rupture in the forecastle deck, and went aft on the
port side. On the well deck he ran into Commander
Lipski.

"Are you hurt, Gunner?" the Commander asked. "No, I just got oil all over me when I fell on the second deck," Horner replied. "I was trying to dog down the doors in the bulkhead forward, but there's water pouring in and fire all around."

Lipski seemed in shock, and Horner knew he was hurt, but couldn't tell how badly there in the semidarkness. "Are you all right, sir?" Horner asked, and Lipski replied, "Yes, go ahead."

Horner continued aft, picked up a life jacket, and passed through the hangar deck as gear began to crash around him. He grabbed the lifeline and crawled out on the hull alongside the motor whaleboat. The boat was still secure in its chocks.

Quartermaster Third Class Vincent Allard left the bridge about twenty minutes before midnight, when Jimmy French, Quartermaster Third Class, relieved him as quartermaster of the watch. When the explosions came, he was already asleep in his bunk, far aft near the chief's quarters. A very deliberate man of thirty-three, Allard dressed quickly but calmly, shifted his money from his locker to his pocket, and prepared to go topside. A shipmate craned his neck out from his bunk and asked what the hell was up, with everybody running around.

"We probably took a couple of fish. You better go topside," Allard replied matter of factly. The man in the sack beat him to the ladder.

The lights were still on all around him, even in the evaporator room, Allard noticed as he made his way forward. In No. 3 mess hall he found a friend whose feet were burned, and they were talking about whether to bandage them or put burn jelly on them when Coxswain Keyes came through the compartment, passing the word for all hands topside.

Allard waited his turn at the ladder, climbed through debris on the hangar deck, and headed for the bridge. On the comm deck he came upon Jimmy French, struggling with a strange type life jacket, one with strings that seemed to tie around the legs.

"How the hell do you get this on?" French asked.

"I don't know, just tie it on any way," Allard replied, and continued up toward the bridge. It had not entered his head that the ship might sink. As he climbed

the last ladder, he found Captain McVay standing at the
head of it. Glenn Morgan, Buglemaster Third Class, was
there, too, even though he was off duty, and they went
around to the front of the bridge. Heavy furniture was
breaking loose in the chart house now, and when he looked
around, McVay was gone from the bridge. Allard dropped
down to the signal bridge, and there the water met him,
along with some men who had been struggling to free rafts.

8

Victor R. Buckett, Yeoman Second Class, then in his thirty-fourth month aboard, rarely slept in his assigned bunk near sick bay. Instead, this night he was sleeping on the desk as usual in a small office in the port catapult tower. This "private stateroom" was his by virtue of seniority and the prerogatives of his rating, yeomen being in the nature of "white-collar" workers aboard warships. The blast below sick bay (thank God he wasn't sleeping in his assigned bunk!) was still strong enough to knock him off the desk. The lights went out.

Buckett scrambled into his pants and shirt in the dark, put his wallet in his pocket, and dropped down the ladder to the office just below his. He was looking for his buddy, Edward W. Alvey, Aerographer's Mate Second Class, the ship's weather man. Buckett had been best man at Alvey's wedding in Vallejo, a few days before the hurried departure. But the lone honeymooner was not in his sack when Buckett got there, so Buckett, thinking possibly a boiler had exploded, went out on the quarterdeck. There he joined the search for life jackets and helped some burned men get into them until the jackets were exhausted. By then Commander Lipski was there and told the men to go over the side, "And make sure you have life jackets." Buckett climbed back to his room, picked up his rubber life belt, and returned to the quarterdeck to follow the wounded gunnery officer over the side.

CPO quarters in the fantail, as far aft as you could get on the *Indianapolis*, still did not escape the force of the blasts far forward. Chief Machinist's Mate Albert E. Ferguson, just finishing a shower after his watch in the forward engine room, was thrown to the deck twice as the lights went out and plunged the head into darkness. He called to another chief in the shower, who said he was okay, and then felt something warm on his leg. He touched it and drew his hand away, knowing even in the darkness that it was blood.

Ferguson hobbled into the berthing compartment, and in the glow of the light still burning could see that glass or jagged metal had slashed his leg in several places, and also cut one foot. Still naked, he scrambled up the ladder to the open deck, looking for rags or something to stop the bleeding. A mess cook noticed his plight, stripped off his white pants and gave them to the chief. Ferguson barely had time to rip them into strips and try bandaging his wounds when the ship rolled over. He slid into the water, blood, pants, and all.

When Coxswain Keyes got to the chiefs' quarters with his cogent message, Chief Machinist's Mate Ralph Lane was still sacking in. The call for "all hands topside" made him conclude there might, indeed, be some place better than a warm bed. He battled his way to the ladder through overturned lockers, bunks half torn from their fittings, and all manner of gear flung at crazy angles. Chief Firecontrolman Clarence U. Benton, 28, heard all the commotion and bounced out of the sack he had just climbed into. The compartment shook violently. Beaming a flashlight around, he saw lockers torn from the bulkhead, their doors flapping open like idiots' jaws. Bunks were thrown across passageways, the wire springs forming barriers as tough as fences. Benton tore his way to the ladder, uprooting the bunks like Paul Bunyan marching through the forest. At the ladder, he recalled the men in the brig below, but when he aimed his flashlight down there, the door stood open.

Turning forward, he passed through the mess room, where the lights still burned, and into the radar room and fire control shop. There was still power on the radars and computers, but every phone in the place was dead. Benton quickly went up to the boat deck, and as he stepped onto the open deck the list increased to forty degrees. Behind him there was an ominous grating within the ship. Outside, shells and ammunition cans rolled and bounced around him.

"Throw 'em overboard," Benton shouted. Fuses had undoubtedly been set on some of the ready ammo. Men around him pitched in for a few minutes, but suddenly there was the final roll and it was all over. In his last glimpse before immersion, Benton saw the No. 4 screw rise from the water and strike a swimmer, splaying him backward and out of sight in the gloom.

When the *Indianapolis* departed Guam, she carried eighty-two officers (including the passenger, Captain Crouch) and 1,114 enlisted men. Around midnight on Sunday, perhaps sixty-five of the officers were in officers' country in the forward part of the ship. Most of them were asleep, but a few were still in the wardroom, or the showers, or reading in their rooms.

The two torpedoes cracking home, each carrying 1,210 pounds of high explosive, bracketed officers' country fore and aft. Well over a ton of explosive was delivered to the cruiser's tender belly within a space of 175 feet. The first hit at about Frame 7, or some twenty-eight feet back from the bow and, if she was running true to her depth setting, rammed smack into the chain locker. There is no telling exactly where she hit, but it was probably not aft of Frame 7. The two tanks for storage of high-octane aviation gas were at Frame 15. Only one was full, 3,500 gallons, but had it exploded the entire bow might have been blown off.

The second torpedo struck a telling blow. With this one shot alone, the *Indianapolis* was doomed. Besides opening a huge hole amidships, it wiped out all communications, lights, and power in the forward half of the ship, and with them went the fire mains, radio, radar, and fire control for the guns. Striking at Frame 50, directly below the bridge, the blast must certainly have opened the forward fire room to the sea, destroying any pretense of watertight integrity that the vessel might have had.

In addition to the officers, many of whom were never seen again, berthed within this area and even closer to the blasts were all the Marines and steward's mates, plus other enlisted men. Not all were in their assigned bunks, of course, but the fact is that of the thirty-nine Marines aboard only nine survived, and of the thirty-two stewards, not a single one.

The blasts wracked the forward part of the ship with tremendous force, and in an instant a powerful, efficient fighting mechanism became a shambles. Torpedo 2 performed with diabolical efficiency. It wiped out Central, with every officer and man there, and along with it all internal communications and every alarm device the ship possessed. It raptured fuel-oil tanks in the double-bottom and scattered the sticky, inflammable stuff all through that part of the ship, reaching incredible places. Sick bay, the ship's offices, the wardroom, Radio I, all were in this area and all suffered, either immediately from blast or within minutes from smoke, fire, fuel oil, ruptured mains, and burning electrical cables.

Within seconds of the two blasts, the forward half of the ship erupted into frenzied life, with men stumbling through darkened passageways, coughing and spitting from smoke and noxious fumes from dozens of sources. Some men floundered aimlessly, like beheaded chickens, others ran silently and swiftly with great purpose. Some screamed and bled, others merely bled, and some did not move at all.

Most men did what they could, to help themselves and to help others. There could be no direction to these efforts, for the ship's nerve center was gone. Every action was strictly local, because no man could know more than his eyes and ears, in their limited range, could tell him. Forward Repair Party was obliterated in the first instant, but even had it been spared, it could have made no contact with the first lieutenant's office or the bridge. No communication was possible except by messenger, over ruptured and tilting decks made slippery by scattered patches of ubiquitous fuel oil

Dr. Modisher, treacherously near the forward blast in the last room forward on the port side, awoke as the porthole cover whistled by his head, torn completely off the bulkhead by concussion. He fought his way to the forecastle by Turret I, and found the deck littered with injured men, cases of burn, fracture, and shock. Medical supplies appeared—probably from the emergency boxes near the gun mounts—and he struggled in the blackness and confusion to give succor with morphine, sulfa, and burn jelly. But it was little use, as men slipped about on the oily deck and the list to starboard grew. Dr. Modisher heard the word passed to abandon ship, but gravity and fuel oil were already executing the order before it was given. Men slid into the water on greased runways, the uninjured trying to ease the helpless into the water as it rose across the forecastle.

On balance, officers and men did the best they could. As the shattered bow plowed into the swells, no longer able to rise with them, the tremendous force of the sea against the exposed bulkheads was too much for man or ship. The transverse bulkhead at the chain locker leaked in a dozen places through split seams, sprung plates, and twisted doors. This alone could have been serious, but it was nothing compared to the amidships hit, which ripped the bottom open laterally—like a giant can opener. The men forward did not know the extent of the damage amidships, but they soon felt its effects. Water pouring in from starboard tipped the mighty ship to that side, and water cascading in forward pulled the bow down, as if to make it easier for her to slake a mortal thirst.

Casey Moore got down from the bridge in time to see some of the reflex actions of scattered knots of men—like ants battling a flood—and he ran back to the bridge. There he reported the disaster he had seen. Captain McVay was resolute. This was a peacetime ship, sturdier than the *Pittsburgh*, and she had lost her bow and survived. He had seen trouble before, and he had known of many a ship saved by calmness in the first panic. He would wait. There was good precedent for this. Earlier in the war, more than one ship had been lost through too hasty abandonment. The Navy recognized this, and the latest "Damage Control Manual (1944)" bore emblazoned on its cover, "Don't Give Up the Ship."

The scene on the fantail was fantastic. Within minutes it was peopled with men crawling everywhere, like flies on a piece of garbage. In the light of the intermittent moon, or flames from forward, they gathered there by instinct, droves of them, over five hundred in all. No one told them to go there, but after all instinct was invented long before thought. And once they arrived, there was no one to tell them what to do. The great bull voice of the

PA system, representing the unseen presence on the bridge, was stilled. No orders, no instruction, no central direction would ever come from it again.

So they gathered and they waited. A few were wounded or burned, most of them were not, and many were naked or wore only the skivvies or shorts they had been sleeping in. Not one in a score had shoes on, or carried a knife, flashlight, or any of the dozen other items they had been instructed to have ready in case of just such an emergency. No one was figuring, even then, on abandoning ship. Some men had already gone over the side, to be sure—blown off the forecastle or driven over by panic —but they were not many. Most of the men were calm, if confused. It was inconceivable that this big ship would sink.

But as the bow slowly sank, and the stern began to rise, the feeling of impregnability gave way to a new thought. The seed of doubt matured rapidly as the list to the right developed. A few officers and leading PO's kept telling the men, "Get a life jacket, get a life jacket." Strange creakings, bangings, bubblings, and cracking sounds rose from below and the ship began to slew around, obviously out of control.

Men began to drop off the starboard lifeline, despite orders by some officers or in response to urging by others. It was all happening so quickly, and there was no word from above. Men acted individually, in response to their own natures. They were dribbling off the side now like peas from a planting machine. When the last great lurch came, there was no longer time for individual decisions. They could only get away from the ship in the best manner open to them. She was clearly going down.

Some were reluctant to go, for they feared the dark, oily void awaiting them more than the ship breaking up beneath them. By some miracle, it might stay afloat. Such things had been known to happen. Ensign Twible screamed for the men to go over the side, but no one moved. They waited until he himself went, then followed him in a rush, like sheep. Some men clung to guns, stanchions, lifelines, any projection, until it was let go or drown. Others, high in the superstructure, plotted it coolly and waited for a hole to drop through, taking no chances on getting tangled in the rigging or dropping into a swarm of debris or flailing men.

Hundreds fought their way up to the port railing, and walked or slid down the hull. Some waited too long and became fouled in the screws, as Nos. 3 and 4 rose from the water. No. 3 was still turning, a terrifying and relentless meatgrinder. In the minds of everyone was the fear of suction when the ship went down. True or not, everyone has heard that a sinking ship exerts terrible suction when it goes down, and can drag anyone near the hull down with it. So once in the water, every man struck out for safety, one thought only in mind—get away from the ship.

And the last ones off had little time, for the ship seemed anxious to go. As the head and midships, now filling rapidly, sank lower, the final hundred feet or so of the giant hull raised straight up out of the water and seemed to stand there for a moment.

Hundreds of men, directly under it, watched in terror as it hung there, fearing any moment it might topple on them. Captain McVay, now a shipwrecked sailor like the lowliest seaman, saw the screws above him and thought, "Well, this is the end of me."

But they were wrong. The *Indianapolis* waited but a moment, then slipped straight down, like a leadline, disappearing quickly and silently, without suction, without anguish. Thus ended her career of twelve years, eight months, and twenty-three days afloat—the last major vessel lost in World War II.

The time was 12:14 A.M., Monday, July 30, 1945, East Longitude date.

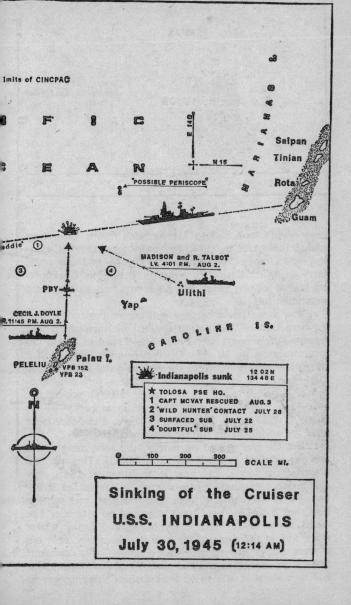

lmits of CINCPAC

F I C

C E A N

MARIANAS

E 140

N 15

Saipan

Tinian

Rota

"POSSIBLE PERISCOPE"

Guam

eddie ①

③   ④

MADISON and R. TALBOT
LV. 4:01 P.M. AUG 2.

PBY

Ulithi

CECIL J. DOYLE
R.11:45 P.M. AUG 2.

Yap

CAROLINE   IS.

PELELIU   Palau I.
        VPB 152
        VPB 23

Indianapolis sunk   12 02 N
                     134 48 E

★ TOLOSA PSE HQ.
① CAPT MCVAY RESCUED   AUG.3
② "WILD HUNTER" CONTACT   JULY 28
③ SURFACED SUB   JULY 22
④ "DOUBTFUL" SUB   JULY 25

N

◎   100   200   300
                                  SCALE MI.

Sinking of the Cruiser

U.S.S. INDIANAPOLIS

July 30, 1945 (12:14 AM)

9

Leyte didn't look bad to MacArthur's troops when they landed there late in 1944, especially after the Solomons and New Guinea. The natives were friendly and they could carry on an intelligent conversation in English. Cockfighting was a popular sport, and houseboys and laundry help were plentiful.

The name Leyte became well-known during the war, for here General MacArthur enacted his famous "I have returned" ceremony, with Provisional President Sergio Osmeña standing by his side. Off the shore in Leyte Gulf a short time later was fought the biggest naval battle in history—the Battle for Leyte Gulf. Tacloban, provincial capital of Leyte and a city of nearly 50,000 population, enjoyed a brief day of glory as provisional capital of the liberated Philippines. Osmeña was there, and MacArthur lived for a while in the former Japanese Club.

But the war moved on swiftly, and soon the generals and the admirals were installed in Manila. The spotlight moved from Leyte, and now in midsummer, 1945, only one major command remained, the Philippine Sea Frontier. Leyte was still a huge and bustling rear-echelon base, but it was all hard work now and no glamour. The island stood in the path of typhoons and heavy winter rains, and in the summer the heat and humidity, only ten degrees above the equator, were stifling. The elements alone were enough to contend with, let alone the confusion and monotony of war in its backwashes. Shipping was so mixed up, Christmas packages were still arriving in May, battered almost beyond identification.

The headquarters of Vice Admiral James L. Kauffman, Commander, Philippine Sea Frontier, was still located at Tolosa, twenty miles south of Tacloban, where it had been set up in January. The Quonsets sprawled over five and one-half acres in a palm grove, and when it rained (did it ever stop?) the place was a sea of mud. But the command had been growing steadily and by July 1, when Admiral Kauffman went back to the States on leave, the PSF had administrative command over a huge area, running from 130 degrees East Longitude all the way west to Indo-China, taking in Malaya, Thailand, Borneo, and Sarawak.

Kauffman's trusted chief of staff, Commodore Norman C. (Shorty) Gillette, took over as acting commander during Kauffman's absence. He often flew up to Manila, completing arrangements for PSF to move up there, and also to confer with Vice Admiral Thomas C. Kinkaid. Kinkaid, as Commander, United States Seventh Fleet and Commander, Allied Naval Forces, Southwest Pacific Area, was the head of what most everyone called "MacArthur's Navy." It was understood that Fleet Admiral Nimitz, from Guam, ran the show east of 130 Longitude, the famous "Chop Line," and MacArthur controlled everything west of there, up to twenty degrees North Latitude, that is. So while Kinkaid ran the "Fighting Navy" for MacArthur, Gillette ran the "Paper Navy" for him.

With a staff of 183 officers and 484 enlisted men, PSF was responsible throughout a vast area for all local naval defense, harbor control, routing, dispatching, and escort of routine shipping, and the myriad details of naval administration. The PSF had 220 vessels under its command, for transportation, escort, salvage, and repair, but had no responsibility for combatant ships. These came under either Admiral Kinkaid at Manila, or Admiral Nimitz at Guam. And while the headquarters of PSF sat on the shores of Leyte Gulf, it did not directly administer that area. The gulf, covering some four hundred square miles, came under the command of Commodore Jacob H. Jacobson, USN, Commandant of NOB (Naval Operating Base), Leyte Gulf. Over 1,500 vessels were arriving and departing monthly during the summer, making Leyte one

of the world's busiest harbors. Besides the forward movement of men and supplies, the port grappled with the tasks
of salvaging and repairing hundreds of ships damaged in
battles or typhoons, routing and escorting homeward-
bound convoys, and receiving, berthing, and servicing hundreds of incoming ships each week.

Handling the arrivals, a routine but taxing occupa-
tion, was taken care of by the port director's office, a sub-
sidiary command under NOB, Leyte Gulf. The port director, in accordance with procedures long standard in the
Pacific, received advice of arrivals from his HECP (Harbor Entrance Control Point). At Leyte this was an LCT
anchored near the entrance to the gulf. The HECP would
identify arriving vessels and pass the word to the port director, with a copy of the dispatch to PSF. The port director would assign arrivals to numbered berths and take care
of their needs, be it fuel, food, or films. The names of the
vessels would go down on the "Ships Present" list, for the
use of any activity desiring such information.

All of this procedure applied, by long practice, only
to merchant vessels and naval auxiliaries. It did not apply
to combatant ships; the rules on that were quite clear.
They had been laid down meticulously in identical letters
to both the "Nimitz Navy" and the "MacArthur Navy."
The letters, known as CINCPAC's 10-CL-45 and Seventh
Fleet's 2-CL-45, set forth in three pages of single-space
type the procedures for routing combatant vessels outward bound from a given area. The matter of arrivals
was covered in one sentence, the last sentence on the last
page. It said: "Arrival reports shall not be made for combatant ships."

The reasons for this were simple: To provide security and to relieve communications. Naval Operations,
which handled the disposition of fleet units throughout
the world, did not want every local naval organization
popping off with long lists of combatant ship arrivals. Not
only would it crowd the air waves but it might tell the
whole world where the fleet was. So port directors everywhere took care of routine shipping and kept their hands
off the fleet, unless asked for help locally.

Thus there was mild surprise in the office of Port
Director, Tacloban, when the *Indianapolis* departure dis-
patch was received from Guam. Lieutenant Commander
Jules Sancho, USNR, had just arrived and was taking over

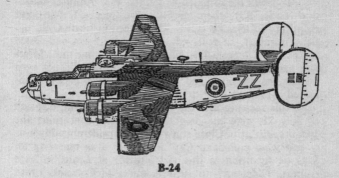

B-24

as Acting Port Director. Sancho, 42, was a former merchant mariner with considerable sea experience. His operations officer, Lieutenant Stuart B. Gibson, USNR, soon to turn 35, had been in the Navy nearly three years, all of the time in port director work, and had been in the port director office at Tacloban since January. When Lieutenant Gibson received the dispatch that the *Indianapolis* would arrive on July 31, he entered the ETA in a log book he kept for the general information of anyone interested in activities in Leyte Gulf. The message then went on through Lieutenant Commander Sancho up to Commodore Jacobson. Neither Gibson, nor Sancho (who had barely had time to unpack or read his mail), nor Jacobson paid any further attention to the matter. It was not the function of a port director or an NOB to plot the movements of combatant ships. Neither office had plotting boards of any kind and was purposely kept ignorant of fleet movements.

CINCPAC's original orders of July 26 to Captain McVay, when he arrived at Tinian, had not been communicated to any command in the Philippines. Those orders had said:

"Upon completion unloading Tinian, report to Port Director for routing to Guam, where disembark Commander Fifth Fleet staff personnel. On completion report to Port Director Guam for onward routing to Leyte where on arrival report to Commander Task Force 95 by dispatch for duty. Commander Task Group 95.7 directed to arrange 17 days' training for *Indianapolis* in Leyte area."

This was the dispatch which the Vice Admiral Oldendorf (CTF 95), then off Okinawa, received, but Rear
Admiral McCormick (CTG 95.7), then in Leyte Gulf, did
not. Or rather, he received it in garbled form and failed
to ask for a repeat. The Navy said later that the address
was garbled and Admiral McCormick's staff did not even
decode the message. Too bad, since he was clearly mentioned in the text.

This message and the Port Director, Guam, dispatch
of July 28 were the only two ever sent concerning the
Indianapolis' trip. Close study leaves considerable doubt as
to just what command Captain McVay was reporting to.
Was he reporting to the port director at Leyte, to Vice
Admiral Oldendorf, to Rear Admiral McCormick, or to
the Philippine Sea Frontier? All of them later disclaimed
any responsibility for reporting the *Indianapolis* overdue.

Herein lay the seed of the *Indianapolis* tragedy. There
was no operational control procedure for reporting combatant vessels overdue. The instructions were explicit on
departures, and they were explicit on arrivals, but they said
nothing about nonarrivals. If a combatant vessel arrived,
it was not to be reported. But what if a combatant vessel
did not arrive? Silence.

When Tuesday morning came and the *Indianapolis*
was not reported in Leyte Gulf there was no consternation,
nor even any discussion, in the port director's office. In
the first place, the port director considered he had no responsibility for combatant vessels. In the second place,
nonarrivals of ships, both combatant and noncombatant,
were quite common. Combatant ships sailed independently,
and there were a dozen reasons why the *Indianapolis*
could have failed to arrive. Captain McVay's orders could
have been changed by dispatch from CINCPAC while he
was under way. (The chance that the port director would
have been informed of this was slim indeed.) The vessel
could have been delayed, by breakdown, by weather, or
dashing off on a sub hunt. Vice Admiral Oldendorf could
have ordered him to come straight to Okinawa, or Rear
Admiral McCormick could have messaged that he would
meet Captain McVay at sea. In none of these instances
would the port director's office have been advised, if past
performance was any guide.

As for Rear Admiral McCormick, he felt no concern
for the *Indianapolis* either. His view was that when the

vessel arrived, he would talk with Captain McVay and
they would decide what kind of training was needed and
agree on a schedule. TG 95.7, or the Philippine Training
Group, was constantly changing in composition as vessels
arrived for training, or departed upon completion. Often
there was no warning when vessels were arriving, and quite
often they didn't arrive when they were scheduled to.
Only on Monday, the battleship *West Virginia* steamed
in from Okinawa. Neither Rear Admiral McCormick nor
anyone else in the Philippine area had any idea she was
coming. If this happened with battleships, why worry
about an overage cruiser?

No one did. Rear Admiral McCormick, with his flag
in the battleship *Idaho,* sailed out of Leyte Gulf on Tuesday morning with a couple of other old battleships, bound
for exercises off shore. The battlewagons *Arkansas, Texas,
New Mexico, Mississippi* and *Colorado* were also in port,
and those that didn't go out for training were left under
command of Commander Battleship Division 4, then in
the *West Virginia.* It was understood informally by him
that the *Indianapolis* might arrive that day. As a matter
of fact, if she had arrived on schedule, the *Indianapolis*
would have passed Rear Admiral McCormick in the *Idaho*
as he steamed out of Leyte Gulf. No one in that flotilla
seems to have marked the fact that the *Indianapolis* was
not sighted. In any event, nothing was done about it. No
dispatch was sent to the *Indianapolis,* to CINCPAC, to
PSF, or anywhere else to inquire where she might be.
There were a dozen reasons why she might not have arrived, all well-known to any fleet commander.

And down the shore at Tolosa, at PSF, no concern
was felt. Obviously, the approach of one particular cruiser
to its borders did not loom very large to PSF, particularly
with a half dozen battleships already standing in the harbor. At any rate, the vessel was not reporting to PSF. It
was a Fifth Fleet ship and it was reporting to a Fifth
Fleet unit for duty. But upon receiving the dispatch from
Guam that the *Indianapolis* had left for Leyte, the surface control office at PSF began a graphic plot on its
operational plotting board. The same thing was done at
Guam, at the headquarters of Commander, Marianas.
Each day, on each board, the line representing the *Indianapolis'* supposed progress was drawn a little farther
along, from Guam toward Leyte. On the day that she was

due at Leyte, the plot was erased from the plotting boards
at both ends. She was assumed to have arrived. This was
standard procedure at that time for plotting the routes of
combatant vessels. Fighting ships departed from one point
and were regularly "assumed" to have arrived at their
destination. It had always worked before. The case of the
Indianapolis was not unusual in any way, except for one
detail—the assumption, in this case, was false.

Tuesday was a usual day at Leyte in all respects.
Thirty or forty merchant ships or naval auxiliaries arrived,
checked in with the HECP, and were assigned berths by
the port director. His office reported the arrivals, as per
long practice, but never reported nonarrivals, with one exception—ships in convoy. No port director's office, up to
this time, reported nonarrival of combatant ships.

Rear Admiral McCormick went blithely to sea, and
the PSF executed its routine tasks. If the Indianapolis did
not arrive at Leyte, PSF might be notified some day as
to why not. More likely, it would never hear anything.
Shorty Gillette, of course, and his chief of staff, Captain Alfred N. Granum, would have no personal concern
with an individual ship. They probably knew nothing
about the Indianapolis at all. They soon would.

10

The Pacific Ocean is the largest single physical feature on earth. It is greater in size than all the land above sea level on the rest of the globe. The extreme depth, about 35,400 feet, lies between Guam and the Philippines.

No one knows exactly where the *Indianapolis* went down, but the Navy accepted the spot as 134 degrees, 48 minutes East, 12 degrees, 2 minutes North. Commander Hashimoto fixed the position as 134 degrees, 16 minutes East, 12 degrees, 31 minutes North, or some 44 miles northwest of the Navy's position. Not that it made any serious difference; the nearest land was still some 250 miles away, directly south, the top end of the Palaus archipelago. Guam was 600 miles to the east, Leyte 550 miles west, and to the north there was nothing for nearly a thousand miles. The water at this point was probably 10,000 feet deep, give or take a couple of thousand.

Some of the men saw their ship go down, but many did not—they were too far away. The ship, making about 15 knots at the time of the hit, slowed rapidly after the first torpedo blunted her nose, and the second one knocked out two of her four turbines. But she continued under way until almost the end, with the result that men were already widely scattered, right from the start. The biggest group, by far, was around the hull when the stern rose straight into the air, poised there a minute, then passed straight down, never to be seen again.

Men reacted in a variety of ways. To some it was a bit of a lark; these would be the young, the high-spirited, the unstable. The badly wounded were already shielded, mercifully, by a protective blanket of shock. It was not long before the sea would close over them, ending their troubles. Fate was unkindest to those rendered unfit for the fight, but condemned to struggle unequally until the inevitable came to call them.

Every man had his immediate problems: getting away from the ship, struggling in the fuel oil, spread incredibly everywhere, finding someone else—for fear of being left alone was universal—finding a life jacket or keeping one, grabbing for a raft, floating debris, anything. Here it was all sheer luck, and each man blessed his or cursed it, in proportion to how he fared in the great last scramble.

Captain McVay was fortunate, though there were times later when he might question this. One of the few who remembered the rudiments of abandon-ship procedure, or who had time for it, he had quickly dressed. As he walked down the side of the hull—his hull, his ship, his command—a soft wave came up behind him and gently carried him into the sea. Above him towered the stern, the giant screws glinting in the fitful moonlight. For an awful second he thought the vessel might fall on him.

And in that moment the thought flashed through his mind that it might be better this way. As an Academy man, a second-generation career man, and a third-generation Navy man, no one had to tell him what faced him if he survived. If the ship falls on me, he thought, I won't have to face what I know is coming after this.

But the will to live was too strong, and he struck out swimming, away from the menacing hulk above him. After only a few strokes, a wave of oil and water washed over his head, and he turned to look. The ship was gone.

The captain struck out again, and almost immediately ran into a crate of potatoes, late tenant of the fantail. He climbed astride this, reached out and grabbed a shattered desk floating by, and almost in the same instant saw two rafts not twenty feet away. Captain McVay quickly swam to them, and as he climbed in one he heard men calling for help.

He called back and soon Quartermaster Allard swam alongside, towing two shipmates who looked more dead than alive. Allard pushed Seaman Second Class Ralph D.

Klappa toward the raft and Captain McVay reached out for him, saying, "You can make it the rest of the way."

"I can't do anything," Klappa said and started to slide. Only eighteen years old, he had been to sea just fifteen days. McVay pulled him aboard and the youngster lay in the raft, vomiting oil and salt water. Meantime Allard helped Seaman Second Class Angelo Galante, 20, over the side and then pulled himself aboard. Galante joined Klappa in retching as they lay in the raft, recovering from fright and exhaustion.

McVay and Allard lashed the rafts together and spent the night investigating their new home. They quickly discovered the rafts had fallen into the water upside down. Paddles, rations, matches, flares, and other emergency gear were all secured to the bottom. By incredible chance, they saw and heard no one else throughout the night. A man low on the water can see practically nothing, even in daylight, and particularly with a twelve-foot swell running. But at dawn they discovered another raft and floater net nearby, with five more men on it. Captain McVay directed them to come over, and soon the three rafts were lashed together with fifteen feet of line between each. This kept the party from straying but allowed enough line so the rafts wouldn't bump.

John James Muldoon, a thirty-year-old New Bedford sailor, was senior man in the second group. A machinist's mate first class, he had served in the *Indianapolis* two and a half years. In his group were Yeoman Second Class Otha A. Havins, and his buddy, Jay R. Glenn, Aviation Machinist's Mate Second Class, as well as John Spinelli, Ship's Cook Second Class, and George R. Kurlick, Fire Controlman Third Class. The twenty-year-old Kurlick was naked, but none of the men was injured. As Captain McVay surveyed his command through one eye (the other was inflamed from fuel oil and nearly closed) he thought he was seeing about him the sole survivors of the 1,196 men aboard the *Indianapolis*.

He was greatly mistaken. There were hundreds of men within a few thousand yards, all struggling for their lives, and none as well off as the captain's group. There were a number of reasons why Captain McVay could not see them, or they him.

Men left the ship in a variety of ways over a period

of 12 minutes, during most of which the ship was still under way. The first off were soon left far behind, mere heads bobbing in a blanket of fuel oil, virtually undiscernible even from a ship in broad daylight. Those who stayed till the last were split into groups determined by the point at which they had left the ship, the swirling and eddying of waters around the hull, their swimming strength, and the impedimenta thrown in their way from the foundering vessel.

And hardly were they in the water than the sea began inexorably to separate them. The swimmers, nearly totally immersed, presented little surface to the wind and thus the prevailing current began carrying them to the southwest at about one knot. But those on rafts, or debris, felt the force of the ten-knot wind and were wafted off to the northeast at varying speeds. By daybreak, the groups were scattered over a line of several miles, on a generally southwest-northeast axis. A man with his eyes six inches above water can't see much in a moderately rough sea, even from the top of a twelve-foot swell. If his eyes are smarting from salt water and fuel oil, and partly blinded by a hot sun, he can see even less. Men on a raft have a better chance, but even on a crest you can't see into the troughs of other waves, and you may be scanning east when a head bobs up to the west, only to subside into a valley as you turn.

It may have seemed fortuitous that Doc Haynes, his assistant, Dr. Modisher, and Father Conway were thrown into the largest group of survivors. Actually, Haynes found soon after he entered the water that there was little medicine could do, though ministrations of the spirit might prove helpful. Hardly had the giant hulk slipped beneath the waves when the night was pierced with screams of "Doctor," "Doc," "Doctor." The thirty-three-year-old physician and surgeon, yearning to respond with the skills at his command, found he could not. For the first time he realized that his hands were painfully burned. He had been too busy to notice until now. Even had they not been, there was the fuel oil. It seemed to cover the sea everywhere, in a great viscose blanket, evil-smelling and irritating to the eyes. Men who swallowed it puked for hours, until it seemed their very stomachs would come up, inside out. Men who got it in their eyes or nasal passages cried in pain and made matters worse by rubbing in a vain effort to get rid of it. The offensive liquid was every-where, in vast, astounding quantities and from this end-less, undulating counterpane the men struggled to get free.

In these first confused and painful hours, mercifully covered by darkness, at least twenty men, already maimed, slipped away beneath the water, unequal to the battle. These were the men without life jackets. For those who had them, but could not long survive, Doc Haynes's role quickly changed from physician to coroner. Paddling from one still form to another, it was his task to lift the eyelid, test the reflex. Finding none, he would nod to bud-dies nearby. They slipped off the life jacket from one who no longer needed it, and passed it to a man who had none. For the receiver, it was a gift beyond price. Fresh and new now, it held him out of the sea from the chest up, and everyone knew they were good for forty-eight hours. These good, gray vests of kapok bought two full days of life, and surely by that time help would come. There was no fighting yet, for life jackets, but no one spurned one, not even the strong brave youngsters.

As dawn came, each man of the perhaps eight hun-dred still alive surveyed a new world. Some things were common in each man's world, and to each some things were different. Everyone saw immediately that there was nothing solid to cling to, only water on all sides and be-neath—everywhere but up. Each man knew already that the sea was harshly saline, the oil sulphurously irritating, the wind and frothing comber a constant burden. Those on rafts, floater nets, or debris, a few precious inches higher than the swimmers, still could not keep entirely out of the sea.

Besides the mass reaction to this peril and discomfort, each man had his own private little problem, the problem of individually living or dying, and each reacted according to his nature. Some whimpered in terror, others were defiant, still others resigned. Many were surprised, not only at their own insouciance, but at the depths of char-acter displayed by others. Courage blossomed in unex-pected places, and cowardice in still less likely places. Now they were all in the ultimate extremity, the God-fearing and the Godless, the evil and the noble, the weak and the strong, and let us see who will survive.

Monday dawned clear and the men welcomed the sun. It seemed at first to warm them spiritually after the cold night, and promise strength and help. They took heart and, as man seems to do in any circumstance, began organizing this new watery world. There was no question of over-all command, for already the groups were widely scattered. Indeed, in most cases each group knew only of its own existence and was fully occupied with its own problems. Some few small groups, finding themselves close together in the morning, did put their meager forces together. Almost from the start they fell into two large groups, and a dozen or more small, isolated clusters.

In perhaps the largest group—some three hundred men that first day—Lieutenant Commander Haynes was the senior surviving officer, and by virtue of rank, training, and force of personality he took charge. Strictly speaking, he was not the senior officer, for Commander Lipski, the gunnery officer, was there. But he was clearly dying. The flesh on his hands had been burned down to the tendons, and his eyes were burned closed. Shipmates gathered round him and tried to hold his tortured body out of the stinging sea and oil, and Doc Haynes looked on in anguish, unable to lessen his pain. From somewhere, a cork life ring appeared, and they used that for the severely injured. It knew more than one tenant. A long piece of line was formed into a large circle, and perhaps a hundred and fifty men clung around the perimeter. With only this flimsy line, they felt better. There were many other arrangements—one man clung to a toilet seat. Schecterle, just out of sick bay minus his appendix, latched onto a lard can, occasionally dipped into the contents to still the pangs, and alternately used the top as a heliograph. Plenty of ammunition cans were in evidence for a while, and the rubber-type, inflatable life belt was worn in several styles. Some put it around their middle, as indicated. Others wore it like a bandolier, lay across it side-saddle, or sometimes floated—using it as a pillow. In any form, it was nearly useless, and the wise man watched for a kapok that might soon be vacated.

Off to the northwest, less than a thousand yards away at the start, was a second large group. Whatever it was at the start, by dawn Monday death had weeded it down to 120 men and perhaps eight to ten officers, senior of whom was Dick Redmayne. Now he found himself in command of three small rafts, one floater net, some 5-inch

ammo cans and other flotsam. His force included one
seasoned warrant officer, three or four green ensigns, and
assorted enlisted men, fortunately including a couple of
chiefs. Among them was Benton, whose courage would
win him the Navy and Marine Corps medal.

To the northeast, capping the triangle, were the
splendid isolationists: the men whose great good fortune
it was to have nearly separate quarters on the rafts. Besides McVay's enclave of three rafts and nine men, the
biggest single floating command fell to Ensign Rogers, a
tall, rangy lad who had been to sea only two weeks. He
had been aboard so briefly that though he was a junior
officer of Turret IV, he still didn't know his duties or even
how it worked. Only the night before, his roommate, the
ever-efficient Ensign Woolston, had let him in on the open
secret that a sub had been reported along their course.
Rogers paid no more attention to this than anyone else.
Anyway, he was busy writing a letter to his bride. It was
their first anniversary (one month, that is), and he didn't
want her to think he had forgotten it.

Rogers was one of the last to leave the ship, and
when he hit the water he went down, down, down. He
thought he would never come up, but he did and right in
front of him was a raft. He grabbed a hand rope on the
side and hung on as the ship reared above him, hesitated
a moment, and then plunged. It was unbelievable that
anything as big and safe and solid could disappear in a
moment, but she did. After the final waves washed over
him, Rogers climbed into the raft and met his new "shipmates," a mountain boy named Willie Hatfield, Seaman
Second Class, from Salt Lick, Kentucky, and Chief Ferguson. During the night they picked up another man. Ferguson was suffering from his leg wounds, and Rogers put a
tourniquet around his thigh. Throughout the night, he
periodically released the pressure, fearing gangrene, and
when dawn came he carefully unwrapped the bandage
made of the mess-cook's pants. There was a deep cut at
the knee, and four or five inches of flesh gouged out below it, besides less serious cuts on the leg and foot. "Doc"
Rogers rewrapped the wound as best he could, and cut
the loss of blood to a slow ooze. Figuring rapidly, he rea-
soned that the ship would be missed Tuesday morning,
when it failed to show off Leyte for target practice.

Search would start immediately and they should be found by Wednesday morning. Ferguson could last that long, he figured. Ferguson never complained.

Daylight disclosed three other rafts nearby with men on them, and in an hour or so of paddling they were brought together. Rogers was now commander of four rafts and nineteen men, including a couple of Marines. All the men were sound, except Ferguson, but the rafts had lost all water and most of the food. One first-aid kit had been salvaged, and Rogers sprinkled sulfa on Ferguson's wounds. They tied the four rafts together for a while, but the constant bumping jarred the chief's leg painfully, and Rogers decided to cut loose from the others. The rafts drifted slowly apart, but remained in sight of each other until the end. As the sun became hotter on Monday, Rogers took off his pants and helped Ferguson wriggle into them, to protect his leg. The ensign shielded his own legs under a life jacket. So here they were, four men in a raft with one can of Spam, which appeared from somewhere. Rogers opened it and they all tried a little. The other two declined a second helping, so Rogers and the chief finished it. Hatfield began trying his luck with some of the emergency fishing gear.

During the night, the McVay rafters became scavengers, snatching from the sea any interesting looking objects they passed. At first light, the captain began to take stock of his possessions. His wristwatch was working fine, and he decided to keep a log, using paper and a pencil stub disgorged from various pockets and wallets. The sun gave an approximate position, and a fish line streaming in the water indicated drift. In spite of the wind, the rafts drifted west, and a few degrees south. The inventory revealed a relatively secure position. There were ten twelve-ounce cans of Spam, two large tins of malted-milk tablets, seventeen cans of biscuits, but no water. At least the food would be ample for some days to come.

Paddles were retrieved from the underside of the rafts, and one carton yielded fifty small packages of Camels. Oh boy, all the comforts of home! Well, nearly. There wasn't a lighter in the crowd, and the matches from the emergency kits were soaked. Cigarettes and no way to light them; they cast the cigarettes back into the water, removing at least that form of small torture.

They also found a first-aid kit—unneeded—and,

very reassuring, a can of Very flares and an emergency signaling mirror. In the can were a small pistol for firing the flares, and twelve flares in all, four each of red, green, and white. Captain McVay began to feel better. With his little convoy stretching out over seventy-five feet of water, and his signaling devices, he was confident they would be sighted by a plane on this heavily traveled track. Kurlick, who had been routed from the shower by the catastrophe, covered himself with life jackets. Allard turned to making cornucopia hats for the men from bits of canvas, and they settled down to wait. The skipper decided that for the sake of discipline they had better set a two-hour watch, and he took the 4:00 to 6:00 morning and afternoon watches. The watches were really only nominal, because everybody snapped awake when a plane went over or the shark nosed around.

He joined them the first day, a four-footer with his large dorsal fin bleached white from the sun. He was a friendly fellow, and refused to leave them, cutting back and forth around the rafts, occasionally bumping them. They flayed him with paddles, but he was not discouraged, and finally they gave up and let him hang around. No one had a sheath knife so they couldn't kill him, and he was a nuisance, scaring away other fish.

They sighted another raft some 1,500 yards away on Monday morning, but the men were all too tired to try to paddle over to it. By Tuesday morning they felt stronger, and began paddling in turns. Four and a half hours later, they overtook the raft and found one man on it, happy to join them. They welcomed him because he had another can of flares. Now they were four rafts, one floater net, and ten men. There were other rafts nearby, they now knew.

They sighted them once in a while, on a wave top, and all the time they were out there they could hear whistling. But the others seemed not anxious to join them, probably because it was too exhausting trying to paddle the cumbersome rafts. Life was becoming a little grim now. The men were tired, and they ached. All soon discovered that the designer of their rafts had never had to sit on them very long. The rounded top chafed on the buttocks and soon wore them sore. Hands blistered from paddling and every cut or abrasion began to develop salt-water ulcers. There seemed no way to keep dry, even in the rafts, and the constant salt-water dousing was irritating, physically and mentally. It was uncomfortable to sit down, but if you stood up and fell, you had a new cut to contend with. Elbows were turning raw from rubbing and the skin seemed tender and sensitive all over.

At 1:00 P.M. on Monday they saw their first plane. It was a twin-engine bomber, flying high, and passed directly over them. Two hours later there was another, a B-24 or B-29, way off to the south. Nobody really expected to be seen by them, but still, it was not reassuring. The planes were pretty high, and of course they weren't looking for anything in particular. At ten o'clock that night, they saw running lights and McVay fired his first flare. The plane never wavered. Other rafts saw it too, because they fired flares plainly visible to McVay's men. One more plane passed that night, about 2:00 A.M. Tuesday, and again the flares sputtered out unseen. Tuesday they saw no planes at all during daylight hours. Toward morning the sea began to moderate, and all day Tuesday and Wednesday it was nearly calm, a blessed relief from the constant pounding and wetting of the first twenty-four hours.

In the long hours of torpor settling over them, there was little to do but think. And Captain McVay had much

PBY

to think about. He was not normally an introversive type; quite the contrary, he loved life. His mind and heart were not of giant stature, and he never pretended they were, but it would be wrong to call him shallow. He loved life and he liked people, and he dreaded to think of what had happened to him, and what he faced.

He had no feeling of guilt. What had happened he had known might happen on one of those many times he traveled alone with no escort to fend for him or give alarm in case of trouble. Every precaution of the prudent man had been taken. Before he retired that night, all conceivable emergencies had been dealt with in the night orders. The ship was blacked out and buttoned as tightly as conditions permitted. The watch was in competent hands, and he himself strayed not a dozen feet from the bridge, available at any moment.

But Captain McVay did feel sorrow. He knew many of his officers were gone, but as bad as he thought it was, he still did not know the true magnitude of the tragedy. When he stepped foot on land again, he would learn that between him and his No. 32 in the chain of command not one officer survived. That of 82 officers aboard, only 15 survived, barely one in six.

For a moment, he remembered the good times ashore, only a few weeks ago, his closest officers around him, and their wives. They would have to be told, and he would have to tell them. And the wives and parents of the others, too. Many of them would look at him with accusing eyes. Some would be angry, some would be numb with tragedy, and a very few perhaps wouldn't give a damn. As the hours ticked by there were even moments, in the night, when it seemed that rescue would never come, and maybe that was just as well. But that was not fair to the men with him, and when the sun rose these thoughts left him and he prepared again to face what he knew he must. He was ready, for a good commanding officer never shirks his responsibility. Captain McVay was a good commanding officer.

11

For the swimmers, the battle for survival began the instant they hit the water. First it was the struggle to get their heads above the water and out of the slimy, choking oil. They sputtered and coughed, some vomited for hours, sprewing out the irritating substance, and many were blinded in one eye or both. Their noses, mouths, and throats smarted from the oil, and membranes became inflamed. And always there was the chop and splash of waves. By dawn, many were already seriously exhausted, but as the sun rose and they began to see others around them, the men took heart.

There was little talk among them, but a question often asked was whether a radio mesesage got off the ship, and how soon rescue would come. Officers who knew nothing about it assured the men around them that the distress message had gotten away. It was the least they could do, and if said with enough authority it even made them feel a little better. Even if no message got off, the ship would soon be missed and planes and vessels would come looking for them, the officers said. Everyone wanted to believe that, so it didn't sound too bad, and if some men had little gnawing doubts, they kept them to themselves.

As the sun rose on Monday, the sea flattened out a little and the men felt better. The kapoks were holding them high, and the worst of the oil bath was over.

"These things'll hold you up at least forty-eight hours," they said, and everybody knew they'd be rescued before then. Some of the fellows began to get a little cocky, and cracked a joke now and then. The men around him got a kick out of Johnny Reid, swimming around in his bathrobe. It was shrinking by the hour. Schecterle pulled out his wallet and found a soggy dollar bill in it.

"Beer for the house," he said, and they all laughed.

But the mood didn't last long. The sun rose steadily, and as it glinted off the oil their eyes began to burn, and pretty soon they were nearly blind again—photophobia, worse than snow-blindness, because, even when shut, their eyes glowed like two red balls in their heads.

Little things began to be important. Doc Haynes discovered he'd tied up his life jacket wrong—higher on one side, so that the collar tilted his head to one side. It wasn't funny, and even less so when he discovered the water-soaked knots wouldn't come undone. He worked for hours picking those knots out with his fingernails until he finally got it undone and tied up right.

As the heat rose, thirst began to bother some men, particularly those who had dehydrated themselves with retching or coughing. But there was no deliberate drinking of sea water that day. The men warned one another about that, and they all knew it was bad for you. Potatoes, canned peanuts, onions, other bits of food floated on the surface in some places, but most of the men wouldn't eat anything. They were afraid of upsetting their stomachs further, or getting even thirstier. A few ate anything that came by, and even hid a surplus in their pockets for later, but hunger was not a real problem yet.

It was some hours before they began to realize that sharks and other rapacious fish were among them. Suddenly a man screamed, his head bobbed for a moment, and he began flailing the water with his arms. Blood welled to the surface, and other men took up the cry. They beat the water with their arms and legs and shouted and screeched in an effort to scare the intruders away. At first they thought only of sharks, because everyone knew about sharks, and the telltale dorsal fin was often in evidence on the fringes of their circles. Gradually word spread from the older men that these warm equatorial waters were also host to carnivorous fish that could not be so easily seen.

"The barracuda has teeth like a razor and swims eighty miles an hour," one man said. "And if he slashes you going by he can cut your leg right off."

"Yeah, and what about the poisonous fish? One touch and you're dead," another man said.

Terror gradually spread, and the sea that once had seemed so friendly now became peopled with great and unknown perils.

Monday was generally a day of hope. Even the timid and the faint-hearted felt that something would happen—a ship would pass by and sight them, a plane would see them in the water, search parties must already be on the move.

"We were supposed to fire at sleeves tomorrow morning," they thought, "and even if the message didn't get off they'll miss us then and come looking." There was really nothing much to fear if one could just stay alive until Tuesday. True, it was a little disheartening when the first planes went over Monday afternoon and showed no signs of seeing them.

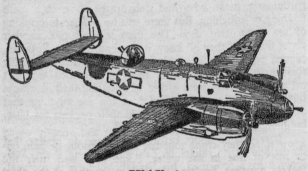

PV-1 Ventura

"I'll bet they saw us but couldn't stop," one said.

"Yeah, they radioed in and other ships will be out to look for us," said another. Nearly everybody believed that. If you could just hold on until Tuesday.

Some could not, of course. The injured who survived the first few hours were weakening now, with the sun high and hot, and the sea and the oil and their wounds all conspiring to sap their strength. It was pitiful to those around them not to be able to help, but there was nowhere to put them, nothing to give them, no way to protect them. They put some in the rafts, but there their bodies were fully exposed to the cruel sun. So they put them back in the water and tried to tie them to the rafts, if they were too weak to hold on. In these last hours of agony, those who had been spared injury gave unstintingly of their strength, their food, even their life jackets to help those who could not help themselves. But in most cases it was not enough. The burned and the maimed slipped away, one by one, and by Monday night nearly all of them were gone.

One of the last to go was Commander Lipski, whose grit had kept him alive despite his ghastly burns. Finally, now blind and nearly incoherent, he gasped out to Doc Haynes, "I'm going now, Lew. Tell my wife I love her, and I want her to marry again." They took the life jacket off his body and committed it to the sea.

It was a relief when the sun went down on Monday, but as darkness settled the wind turned cold and the men felt it as you do only in the tropics. After the blasting heat of the day the effect is devastating. It was black again now, and the men knew the full terrors of the deep. It was hard to see the man next to you, and there was the paralyzing fear of getting lost, getting separated from the group, dozing off and waking to find yourself alone in this vast sea. Sleep was becoming a peril now. During the day, many of the men had napped briefly, knowing that buddies would awaken them if their heads got too near the water, or a slap from the sea would shake them up. At night, you might slip away or go under and nobody would know it. So they clung together in little knots, or held on-to bits of line in the water. Some men tied their life jackets together, knotting the strings together at the chest like Siamese twins.

The strongest and the bravest tried to stay alert, even riding herd on the group like swimming cowpunchers, bringing back the strays and holding the men together. More than one, in this way, used up the reserves that might have kept him alive in the final hours of agony. They were, in truth, laying down their lives for their friends.

For most men, the night was worse than the day. Man's spirit normally sinks at night, and during the long, dark hours they fell prey to fears forgotten by day. It was a grim band, indeed, that struggled through the first

twenty-four hours in the water, and in the hours just before dawn a few men began to ask themselves why they
fought on. A few, weak and dispirited, perhaps impelled
by some previous purposelessness in their lives, may indeed have succumbed to the lassitude of despair. It was
so easy just to slip down, to let go, to sink, and in a few
moments it was all over. But the first streaks of morning
light in the sky revived the great majority of them, and
they prepared to meet the day of rescue. For surely help
would come on Tuesday.

The wind dropped and the sea moderated Tuesday,
and the men took it as a good omen. They were weaker
than the day before, but they had hope. They realized that
the kapoks were becoming logy, and their chins were
nearer the water, but they could last the day out, and
before nightfall they could expect to be warm and dry
aboard some ship. Some were beginning now to indulge
in little orgies of just thinking—a dry sack, a warm place,
a steak, a cold beer. A man could devote hours just to
putting the trimmings around the steak, or thinking of his
own bed at home and his mother saying, "Oh, let him
sleep a little longer." Older men might realize that madness
could lie in thoughts like these, so they tried not to think
at all, or to think of something useful, or helpful, or immediate. Married men could think of their wives and children, of the good times they had known and would know
again, must know again. A father couldn't afford to die,
his family needed him.

Tuesday was hot again, hotter than Monday, but nobody wished for night to come. Besides the fears of the
dark, ships and planes couldn't see you at night. Night
was a foe. But as the daylight hours passed, nothing happened. No plane passed overhead, and no ship came plow-
ing down on them. The strain began to show. There were
quarrels at the rafts and the nets. Men were irritable and
they began to bicker about turns on the raft, a fair share
of the rations, where there were any. Some men said the
officers were hogging the rafts, or hiding food, or eating
secretly. The man who was your friend yesterday was your
enemy today, because he had some potatoes and wouldn't
give you any. The bosun you thought was such a good egg
had been in the raft for hours and wouldn't let you in. The
guy over there had two good life jackets and yours was
shot, but he wouldn't give you one. Some of this was

true, but much was only imagined. But my God, how much did they think a man could stand, out here in the water all this time and nobody giving a damn. Probably haven't even missed us.

Almost from the first, men began discovering that life-jacket design was an art not yet mastered. The rubber life belts were the worst.

In the first place, many refused to inflate, for a variety of causes. Even if they did, they gave little support when worn around the waist, as intended. For one reason or another, perhaps because some were old or the sea water and oil affected them, many burst in a matter of hours. They were better than nothing, to be sure, but not much. The kapok jackets, of the so-called horse-collar type, gave good support, but the collars soon began to rub the men's necks and chins, increasing their suffering as the salt water and oil inflamed the irritated parts. Salt-water ulcers set in around the skin rubbed raw by the scratchy canvas. For that matter, men soon found ulcers developing at any spot where their skin had been cut, burned, rubbed, or otherwise injured during their ordeal. Although they were painful, the ulcers did not strike them as serious at the time, but some men suffered for months afterward if, of course, they were lucky enough to survive at all.

From the first dawn, the ingenious among them— there were many—tried to devise ways to beat the sun. The fortunate, who had left the ship clothed and wearing hats, were best off but most men had plunged into the water in the sketchiest of clothing—shorts only, shorts and skivvies, or nothing at all, if that's the way you preferred to sleep or you were caught in the shower. Those who could lay their hands on bits of cloth—pants, shirt, underwear, even socks—tore them up and tried to fashion hats, eyeshades, noseguards, or collar pieces to protect their necks from the rubbing life jackets. But the best efforts were to little avail. Men's lips began to puff and crack, their eyelids swelled, their faces burned and burned again. The oil helped some on the upper body, but around the head it was highly irritating to delicate membranes of the eyes, nose, and mouth. By Tuesday night the swimmers were in pitiful shape. Most were nearly blind, and it was difficult to see the man nearest you, let alone recognize him, his face swollen and distorted as badly as your own. This may have accounted for some of the events of the

next two days, for the man you didn't know was not
merely a stranger, he was an enemy.

Thirst was more of a problem than hunger. Some
men were quickly in an acute condition from deyhdra-
tion, either because they had swallowed large quantities
of salt water in fighting to survive the sinking or because
the fuel oil and water forced them into long spells of
vomiting or coughing. This dried out their systems ab-
normally and they began to contemplate the water all
around them with more than ordinary interest. As the sun
rose higher and hotter on Monday, some men began thinking of schemes for making the sea water potable. At this
stage, before dementia had set in on a large scale, and
their bellies began to hurt, they talked a little of "strain-
ing" the water, or "evaporating" it.

"How about it if you hold some water in your
hands? Won't the sun evaporate the salt out?"

"What do you say we strain some water through this
hat a couple of times? We can catch it in this handker-
chief and squeeze it through again. That ought to do it."

"Knock it off, it'll still kill you," said the clearheaded
around them. But pretty soon even the clearheaded had
problems of their own, and they became less careful or
less watchful. Then the men who could stand it no longer
took first a little drink, then a bigger one, and a still
bigger one. It is a horrible death, but soon over. During
the last paroxysms, friends about them sought either to
hold them or to escape from their wild thrashings, until at
last the bodies subsided and became still. It was time then
to salvage the life jacket and knife, mirror, or any other
potentially useful object and let the body sink slowly out
of sight.

If Tuesday was a day of hope, that hope died when
night fell and not a single plane had flown over during
daylight. It was then that men truly called upon the well-
springs of strength and courage within them. This was the
night they began to see things. Some saw planes barely
skimming the surface, others saw the running lights of
ships bearing down on them. The latter image terrorized
some men, for they thought the Jap sub had surfaced to
machine-gun them. And at the night wind chilled them,
their teeth chattered and their bodies shook with violent
seizures. This was the night that most of them passed from

the world of sanity into the world of fantasy. Many of them ceased to suffer in the usual sense, even as the asylum inmate may no longer suffer from a world that is too much for him. No gong rang early Wednesday to signal the end of two full days in the water, and few men even thought of time any more. Only later did they realize that by dawn they had been fifty-five hours in this macabre world, specks on the surface of the world's largest sea, floating helpless and unhelped, as if no one knew or cared.

Wednesday was a delightful day for the swimmers. It was the day they learned the *Indianapolis* had not sunk after all. She was lying just below the surface of the water, and the gedunk stand was open, featuring six flavors of ice cream, and the scuttlebutts were pouring forth pure, sweet water as usual. The first man to discover this was so delighted with the find that he urged all those around him to go down with him and slake the terrible thrist that was driving them mad. As the word passed, a sort of frenzy ran through the swimmers and in a short time many were diving like swans, using up the last resources of strength that might have saved their lives. Some men who had not yet passed fully into the world of fantasy tried to restrain them, but it was useless.

Also, on this day, the island was discovered. It was amazing no one had seen it before, but suddenly, there it was, a nice little island, with an airstrip and a hotel. Some of the men were skeptical. Lieutenant McKissick called one of the men aside and asked him, honestly, if the island was really there. The fellow said sure, he knew the Chinese who ran it, but he had swum over and the Chink wouldn't give him any water, or even let him come ashore.

The lieutenant bided his time until nightfall, then he and his buddy started to swim over. On the way, some of the men tried to take their life jackets. The pair fought them off and swam on, but the island had moved and they became exhausted. They tied their life jackets together and slept for a couple of hours, but when McKissick awoke his buddy had gone, leaving an empty life jacket. McKissick heard him in the distance and called out, but his buddy kept going. The lieutenant never saw him again.

At dawn, McKissick started out alone for the island but soon met a couple of kids and gave them the extra life jacket. Then they passed a couple of Marines on a potato crate and invited them to come along. No thanks, said the Marines, they were swimming to Leyte.

"Well, why don't you come over to the island first and have a cold drink, then swim to Leyte?" McKissick asked. That seemed like a good idea and the Marines fell in with the party. But when they got to the island, it was under water. One boy said his mother ran the hotel, and they'd have to wait until it was open for business.

"My room's over there," he said, pointing. "My mother runs this place but I'm not very familiar with it. She's just taken it over."

He called the hotel on the telephone. A steward who used to be on the *Indianapolis* answered and said the hotel was full, but McKissick said, "Here, let me talk to that guy."

"No, he won't talk to you. He won't even talk to me, and my mother owns this place."

Then a lot of planes flew over, and the boys pointed out the airstrip, but the stupid aviators just kept going. It made the sailors mad, but they decided to lie there in their life jackets and wait for rooms at the hotel.

Another bunch of men tried to get ashore on the island, or maybe it was another island, but the Seabees wouldn't let them. So they, too, got mad and swam off. Wouldn't tell anybody where they were going, but just disappeared.

One fellow, after thinking about it steadily for a long time, announced he had figured out that he could swim to Leyte in two and a half days. With a wave of his hand, he struck out toward the west. Some fellows were quietly content where they were. Yeoman Buckett spent all day in a store filled with ice-cold watermelons. The fellow in charge told him he could eat all he wanted to. Watertender Wilcox spent Wednesday quietly, praying steadily most of the day, and crying some when he remembered his wife at home. He was determined, however, that if anyone could survive, he could. Toward nightfall, Wilcox thought that the fellows who did a lot of talking seemed to be doing better so he started to jabber to the man alongside him. The other fellow didn't mind; he was out of his head.

Lieutenant Reid dropped his car keys and dove frantically for them. He simply had to have them, so he could drive over to his farm in New Hampshire, and get some cold milk. He never did find the keys, but he noticed that his ring had slipped off his finger and gone down.

Seaman Second Class Joe Dronet, a quiet kid of seventeen from Cameron, Louisiana, remembered his boot training well, so when the sharks came around he didn't kick and scream like the others. He lay on his back quietly, and they never touched him. Others around him were slashed and bleeding, but the sharks never came near him. And then he felt that he really couldn't die. His mother had worked so hard to get him through high school and it nearly broke her heart when he went away, what with her four other boys already in service. So Joe just made up his mind he wouldn't die, and when the deck officer and twenty-five men swam off for that island, Joe just clung to his floater net. There was a time near the end when he'd take a little salt water in his mouth, but he always summoned up enough will power to spit it out. Lack of sleep was a torture, but he had seen too many men go that way, so he resolved never to shut his eyes.

Some of the life jackets were reaching the saturation point now, and every once in a while a man would fight to get out of his before it sank, only to find that he was fatally trapped in his "life" jacket. It was horrible for the others to watch, but what could they do? There was no way to get the sodden jacket off, and they couldn't hold someone else up when their own chins were now in the water.

In truth, for the swimmers, Wednesday was a day of horror. It was a costly day in lives, for many men swam off and never came back or dived down to the ship and never came up. Still others gave their lives trying to prevent these suicidal jaunts. The big Marine, Captain Parke, swam around and around his group trying to hold it together, but toward evening he quietly sank beneath the sea, exhausted. Father Conway wore himself out in similar solicitude and on Wednesday night collapsed in delirium and expired in Doc Haynes's arms.

By contrast, Wednesday was a good day on the rafts. The sea was calm and flat, the men were well-fixed for food and shelter from the sun and they had settled down for the long wait. Captain McVay from the start had put his faith in ships finding them, not planes, and had figured that Thursday would be the earliest they could be expected. While they had seen no planes on Tuesday, Wednesday was a big day, with eight or nine passing over. McVay's group gave them the works—Very flares, the signal mirror, two signaling flags waving wildly, yellow bunting streaming over the waves, and every available leg splashing water. But it was no good, the planes were too high.

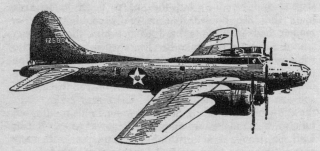

B-17

They aren't looking for anything down here, you know," Captain McVay told his men, trying to reconcile them. "They're busy with their radar and instruments, and even if they did look down they wouldn't see much from that altitude." The men acknowledged this, but the thought didn't make them feel any better.

The emergency fishing kits delighted McVay, an ardent fisherman. The cans contained lures, hooks, a small spear and other equipment, a knife with a one-inch blade, and line. Whitey, the shark, scared most of the fish away, however, and they caught only some small, black fish. The meat was fresh and white, but Captain McVay was afraid it was poisonous and would not let the men eat it. Off in the distance they could see schools of bonita and mackerel, but Whitey kept them away from the raft. On this day the captain decided to cut the rations in half, to make them last twenty days instead of the ten he had originally planned for.

As the sun sank Wednesday, the men's spirits began to decline also. They had been sleeping or quiet most of the day, except Glenn and Havins, who chatted cheerfully. One man took to moaning, but when Muldoon asked him if anything was wrong he said "No," and quieted down. The captain kept telling the men that Thursday would be their day.

"They probably missed us on Tuesday, and began looking for us today," he said. "Figuring twenty-four hours to get here, they should reach us tomorrow."

At other times he told them, "There's really nothing to worry about, men. Our chances are very good. We can hold out for a long time on these rafts, and they certainly must be looking for us by now." In this way the third day ended and they passed into the fourth day on the open sea.

But among the swimmers, morale was deteriorating rapidly. There had been some fighting on the lines Tuesday night, but Wednesday night was a night of terror. When darkness fell the demented men were the victims of stark fear, and every shape became an enemy.

"There's Japs on this line," someone screamed and a little knot of men would be plunged into a melee, fighting with fists, cans, cork, anything that came to hand. Now and then a knife blade flashed in the moonlight, followed by a groan and then a struggle for a life jacket whose recent owner needed it no more.

"Here comes a Jap, he's trying to kill me," a sailor shouted, "Help! help!" The frenzied men took up the shout and began swinging wildly at anyone near. Two men climbed on Doc Haynes and dragged him under. When he struggled to the top again he tried to calm the men, but it was no use. They were too far gone for reason. Those who still possessed their senses could see the toll was terrible.

Toward morning, calm slowly returned and it was obvious the men were falling into the final stupor that precedes death. Haynes moved among the pitiful survivors, trying to rouse them for one last day's fight. He lifted head after head from the water, rolled back an eyelid and, in some, detected signs of life. These men he slapped and cajoled into consciousness, trying to pull them back from the brink.

"This is it," he thought. "Today, or never." Looking around at what had been his three hundred men, he counted less than a hundred left, and of those still in sight not all were viable. Some floated face down and would never lift their heads again. Lieutenant Redmayne's sector was the same. In the rafts, men were piled all over each other, and those at the bottom of the heap, too weak to protest or move, were smothered by bodies above them. Bitterness among the dozens of men trying to get on or near the three small rafts directed itself, rightly or wrongly, but certainly naturally, toward the officers.

"Goddam officers, hogging the rafts and all the food," some muttered. "I'll kill that son of a bitch when we get on shore. Drinking up all the water, and we got none."

Thursday began as a day of calm—the calm of death for the swimmers. With all strength gone, all emotion spent, they seemed nearer death than life, and indeed they were. There was little talk or movement, just a quiet waiting for the end to overtake them. Hanging in their water-logged life jackets, their mouths and noses nearly in the water, they no longer wished nor hoped for anything, not even death. The inevitable sun rose, higher and hotter, and still no complaints. They were not capable of caring any more. A few, slightly stronger than the others, looked up occasionally or even strained to listen when they thought they heard a plane. A little before noon, with the sun still mounting, a few looked up when a plane droned by, high overhead. There was a scattering of muttered curses, even a doubled fist raised weakly out of the water. The plane passed over, to the north. They had known it would.

Then, here and there, a heart fluttered. The plane seemed to pause, to turn. Some thought it was starting down. It was, it was!

"He sees us, he sees us!" someone screamed. Others joined in, and arms and legs began to splash.

"They're coming, they're coming!" "He's turning, he's turning!" "Here he comes!"

Like sleepers roused from stupor the men began to come alive, joining in the chorus one by one. Where they got the strength no one can say, but soon the ocean was kicked into a froth, and cries echoed from many throats. Some men could only croak or grunt, their gullets swollen nearly shut, and some men didn't move or utter a sound. Too late, too late.

It was almost exactly three and a half days—eighty-four hours—since the *Indianapolis* had gone down.

They watched the plane, the blessed plane, as it

came down low and circled, and some men cried and prayed, "God give us strength." They realized gradually that the plane alone could not save them. There was no telling how long it would be until ships arrived, and each man made his own plans for hanging on for the next few minutes, or hours. Now was no time for dying, help was too near. Mustn't fall asleep now, or lose your head. Just wait and be calm, be calm. Save your strength, stop kicking and shouting. He sees us, he'll get the others, the ships will come. Just hold on. Oh God, give me strength.

The big friendly plane circled slowly and then—over the southernmost knot of men—a raft, some life jackets, and other gear spewed from the plane and fell nearby. Grateful men swam out to get the raft, careful not to overtax their strength, and when they reached it clung to the sides, too weak to climb in. Others grabbed the fresh dry life jackets to replace their waterlogged ones. Men for miles around watched as the plane slowly climbed away from them, and held their breath until they saw that she was not going away. It was comforting to have her there, even though she could do them no immediate good. As long as she stayed they knew she was helping them, telling someone by radio where to look, calling others to their aid.

The second plane, a PBM, arrived from the northeast a little after noon. She didn't stay long, but she dropped three more life rafts and then hurried on to the west, toward Leyte. Hope was getting stronger now; other planes would be coming, and ships. Another plane, a Ventura like the first, arrived a half hour later, and also from the south. The two Venturas orbited overhead and seemed to be talking, or planning, and watching. Then the first Ventura, their friend, their savior, took off southward, obviously going back to base to get more help. The second Ventura remained overhead, but it wasn't until nearly four o'clock, with the sun already starting down, that the next plane arrived. This was a big amphibian from the south, and after a look around she began to drop things, like an elephant littering the track at the circus. Out came rafts, one after another, and cartons of rations, dye marker, life jackets, casks of water. Some of the water casks split on hitting the water, some of the gear sank, and some was useless, but it was all welcome, if only as a symbol that help was on the way.

But day was definitely waning, and the men in the
water began to wonder if still another night in the water,
their fourth, would be required of them. To make matters
worse, the sea was beginning to make up again. Toward
sunset those few left in the southernmost group, the
Haynes group, watched in wonder as the PBY slowly
glided down as if to make a landing run. It looked like
suicide, with the swells running nearly twelve feet high by
this time. But the giant plane kept coming down and suddenly it pancaked into a trough, took three mighty
bounces in a towering spray, and came safely to rest on
the water.

Strangled cheers broke through sore and swollen lips
and throats as the PBY began to taxi slowly around the
periphery, pausing now and then to scoop a lone swimmer
into its belly. Those who now had rafts, nets, or other
means of support cursed at the plane as it passed them
without stopping, but it was obvious what the pilot was
doing—as darkness fell he was hurrying to pick up the
lone swimmers, those with nothing to cling to.

It was very nearly dark now, and just as the last light
began to fade a second PBY came in from the south, low
and slow. This one, bearing Army markings, quickly came
down to wave-top height, knifed through the tops of
several swells and cut her power, disappearing in a trough.
Soon she appeared on the crest of a wave, safely landed.
She seemed quite a way off from any swimmers, but maybe some could find her in the dark. Those still in the
water, and there were hundreds, were alone again now,
but at least they had hope, and perhaps a raft, to sustain
them through the darkness.

Eight or ten miles to the north, Captain McVay and
the other raft parties could see the plane activity through
the afternoon. McVay was greatly cheered, not only because rescue seemed near but because the concentration
of activity far south indicated there might be many more
survivors than he had believed. But as the afternoon
waned and the planes seemed to be working ever southward, the raft crews began to worry that they would not
be seen.

Again at dusk, as he had each night, Captain McVay
led the men in reciting "The Lord's Prayer." It seemed
more helpful than usual this night.

McVay began to think his group must be north of the northern limit of the search area.

"We're in a fine fix now," he thought. "If they're going south all the time and we're going north, they are going to miss us."

Naturally he did not express these thoughts to his men, but they were no fools, they could figure as well as he could.

McVay's eye fell on the 40-mm. can they had retrieved at great effort, thinking it might contain provisions. It was empty, but they had kept it, and now was the time to put it to use.

"We'll make a fire in the can and see if we can't attract the planes," McVay said. They quickly tore the collars off a couple of life jackets, and cut up a rubber life preserver. These were put in the can, and McVay fired a Very rocket into the pile. The cloth and rubber began to smolder, and shortly they had a good smudge pot going. They kept it burning well past nightfall, but it seemed to have no effect. The men's spirits sank, and they began to doze.

But this was not to be a night like the others. About 9:30 some of the swimmers and rafters began to notice a light far to the south. At first it seemed it might be an illusion or a faint moon rising behind the clouds. As time passed, however, the light became stronger and within a half hour it seemed pretty definitely to be a searchlight, reflected off the clouds. By the time an hour had gone by, the light was unquestionably brighter, and coming closer, although still a long way off. By 11:00 they were sure—it was a ship coming at them, fast, and with all lights on.

One of the most powerful—and subtlest—enemies had been sleep. The human body can survive many days without food or water, under severe physical conditions, but the brain demands rest. After the first day in the water, the men passed into a sort of drunkenness of fatigue. They feared sleep and they fought it, because it separated them from the world of reality, the world in which they might be saved, and placed them at the mercy of the sea and its unknown terrors, both on the water and below it. They all dozed at times, some in the safety of a raft, others in private little havens they built of kapoks, cans, crates, anything they could put together to give a measure of safety. Others merely dropped their heads from sheer exhaustion as they bobbed up and down in the ever-lowering life jackets.

Now that help was so near, they feared sleep more than ever and were less able to fight it, being on the outer edges of oblivion.

"I mustn't sleep, I mustn't sleep," they told themselves. Men who had not once slept in eighty hours, or so they believed, vowed they would not succumb now, with help so near, so near. But the sea was rougher Thursday night, security so close, and they were so tired—not every man kept his vow.

On the rafts to the north, the men could see the searchlights off to the south, first one, then several, and finally by dawn there was great activity. But it did not move north, or so it seemed.

For the swimmers, actual rescue in the form of help from surface vessels began shortly after midnight on Thursday, exactly four days, or ninety-six hours, from the sinking of the *Indianapolis*. By chance, the first vessel approached from the south. Had she come from the north, she might have seen the men on the rafts first—the men who could wait—and delayed long enough to cost even more lives, for with the swimmers minutes counted. But the planes on the water and the accident of approach led the ships directly to the men who needed help the most, and through the black hours from midnight to dawn the rescue vessels picked up one of the most pitiful bands of men ever to escape the sea. Men suffered from burns— sun or flame—fish bites, salt-water ulcers, inflammation of the nose and throat, acute dehydration, pneumonia, fractures, and cuts and bruises from a thousand sources. But hearts still pumped and blood still flowed and from now on it would be up to medical science.

At dawn the rescue vessels began to see what they had been doing and to realize the magnitude of the appalling tragedy before them. Command and planning took over from the frantic and haphazard methods of the dark hours. They began to take stock of how many men they had aboard, how many might still be in the sea, and how best to comb the area for the last remaining survivor. On orders now, the vessels spread out in search pattern sniffing for the living among this welter of oil, debris, and bodies.

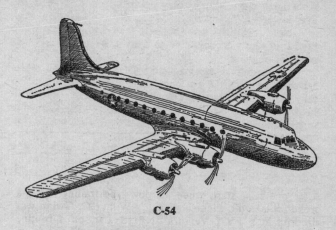

C-54

Last to be rescued were the rafters, at the north of the group. Their most anxious moments came in the last hours of Friday morning darkness, when it seemed the ships were so near and yet would miss them. But at dawn they saw planes to the north and hope rose again. The planes were obviously on box search, and coming ever closer.

At 10:00 A.M. they saw ships, and suddenly someone shouted, "My God, ships bearing down on us! The hell with the planes, we know these guys will pick us up."

Later they learned that neither planes nor ships had seen them, but one of the APD's picked up a radar pip at 4,046 yards. It was the trusty 40-mm. can, McVay's smoke pot. The vessel maneuvered skillfully alongside and gathered in the men—one hundred and seven hours after the sinking.

It was the end of one of the strangest, most dramatic battles of men against the sea. It was the end, and also it was the beginning, for with these suffering and exhausted men lay the answer to the question: What happened to nearly 900 of your shipmates?

12

After one false start, when his new-type trailing antenna broke on take-off, Lieutenant (j.g.) Wilbur C. Gwinn was airborne in a PV-1 Ventura at 8:15 A.M. on a routine "negative patrol" north from Peleliu. He could not know it, of course, but perhaps the most dramatic sea rescue in history was under way. And the trailing antenna, which he was testing as assistant engineering officer of squadron VPB-152, was to play a vital part in the saving of 316 lives.

On the tarmac runway to watch the take-off were the squadron commander, Lieutenant Commander George C. Atteberry, and his air combat intelligence officer, Lieutenant Malcolm S. "Pappy" Langford. A lawyer before the war (and still), Langford was an "old man" of thirty-nine, hence the obvious nickname from the fly boys. VPB-152 was a close-knit squadron of 18 crews, welded into a keen, proud team by Atteberry's leadership and a common, exciting experience. For some months they had trained at Clinton, Iowa, in a "top-secret" weapon which might have been of vast importance but in the end was scratched for something better.

When the project was dropped, VPB-152 gradually staged out to San Francisco, Hawaii, Midway, and finally Peleliu. The job was pretty routine now, but important. Tens of thousands of Japanese soldiers were cut off on the islands of the Palau group. VPB-152's job was to help them along by preventing food, supplies, and reinforcements from reaching them or evacuation vessels from removing them from the jungle prison.

Atteberry and Langford had laid out five search sectors north of Peleliu, Victor 22, 43, 19, 35, and 26, and each crew flew one mission daily. Theoretically, that is. Actually, the planes were up more than they were down, with special missions for air-sea rescue, weather, or un-evaluated sightings. Every time someone reported a tree stump floating in the water, a crew went out to probe around, for pilots were splashing regularly from the heavily traveled airways over those vast waters.

As Gwinn and his crew of four took off on Thursday morning, August 2, the weight snapped off the trailing antenna. The Ventura, a twin-engine land plane, returned long enough to have another weight affixed and was off again in a few minutes. Victor 19 was a dog-leg sector, starting out northeast, then turning north to northwest and back to base on the hypotenuse. Flying into the sun on the outbound leg, the crew could see virtually nothing on the smooth sea. But these were not visual patrols anyway. Primary reliance was on radar pips, with the crew seldom looking down at the empty water.

The flight droned on for nearly three hours, and around 11:00 A.M. an overcast commenced to form above 10,000 feet. Near the northern extremity of Victor 19, Gwinn dropped the Ventura down to about 5,000 feet to get a better combination of radar and visual observation. Chief Radioman Hartman, bored with routine patrols in the backwash of the war, was thankful for something to do when Gwinn suggested a test of the new antenna weight. Ordnanceman H. Hickman reeled the wire out behind the plane, and for the second time that day the weight separated. If this was supposed to be an improved type, give me the old one, Hartman thought.

The wire whipped around like a tomcat's tail in an alley fight as he and Hickman tried to reel it in. It wasn't very funny, either, for the wire might damage the tail surfaces. So after a while the boys called for Gwinn. He turned the plane over to co-pilot Lieutenant (j.g.) Warren Colwell, and began scrambling aft.

Together, Gwinn, Hartman, and Hickman tamed the wild wire and reeled it in. Gwinn started to fasten a piece of rubber hose to the end, for another try.

He was on the edge of a great discovery. As his gaze wandered down through the tail-gunner's blister, a perfect combination of sun and sea showed him an oil slick. Hartman and Hickman saw it at almost the same instant. They let out a cheer. Here, at last, was some action—an enemy sub!

Gwinn ran back to the cockpit, gave Colwell a quick fill-in (he couldn't have seen the oil slick from where he was), and immediately turned the Ventura to put the sun at his back. Hickman and Mechanic J. K. Johnson opened the bomb-bay doors and the jubilant crew was ready for anything. Everybody saw the oil slick now and Gwinn dived to 1,000 feet for a run over it.

Suddenly Gwinn saw a head sticking out of the slick. Colwell saw another, then another and another, until in a few seconds there were at least thirty. The fly boys were dumbfounded. Langford had mentioned no ships in the area at morning briefing. Gwinn shouted over the intercom for the men in the belly to shut the bomb-bay doors, and the Ventura made a low pass over the slick.

In the water, there was absolute delirium. At last, dear God, help at last! Even as the weakest died at that instant, the stronger cheered, whistled, shouted, slapped the water, smiled, laughed, chortled, or burbled. Some only moaned, and a few, face down in the water, saw nothing.

Gwinn was twenty-four, a California farm boy, quiet and modest but utterly competent. He knew exactly what to do, and did it. First he made several passes over the area, while his crew dropped the plane's life raft, life jackets, and two sonobuoys. Maybe someone will talk to us over them, Gwinn thought.

Then he pulled up to get altitude for radio transmission, and the first message went out at 11:25: "Sighted 30 men in water, position 11-30N, 133-30E." The damned trailing antenna was only part way out, but maybe the message would get through. Circling for more altitude, the astounded crew now counted 75 heads in the water, and Hartman keyed out a second message to Peleliu. And a few minutes later another message—150 men now. Wow, this is big stuff, the boys in the belly thought.

But there was no such excitement in Peleliu. Gwinn's first message came through badly butchered, thanks to that antenna—but without it there would have been no sighting, and perhaps not a single survivor. When the Communications Center got through, it had something like "Am circling life raft," a report about as common as chow call in those days.

However, the second and third messages came through better, and Communications realized quickly it had something big. They rang up Operations at the nearby headquarters of Rear Admiral Elliott Buckmaster, who had command of this whole area under the title Commander, Western Carolines Sub-Area. The operations officer, Commander Marshall A. Anderson, granted permission to put every available plane in the air, and immediately telephoned over to their quarters for Admiral Buckmaster and his Chief of Staff, Captain Eugene T. Oates. They jeeped down to Operations and set in motion a giant rescue operation. Charts were whipped out to plot the location of the men in the water, and junior officers scurried to find and report the position of every plane and ship for hundreds of miles around. They all might be needed.

Lieutenant R. Adrian Marks had the standby duty that morning with VPB-23, a PBY squadron. He topped off his gasoline load to a full 1,250 gallons, enough to keep him in the air for twelve hours. Crewmen checked to make sure the full load of survival gear was aboard, including droppable life rafts and ration kits, and at 12:40 P.M. the giant amphibian waddled down the runway. With good luck it would reach the scene in about three hours, lumbering along at about 100 knots.

Right behind him down the runway came Atteberry, off for the scene, too, in his much faster Ventura to relieve Gwinn, whose gas was running low. As he passed Marks, Atteberry called over on voice radio: "Gambler Leader to Playmate Two, Gambler Leader to Playmate Two, pardon my dust but we've got business up north." The Ventura disappeared ahead and the PBY droned on, trying its best to look dignified.

Atteberry found Gwinn about 2:15 P.M., and the latter already had company. An unknown PBM (serial K9244), en route from Guam to Leyte, had happened on the scene about 1:45, sent three hot dispatches to Guam, dropped three life rafts, and continued on to Leyte. As he was leaving, Atteberry was already telling Peleliu "One fifty survivors, Lat. 11-54N. Long. 133-47E." Marks

Purple Heart

eavesdropped on that message, and was shocked. "One fifty" must have been an error in coding, he thought, as he changed position to the new location.

There was another rubbernecker, this one on the surface. The *Cecil J. Doyle* (DDE 368), a trim new destroyer escort commanded by Lieutenant Commander W. Graham Claytor, Jr., a Washington lawyer, was loafing along on a nice summer afternoon about fifty miles north of Babelthuap, the largest of the Palau islands. The *Doyle* was stationed at Kossol Roads, at the north end of Babelthuap, and to relieve the boredom, occasionally lobbed shells onto the island to stir up the 40,000 Jap guests.

As he steamed south about 2:30, Claytor saw a PBY on opposite course. Friendly-like, he called the plane on voice radio when it was overhead and discovered that the pilot was Marks, his Indiana-lawyer acquaintance from Peleliu. Marks quickly told him all he knew and volunteered that he assumed the *Doyle* would soon get orders to reverse course.

With cynicism born of experience, Claytor knew it might be hours before such orders got through the constant communications jam to him. Why wait? So the *Doyle* made a 180-degree turn and Claytor rang for full speed ahead. He laid her flat out and the new Westinghouse turbines soon gave him 22 knots. Official orders came through an hour and a half later. It is not possible to say how many lives Claytor's stolen ninety minutes saved, but not one who lived would have wanted to risk it.

At about the time Claytor was talking to Marks, things were beginning to happen on Leyte, far to the northwest, and Ulithi, to the northeast. Messages from Gwinn, Atteberry, and the unidentified PBM were beginning to make an impact. Nobody knew quite what was up, but obviously it was something big, with the lonely sea scattered with at least 150 men, a tremendous oil slick some ten miles long, and debris of almost every kind.

Lieutenant Commander Albert H. Nienau, erstwhile circulation man for the *Seattle Star*, got a foggy picture from messages around 12:30 P.M., something about unidentified debris in the water east of him. He was in command of the *Dufilho* (DDE 423), on routine antisubmarine box patrol about 150 miles east of Leyte Gulf.

Upon receiving orders from Commodore Gillette to "proceed at best possible speed and investigate" he laid on about 21 knots. Upon checking fuel gauges, he cut this to 18 to conserve oil in case of extended search needs.

To the north of him, also on routine patrol out of Leyte, lay the *Bassett* (APD 73), and also about a year old. On the bridge was Lieutenant Commander Harold J. Theriault, bushy-eyebrowed son of a Gloucester fisherman and a deep-water man himself. Though no one knew it yet, rescue honors would go to the *Bassett*, for picking 151 men out of the sea. Theriault's first message, received at 2:16 P.M., directed him to proceed to about 12N. 134E. and he opened to flank speed of 21 knots. The position given him was some twenty miles north and west of the *Dufilho*'s orders.

As Theriault hit the course, two other vessels laid in behind him. These were the *Register* (APD 92) and the *Ringness* (APD 100) en route to Leyte after escorting the carriers *Chenango* (CVE 28) and *Gilbert Island* (CVE 107) to Ulithi. On orders from CINCPAC, they were turning back to join the search.

On *Register,* in commission only six months, Lieutenant Commander John R. Furman licked his lips and welcomed a chance for some duty to break the convoy monotony. The *Register* had been blooded at Hagushi Beach, Okinawa, when a kamikaze hit one of the kingposts during a suicide raid on May 20, but life had been pretty dull since in the backwaters of the Philippine Sea. Furman, a genial New Englander recently out of Cornell, was a team man so he talked over the problem with his exec, Lieutenant Arch R. Winter, an architect from Mobile, Alabama, the ship's doctor, Lieutenant Louis Hamman, Jr., of Baltimore, and the chaplain, Lieutenant (j.g.) Kenneth N. Bragg of Olympia, Washington. When the *Register* reached the scene she was ready, right down to a movie camera on the bridge.

The *Ringness,* under command of Lieutenant Commander William C. Meyer, had had a hot time in her nine months in commission. In the Forward Area only since March 1, she spent April and May in the heart of the Okinawa campaign fighting off kamikazes and, on April 27, exploding a Japanese submarine with depth charges.

On May 11, she raced out to the famed "hot corner," Radar Picket Station 15, to aid some destroyers in a bitter battle against kamikaze waves. On that mission she had logged over 25 knots, believed a record for APDs. Now in the rear escort group, she was to add still one more honor—rescue of Captain McVay and thirty-eight enlisted men.

Ulithi had seen the greatest concentration of fighting ships in history when the fleets marshaled there for the Okinawa invasion. She was still busy with heavy transport traffic moving up, but there was very little enemy action left around there. On radar picket station north of Ulithi were the *Ralph Talbot* (DD 390) and the *Madison* (DD 425), bearded veterans of the war. The *Talbot* had been in the thick of the Pacific campaigns since the first gun at Pearl Harbor, and the *Madison* knew virtually every sea lane in the North Atlantic and Mediterranean.

The word reached Commander Winston S. Brown, USNR, in the *Talbot* at 4:01 P.M. (Zone-10), just an hour after he had taken station at Able 6, relieving the *Rhind* (DD 404). Commander Brown (USNA 1929) immediately laid on 32 knots on a northwest course and cranked up the TBS to talk to Commander Donald W. Todd, USN (USNA 1931), who was on the same mission in the *Madison*. They settled between them that on arriving at the scene Todd would take charge as SOPA.

Thus by late afternoon seven ships were converging on the survivors, but not one was less than two hundred miles away. Hashimoto could not have chosen a better spot. There had been no policeman on duty at what he called "the crossroads," where the Peleliu-Okinawa and the Guam-Leyte tracks crossed. Come to think of it, with all the escort vessels then available, it might have been a sound idea to put one on duty at the crossroads.

Meantime, the fly boys were not idle. Atteberry sent Gwinn back to Peleliu before his gas gave out and then set out on melancholy inventory of the whole area while waiting for Marks to arrive. It was an amazing sight, with oil-covered heads appearing like blisters on a hot tar road. Atteberry hardly knew where to drop his life-saving gear, but finally let it go in spots that looked as though they needed it most.

When Marks hove into sight at 3:50 P.M., Gambler Leader told him on voice to follow him on tour before making drops. The big PBY winged over the whole area, which Marks figured was ten miles long and five miles

wide, oriented north and south. Some men were on rafts
or flotsam, but the majority had nothing but water-soaked
life jackets. Marks felt that the ones in bunches had the
best chance of staying afloat, while the singles and strag-
glers needed help the most, so to the latter he dropped
three rafts, one shipwreck kit, one emergency-ration kit,
and some cans of dye marker. To the boys in the water,
just seeing something fall was a help because it made them
feel rescue was that much nearer.

But it was pitifully little help, and Marks and Atteberry knew it. At 4:25 P.M. Marks messaged his base in
plain language, "Between 100 and 200 survivors at position reported. Need all survival equipment available while
daylight holds. Many survivors without rafts." Five minutes later, feeling desperate action was called for, he decided to land the PBY on the water and radioed the base,
"Will attempt open sea landing. PV circling area."

The PBY was a sturdy plane but was never designed
for landing on rough water.

Marks's message caused temporary consternation at
VPB-23 headquarters. The squadron commander, Lieutenant Commander Max V. Ricketts, was just back from
a patrol over Babelthuap and the limited information
sifting down to his level indicated no such drastic action
to save one man, or even several. Ricketts was a conserva-
tive type, who had grappled his way up from apprentice
seaman in twelve years in the Navy, and there were strict
orders against endangering expensive planes and the lives
of the crew needlessly.

Later in the afternoon, however, when the true magnitude of the emergency became known at his level, Ricketts and his air-combat intelligence officer, Lieutenant J.
L. Blackman, lined up plans to throw the whole squadron
into the rescue.

At Operations, the full picture had begun to emerge
about 2:00 P.M. and Admiral Buckmaster had acted en-
ergetically. Orders crackled over to the northeast, to
Ulithi, to send her fastest and nearest vessels, and the
Talbot and the *Madison* were soon underway. Every plane
on Peleliu, including the Admiral's own, was ordered
readied, to be dispatched on schedules that would keep a
constant shuttle service operating to the rescue area.
Ulithi was ordered to send over all planes possible, loaded
with survival gear for air drops at the scene.

With no authority save urgency, Admiral Buckmaster issued orders to any units he could reach, thereby severing miles of red tape. No questions were raised then or later, proving that on rare occasions red tape can be snipped with impunity. Admiral Buckmaster's staff believed at first that the men in the water might be survivors of a Japanese submarine. There had been reports recently of attacks on Jap subs in that area. As the afternoon wore on, however, someone recalled the Guam dispatch of last Saturday about the *Indianapolis* leaving for Leyte. This information, together with a dispatch received only that morning from Leyte, asking news of the *Indianapolis*, raised some strong fears that a major disaster might be unfolding. The same chilling thoughts, you may be sure, had now occurred at Leyte and Guam.

Lieutenant Marks's problem was how to land a multiton plane in the twelve-foot swells running from the northwest. Fortunately, they were long and widely spaced, and the wind was a moderate 8 knots from the north. Picking a spot where he might be of most aid to single survivors, Marks headed into the wind and put the giant plane in a power stall. It came to rest in three big bounces, the first one fifteen feet high, with what at first seemed to be only two popped rivets and a started seam.

Co-pilots Ensign Irving D. Lefkovits and Ensign Morgan F. Hensley immediately plugged the rivet holes with pencils, and stuffed cotton in the seam, but the radio and berthing compartments were taking water slowly and gasoline began seeping from a wing tank. She stayed afloat, however, and with occasional pumping it looked as though she would be good for some hours.

Overhead, Gambler Leader began playing his part as "eyes" for the PBY whose crew could see only briefly when the plane rode the top of a swell. As Atteberry called the shots, Marks taxied over to the indicated spot and Ensign Hensley reached out of the port blister for the exhausted survivors. Fortunately for them, Hensley was an amateur wrestler and he reached out and hooked them in like gaffed fish.

The first man aboard gasped out the news that the *Indianapolis* had gone down. Lieutenant Marks and his mates were stupefied. They were sitting on one of the biggest stories of the war, and dared not tell it. Marks had only a confidential code book aboard his plane, and he decided not to use that for fear of the Japanese learning something they might not know. It was eight hours later, when the *Doyle* arrived around midnight, that Lieutenant Commander Claytor carefully sent the news in secret code for a shocked Navy hierarchy to ponder.

And there was a double shocker in it for Claytor. Captain McVay had recently married his cousin Louise Claytor. It would be still more hours before Claytor would know that McVay had survived.

Short of letting out the big secret, Marks sent out numerous voice messages to Atteberry and the approaching *Doyle* indicating that the situation was truly grave and begging immediate assistance. But the only material help to arrive before nightfall was an Army PBY of the 4th Emergency Rescue Squadron based on Peleliu.

Army Lieutenant Richard C. Alcorn and his PBY crew were well south of Peleliu when they got word to cease their present mission and head for the disaster scene. Alcorn made best possible speed back to Peleliu, gassed up and loaded rafts and other survival gear. He was airborne northward by 3:00 P.M. The Army PBY waddled onto the scene just before sunset, quickly dropped its lifesaving gear to isolated men, and prepared to set down on the water.

Like Marks before him, the twenty-four-year-old Alcorn came in slowly, skipped several swell-tops and cut the power just in time to stall down into a trough. Nothing popped, but the sun set. Before darkness desecended, Alcorn's crew had pulled only one man from the water.

Alcorn nearly ran him down in the half-dark, but one of the boys in the blister scrambled up onto the high wing and dangled a rope. The survivor grabbed it and the crew led him into the blister like a dog on a leash. Only one man saved, but to him at least the trip was definitely worthwhile.

It was really dark now, and Alcorn turned off his engines for fear of chopping up exhausted men. In the quiet that followed, they could hear men calling in the darkness but could not help them. Fortunately the ships were on the way.

Meantime, Lieutenant Marks had hit the jackpot. Before darkness set in, he taxied into the Haynes group, the largest single group of survivors. By the time Marks arrived perhaps 100 were still alive, but even that number would shrink in the few hours left before the ships arrived. Every added hour was an eternity, and some men who saw rescue near just couldn't wait for it.

With men all around clamoring frantically for help, Marks and his crew had the agonizing task of choosing whom to help and whom to pass by. They decided priority should go to the lone floaters. Those in clusters had at least the moral and material strength of others to help sustain them. Despair came quickest to men alone, but those in the groups were outraged when Marks passed them by.

Some cursed him, shouted, shook their fists but Marks went on, picking up those he felt were in greatest need. They filled the plane, and then clambered onto the wings. The plane looked like a casualty station. As each man came aboard the crew gave him a half cup of water, and a little while later some more until the whole sixteen gallons on the plane had been gulped by the dehydrated survivors.

As darkness set in and shouts were heard, Aviation Radioman Third Class Roland A. Sheperd and Seaman First Class Warren A. Kirchoff volunteered to go out in a raft and look for more. They picked up two more men, for a total of 56 clinging to the plane, which now had holes kicked in the wings and fuselage by frantic men piling aboard.

Planes were coming over steadily now, including three B-17's sent down by Commodore Gillette from Samar, planes of several types from Guam, and the Venturas and PBYs from Peleliu. The B-17's, after dropping survival gear, continued on down to Peleliu and made another drop over the area on the way back to Samar the next morning. Lieutenant Alcorn, his PBY floating ducklike, put on his wing lights for a while during the evening, but quickly doused them. Planes flying over had sighted on his lights, and heavy gear whistled down around him like bombs. A direct hit could have wiped out his plane, his crew, and his survivors.

Surface craft were closing fast from south, west, and east, and the *Doyle* was the winner. Claytor's engine-room gang coaxed the vessel up to a miraculous 24 knots, while the radio room kept in constant touch with Atteberry and Marks, relaying their messages to Peleliu. As they raced on, Claytor began to worry about running down men in the water, for it was obvious they were scattered over a wide area.

About 9:30 P.M. he came to a difficult decision. Despite warnings of submarines in the area, Claytor ordered one 24-inch searchlight beamed forward, with bow lookouts to watch for survivors, and the other 24-inch light pointed skyward, as a beacon of hope for those in the last extremities. And it was, for men sixty miles away saw it shining on the clouds. It gave them the last ounce of courage they needed.

Other skippers reacted differently. Theriault, who ran a taut ship, ordered that no lights be shown as the *Bassett* approached. No telling who was out there in that dark sea, and if those black, oil-covered figures in the water were Japs, enemy forces might be nearby. From experience, he knew the Japs were not averse to sacrificing their own men to increase their bag.

So the *Bassett* made the run-in dark, as did the *Dufilho,* coming up on parallel course somewhat south of the *Bassett.* The *Dufilho* saw the *Doyle*'s searchlights and headed on them. As they neared, Lieutenant Commander Nienau cut his speed and ordered all men not otherwise engaged to act as lookouts. About 8,000 yards from the *Doyle,* the *Dufilho* men spotted a lone survivor. The motor whaleboat shoved off and picked up Seaman Second Class Francis N. Rineay, Jr., of New Orleans, who was completing four full days alone in the water without food or drink. He was burned a ruddy brown from the tropical sun. Using life jackets taken from bodies around him, he had fashioned a sort of mattress which not only kept him afloat but safe from sharks and from drowning while dozing.

But once in the boat, Rineay still had another ordeal ahead. The *Dufilho*'s sonar picked up a strong submarine contact, within 900 yards. Lieutenant Commander Nienau used the loudspeaker to warn his boat away, and after consulting with his officers decided an attack was necessary despite the possible danger to men who might be in the water. It was a tough decision to make, but the *Doyle* lay close by, lit up like a nightclub. So the *Dufilho* headed out from the area and laid down a pattern of hedgehog and depth charges. After twenty minutes, with results negative, the *Dufilho* closed in and picked up her boat. Surprisingly, Rineay was able to help himself aboard the *Dufilho* and after a short rest to give a fairly lucid account of his experience.

About this time Lieutenant Commander Claytor called over the TBS and asked Lieutenant Commander Nienau to provide sound screen for him. The *Dufilho* commenced circling at about 4,000 yards, her searchlights helping the *Doyle*'s boats in their search.

Lieutenant Commander Claytor's radar had picked up Lieutenant Marks's plane about 11:00 P.M., and headed directly for it. Just before midnight, the *Doyle* pulled up a short distance from the PBY and sent her boat over to see what was up.

Until this time, Lieutenant Commander Claytor and his officers still had no intimation that a major vessel had been lost. The most logical assumption seemed to be that several B-29's returning from a raid on Japan had missed their Marianas bases and ditched in this area.

When the boat came back with a load of survivors, one of them made his way to the bridge and announced:

"This is all that is left of the *Indianapolis*. We have been in the water four days." It was Dr. Haynes.

Claytor and the men around him were stunned. When Claytor recovered his voice he blurted out that Captain McVay was married to his cousin.

Dr. Haynes said he had glimpsed McVay soon after the vessel went down but hadn't seen him since.

Claytor immediately summoned the communications officer, Lieutenant James A. Fite, Jr., and dictated the following message for Commander, Marianas, Vice Admiral Murray:

"We are picking up survivors of U.S.S. *Indianapolis*, torpedoed and sunk Sunday night. Urgently request surface and air assistance."

"And make it secret and top priority," Claytor said.

In five minutes Lieutenant Fite was back to report that Guam could give him a position on the top priority waiting list that might be reached in an hour.

"Make it urgent," Claytor said. He did, and Guam cleared the air and took it in at once.

This was the first definite word to get through, and a shocker it was.

13

There was plenty of work to do at the scene, and the *Doyle* set about it. Time and again the motor whaleboat went over to the PBY, transferring the 56 casualties to the ship in an operation that took some two hours. And a marvelous job of seamanship it was, in the darkness with the sea and the wind making up during the night and a slight drizzle setting in.

Each time the boat came alongside Lieutenant Marks's plane, the gunwales battered the PBY's hull while the rescuers battled to shift the sick and weak survivors into the heaving boat. Back at the *Doyle*, strong and willing hands lined the rail to pull the exhausted men aboard and help them below. To the men of the *Doyle* it was a heartrending sight to see the sore and bloated bodies, coated with black oil or severely burned by the sun.

Lieutenant Marks and his crew stayed aboard the PBY after the last of their "guests" had departed, and spent the remainder of the night detaching gear that could be salvaged. It was obvious the PBY would never fly again. And the crew of the *Doyle* spent these hours nosing about in the dark, answering calls, shouts, and whistles from men in the sea, until at dawn she had 93 survivors aboard.

This included the one man taken from Lieutenant Alcorn's Army PBY.

After dawn, the *Doyle*'s boat made one last trip and took off Lieutenant Marks, his crew and their salvaged gear. Then the *Doyle* trained her guns on the PBY and sank it. Farewell to the "temporary island," to which 56 men owed their lives.

Lieutenant Alcorn watched the sinking and called over to the *Doyle* that his plane seemed airworthy and he would try a take-off. The *Doyle* gave him a wind reading, Alcorn gunned the motors, and the PBY achieved a bumpy take-off and headed back to Peleliu.

As the *Bassett* raced to the scene from the west, Lieutenant Commander Theriault received a dispatch about 11:00 P.M. from Commodore Gillette, directing that the first vessel to reach the scene notify him what ship the survivors were from and the cause of the sinking. Theriault would send that message in about three hours, and it was destined to haunt Gillette. For years to come he would be fighting to remove a black mark placed against his name by the Navy, the only one incurred in a long career.

About 1:30 A.M. Theriault picked up lights on the horizon and began readying the LCVP's in their davits. He, too, finally turned on his lights and in no time at all was in a swarm of men. Ensign Jack Broser, twenty-seven-year-old New Yorker, took the first boat away and ordered it over to a raft with four or five men on it. As they closed, Broser drew his pistol, unsure in the dark who the oil-covered men were.

"Who are you?" he shouted, and the word came back: "We're from the *Indianápolis*."

The incredulous Broser snapped, "Quit your kidding. Who are you?"

Broser could see now that some of the men were white (in places) and not Oriental. He turned and called the news out to the *Bassett*, and then began a long night's work.

It is practically impossible to climb from the water into an LCVP except at the stern, and even that is pretty high out of the water. But the boat crew heaved those men off the raft and went after dozens more in the water. Broser and Seaman First Class William E. Van Wilpe dived into the water as the survivors, anxious for rescue, deserted their rafts, nets, flotsam, or life preservers to flounder toward the boat. Broser and Van Wilpe herded them to the stern, then lifted them by legs or buttocks and pushed them up to waiting hands above. As soon as the boat was loaded, Broser took it back to the *Bassett*, where the doctor, Lieutenant (j.g.) Royce Pruett, and the pharmacist's mates were waiting.

Lieutenant Commander Theriault coded and sent off at 1:53 A.M. the message that rocked Commodore Gillette and the staff of Philippine Sea Frontier:

"U.S.S. *Bassett* sends. Survivors from U.S.S. *Indianapolis* (Charley Able 35) which was torpedoed 29 July. Continuing to pick up survivors. Many badly injured."

Ensign Broser brought the LCVP up to the stern of the *Bassett* and put the men aboard over the fantail. Those for whom rescue came too late were laid out there, while the living were hustled below to the berthing quarters for first aid. During one of the ten or twelve trips that night, Broser came upon a youngster astride a pyramid he had constructed of the cork rings on floater nets. He rode it like a horse, in seeming comfort, and when the ensign urged him aboard he said:

"No thanks, I'm waiting for a friend to come by and I don't want to disappoint him." Despite delirium, he was docile enough when they lifted him into the boat.

One wild-eyed boy climbed onto the *Bassett's* fantail without aid but then sat down and announced:

"I can't walk. A shark got my leg."

Assured that both legs were in the right places, he surveyed them for a moment, shrugged his shoulders, rose, and walked to the hatch.

Counting heads as the stream of survivors kept coming aboard, Lieutenant Commander Theriault began looking for help from other vessels. Shortly after 4:00 A.M. the *Madison* arrived on the scene. Having no survivors of his own, Commander Todd sent his doctor, Lieutenant (j.g.) H. A. Stiles, over in an LCVP to help Lieutenant Pruett.

The *Talbot* began searching on its own, and Commander Brown's crew soon had twenty-four survivors aboard. At 5:58 A.M. the *Talbot* picked up six men from a rubber raft, eight more from another raft at 7:05, and ten more from a third raft at 7:21. The twin ships, *Register* and *Ringness*, came in behind the *Bassett* about thirty minutes later. Lieutenant Commander Meyer in the *Ringness* began finding men almost immediately, but it wasn't until 10:20 A.M. Friday, near the northern rim of the search area, that he came on a convoy of four rafts tied together, with a total of nineteen men aboard.

In command of this island in the sea was a short, fair-haired man with bushy black eyebrows and a bad sunburn—Captain McVay. Fairly well protected from the rigors of sea, sun, and sharks, the captain and his group had come through in good shape except for one man, who became slightly delirious the last night. Perhaps the strain of watching others being rescued only a few miles away had been too much for him.

Captain McVay made his way to the bridge and reported to Lieutenant Commander Meyer, who in due course radioed Guam: "Have 37 survivors aboard including Captain Charles Butler McVay 3d, USN, commanding officer. Captain McVay picked up at Lat 11-35 Long 133-21 with nine other rafts within radius of four miles and states he believes ship hit 0015 sunk 0030, 30 July position on track exactly as routed by Guam speed 17 knots not zigzagging. Hit forward by what is believed to be two torpedoes or magnetic mine followed by magazine explosion."

Lieutenant Commander Meyer later picked up two more men to make his total bag thirty-nine.

The *Register* was a proud and happy little ship, so when it reached the scene about 2:00 A.M. every man aboard not needed below was at the rail, plumbing the darkness with eager eyes. There was no luck at first, and it was shortly after daybreak on Friday when Mailman H. E. Anderson spotted the first survivor, a lone youngster on a raft. The *Register* quickly gathered him aboard and all he could do was mutter, "Thank God, thank God," as Doc Hamman went to work on him. He was in severe shock, his skin cracked and parched from the sun and salt. They bedded him down in the trooping quarters and began restoring liquids to his dehydrated system.

The *Register* quickly found more casualties and soon was bringing them aboard in singles, twos and threes. Some were strong enough to stand and wave in their rafts, others sat in semistupor, and still others were unconscious. But all were soon aboard and under the care of Doc Hamman and two aides, Chief Pharmacist's Mate Murray F. Moyles and Pharmacist's Mate Second Class

Robert E. Johnson, Jr. Nearly every member of the crew
tried to pitch in in some way, a couple of men standing by
each bunk giving aid and comfort as plasma and glucose
were administered.

By daybreak Lieutenant Commander Theriault, still
working alone on the western fringes of the area, had
nearly a full load aboard the *Bassett* and with the no-
torious independence of the Seventh Fleet Navy decided
to leave without consulting other vessels present. At 6:00
A.M. he merely notified Leyte: "Departing scene for Leyte
with 200 survivors aboard. Request go alongside hospital
ship. Ninety per cent stretcher cases."

Actually he had 151 survivors aboard, the largest
group rescued by any one ship. There could be no quarrel
with his decision to leave, as plenty of help was now on the
scene, but the abrupt manner of departure did nothing to
allay the feeling that the "MacArthur Navy" was sort of a
third force in the arena with the U.S. Navy and the Imperial Japanese Navy.

As it was, the *Bassett* was the only rescue vessel to
head west, all others taking their casualties south to
Peleliu. It seemed almost as if some powerful force were
pulling him back behind the 130th Parallel, the Chop
Line. As one Peleliu-based rescue skipper put it later:
"Certainly at my level, our liaison with them (Seventh
Fleet) was at best that of rather unfriendly allies; we
never knew what they were doing or why." This lack of
cooperation and communication between the two great
forces ". . . was particularly bad with respect to ships
going between the Seventh Fleet Areas and the Pacific
Ocean Areas," he said. It was in precisely that area, of
course, that the *Indianapolis* tragedy occurred.

But Leyte had been shaken fully alert now, ever
since Lieutenant Commander Theriault's first message had
brought Commodore Gillette springing from his bed at
2:00 A.M. So at 9:30 A.M. Theriault received a copy of
this message from Commander, Naval Operating Base,
Leyte, to Chief of Naval Base, Samar:

"Have 10 doctors, 50 corpsmen, 1 harbor pilot
board APD 73 off Homonhon Point at 0500 Saturday.
APD 73 proceed direct to Guiuan, Samar, and berth as
directed about 0700. Discharge injured personnel, all
available ambulances to be on hand to transport patients
expeditiously."

So at least some of the *Indianapolis* men would finally see Homonhon Point, but on Saturday morning instead of Tuesday morning, and under conditions none could have imagined in advance.

A mere 151 casualties was nothing for Base Hospital No. 114, seven miles inland from Guiuan, on the southern tip of Samar, neighbor island northeast of Leyte. The hospital had been open only a month and had 3,000 beds, most of them empty, and 101 nurses. On receipt of orders from Leyte, Captain E. B. Taylor, MC, USN, immediately set about preparing to receive the survivors.

The *Bassett* plowed westward all day Friday, and at dawn Saturday steamed into the harbor of Guiuan. Pontoon barges were ready to come alongside, and quickly ferried the men to shore. Some were able to walk, but many were still on stretchers, and as they reached shore ambulances quickly carried them away up into the hills.

At the hospital, Ward E-9 had been set aside for them, and Marine guards kept all those without official business out of the area. Even the regular medical corpsmen had to show identity cards to get in. Doctors and nurses swarmed over the survivors, treating dehydration, shark bites, salt-water ulcers, exposure, shock, and burns. In some cases, skin had become so tough and coarse, extragauge hypodermic needles were needed to puncture it as injections were given.

To combat dehydration, half a dozen GI cans were set up in the ward and kept filled night and day with iced fruit juice. Even during the night the cans had to be replenished as dried-out bodies soaked up liquids.

And over everything there was an air of secrecy. Nurses and corpsmen were ordered not to discuss the events off the ward, and official questioning of survivors began as soon as the men were able to walk. One by one they went into a closed room for interrogation, each being asked to tell in his own words everything he could recall of the events of the past few days. In this group were five officers, Lieutenant Redmayne, the engineering officer; Ensigns Blum, Howison and Twible, and Gunner Horner.

Most of the men responded quickly to treatment, but two died at the hospital. At Guam there was a great ferment on to find out what had happened. So on Sunday morning, August 12, the men able to be moved were

taken to the air strip at Guiuan. C-54's with nurses aboard
flew them to Guam, where a court of inquiry was convening the next morning. Not all men went, because some
simply were in no condition to travel. Even those who
did go were taken immediately to Base Hospital No. 18 at
Guam.

At the rescue scene a great many planes were overhead, and by Friday morning Commander Todd in the
Madison took over as SOPA. The airwaves were blue
with chatter as the planes and ships shot messages back
and forth in a race to pick up the men disclosed by daylight. For the moment, the dead were passed by as the
ships darted about. Planes dropped smoke bombs wher-
ever a sign of life remained, and called for ship cover,
and by noon the job was done.

As Commander Todd took stock by TBS, he found
the score as follows: the *Doyle* had ninety-three men
aboard, the *Register*, twelve, *Dufilho*, one, *Ringness*,
thirty-nine, and *Talbot*, twenty-four, a total of one hundred and sixty-nine.

Since it was obvious that the job was about over and
several of his men were in very serious condition, Lieutenant Commander Claytor asked permission to leave
about noon. Commander Todd granted permission, and
the *Doyle* made off southward at 22 knots.

Commander Todd decided to send the two APDs to
Peleliu also, since they were best equipped to handle the
casualties. So at 2:45 P.M. he ordered Commander Brown
of the *Talbot* to put his twenty-four survivors aboard the
Register and Lieutenant Commander Nienau to transfer
his one man to the *Register*. The *Register* and the *Ringness* then shoved off at 4:15 for Peleliu, with thirty-seven
and thirty-nine casualties aboard, respectively. The *Dufilho* was released and returned to Leyte.

The *Madison* and the *Talbot*, aided by planes, remained to scour the area the rest of Friday, and shortly
after midnight the *Alvin C. Cockrell* (DDE 366) arrived
on the scene. She was commanded by Commander M. M.
Sanford, USN, CTU 94.6.1, the Palau Surface Patrol and
Escort Unit, which also included the *Doyle* and the *French*
(DDE 367). The *French*, commanded by Lieutenant
Commander Reginald Chauncey Robbins, Jr., had been
about one day south of Peleliu when she received orders

to go to the scene. She finally arrived on Sunday, after refueling at Peleliu.

At dawn Saturday, two more destroyers arrived from Ulithi—the *Aylwin* (DD 355) and the *Helm* (DD 388), commanded respectively by Commander K. F. Neupert and Commander A. F. Hollingsworth. But after noontime Friday, it was just a question of destroying debris and attempting to identify bodies, for there was no one left alive. The *Doyle, Register,* and *Ringness,* after leaving their survivors at Peleliu, returned to the area by Sunday, and the ten ships and countless planes continued the search through Monday. Thereafter, all departed except the *Doyle,* which stayed alone until Thursday, August 9. She found only a Japanese floating mine, Type 93, which she destroyed on Wednesday. After that, the seas closed forever over the remains of the *Indianapolis,* some 10,000 feet below.

The mop-up was a macabre affair but most necessary, not only to render decent burial to the dead but also to sponge the sea clean of all marks of the tragedy. As soon as it was obvious that no more men remained alive, the order was given to dispose of surface material either by taking it aboard or sinking it. Gradually the sea was cleared of rafts, nets, line, cans, clothing and bodies.

Here the men in the motor whaleboats had trying times. As bodies were found, identifying marks such as scars, tattoos, and dental work were noted, and dog tags, rings, watches, wallets, and other personal belongings were salvaged. In more than one case only skeletons were found, stripped by voracious fish. Some bodies that had been exposed in life rafts were so burned the fat had been rendered from the skin, leaving it as tough as bacon rind. Decomposition was far advanced in some cases.

But the work had to be done, and eventually all bodies had been disposed of by weighting with 5-inch shells or other heavy objects. As the final act, the ships formed a line 10-abreast and thoroughly combed an area within a 100-mile radius of the first rescue. When the ships and planes finished, it was unlikely that anyone had been missed.

Peleliu, as the Marines found out in some of the bloodiest fighting of the war, is surrounded by shallow

water extending far out and cannot be approached by
large vessels. So when the island was informed that rescue
vessels with 169 survivors were headed for Peleliu, the
Seabees turned out to build a ramp to help get the casualties ashore. They quickly constructed a wooden runway
from the nearest road, across the sand and down into the
water. Across this the stretcher cases would be quickly
trundled to ambulances for the three-mile trip to Base
Hospital No. 20. The hospital, with nearly 1,000 beds,
prepared for the emergency by mustering ambulances,
nurses, corpsmen, and supplies. The Supply Officer rounded
up blankets, clothing, and shoes for the men who had
lost everything, except their lives.

Lieutenant Commander Claytor kept the *Doyle* at
22 knots southward toward Peleliu and arrived off Orange
Beach just after midnight on Saturday morning, August
4. As he moored to a buoy, LCTs and LCVPs were already hovering around and willing hands soon began the
task of transferring the men to shore. Many of Claytor's
patients were in serious condition, and at least two were
in critical condition—Ensign Woolston and Seaman Second Class (QM) Fred Elliott Harrison. Woolston gradually recovered, but exhaustion had so weakened Harrison
that pneumonia developed. He died at 9:30 A.M. Wednesday, August 8. With vehicles commandeered from all
over the island and men from many outfits helping, the
wounded had all been brought ashore and moved to the
hospital by 5:00 A.M.

After a brief respite, the men went back to work
again as the *Register* and the *Ringness* arrived with the
rest of the survivors. As the LCTs came alongside in the
morning sun, the rescuers got a laugh out of one that
had a palm tree scene painted on the side. Under it was
lettered "Sons of the Beach." But it was a grim business,
with many of the men litter cases and at least one beyond
help. Gunner's Mate Third Class Robert Lee Shipman,
who had served on the *Indianapolis* nearly three years,
had survived the watery ordeal but it took more from
him than he could give. He, also, died early on Wednesday morning, August 8. Funeral services for him and
Harrison were held on the same day in Purple Beach
Chapel, a beautiful little stone and timber structure designed and built by the 73rd Seabee Battalion. As an
honor guard of enlisted men from the island detachment

accompanied the bodies down the coral road to the cemetery, chimes made of Japanese and American shell cases pealed out from the chapel tower. The bright sun, the quiet water, the war so nearly over—it was an oddly affecting scene even for these men, who had never known these dead.

Captain McVay had hardly put foot on land before a tall figure came striding down the low beach, hand outstretched, face wreathed in smiles. It was "Tommy" Oates (nobody called him Eugene).

"Thank God, Charlie, it's good to see you alive," he said, and put his arm around the little Irishman, who really needed no help. But they hadn't seen each other since 1940 in Manila, when Oates was president of the Army-Navy Club and McVay was secretary. Captain Oates was chief of staff at Cavite then, and McVay was naval aide to the U.S. High Commissioner in the Islands. The men were good friends, even though Oates was ten years older than McVay.

"You're coming up to my place until you get your feet on the ground," Tommy said, and led McVay off to Hut No. 2 at the northern end of the island. This was a Quonset on raised concrete piers, with one side opening out onto a wide porch overlooking the water. This Quonset, and Admiral Buckmaster's next to it, was set in a grove of palms. Leading up to them were winding walks, bordered by low coral walls and beds of tropical plants. There wasn't much to do on Peleliu these days, so the grounds in the palm grove got plenty of attention.

Tommy made his guest comfortable in these pleasant surroundings. He asked no questions and he wanted to keep Charlie there overnight so no one else could bother him. As they passed the hours talking on the porch, only the infamous Palau gnat broke the serenity. *Culicoides peleliuensis* bred in great swarms in the swamps of Peleliu and no effective defense had been found against them. Some men, nursing great welts, swore they were worse than the Japs, and even wire screening couldn't stop them.

On Sunday, August 5, a planeload of newsmen arrived from Guam, and Captain McVay agreed to receive them in the hospital. With a stenographer present, he recounted for them the nightmare he and his men had experienced in the preceding days.

Near the end, one of the reporters asked the crucial question:

"What would be the normal time before you would be reported overdue?"

For the first and only time throughout the long ordeal of investigation, Captain McVay publicly drew the veil, ever so slightly, from his private feelings as he answered:

"That is a question I would like to ask someone. We were to be thirty miles off Homonhon at 0600 Tuesday morning. We had asked for plane services so we could have gunnery practice. If the plane did not intercept, that probably would not have caused suspicion, as they might have thought they missed us. We were due at our anchorage at 1100. I should think by noon or 1300 they would have started to worry. A ship that size practically runs on train schedule.

"I should think by noon they would have started to call by radio to find out where we were, or if something was wrong. So far as I know, nothing was started until Thursday. This is something I want to ask somebody myself. Why didn't this get out sooner? Maybe it did, I don't know. I don't believe Rear Admiral Buckmaster knew that we were missing until Thursday."

(Captain McVay apparently erred in saying planes had been requested for Tuesday morning target practice. The *Indianapolis* was to have asked for planes, but as far as is known no dispatch of any kind was sent from the vessel after it left Guam. It seems more likely that this dispatch was to have been sent Monday, but of course the sinking intervened. Had this dispatch been sent on Sunday, or had it been handled in the sailing dispatch of Port Director, Guam, a search might have gotten under way Tuesday, when the *Indianapolis* did not keep a rendezvous with the target planes.)

The hospital ship *Tranquility*, gleaming white and brightly lighted, arrived off Peleliu at nine o'clock Saturday night and the commanding officer, Captain Bartholomew W. Hogan went ashore to see what was up.

Sunday passed quickly in the hospital and on Monday morning transfer of the men to the *Tranquility* began. About half the men were stretcher cases, but even for the eighty-six ambulatory survivors the transfer was an ordeal. The morning sun beat down on them as they waited first on the beach to be ferried out to the side of the great white vessel and then to be hoisted aboard. But once inside, they reveled in air-conditioned wards, soft beds, and the sight of nurses moving among them. At 1:00 P.M. the hospital ship steamed out for Guam, leaving behind three men, of whom only one would survive.

Just before the survivors left, a touching incident occurred. Atteberry, Langford, and some of the others from VPB-152 took Gwinn aboard the *Tranquility* and introduced him to the men with the words:

"Boys, here's the guy who found you."

Men in all stages of recovery, some weak and hollow-eyed on their beds, shouted, cheered, and whistled. Those who could, crowded around and thumped him on the back, laughing and jumping. Some merely turned their heads on their pillows and cried softly. Quiet, reticent Gwinn himself broke down under the flood of emotion, the most treasured moment of his life.

The hospital ship was waiting, however, and so was the Navy. The Hiroshima bomb had been dropped and the war was obviously near the end. The loss of the *Indianapolis* could not be kept secret forever, and it was necessary to be prepared to tell something.

The *Tranquility* arrived at Guam on Wednesday and the Peleliu survivors were reunited a few days later at the hospital with their shipmates flown in from Samar. The following week, those able to stand were drawn up in parade formation on Davis Field, and as the NOB band played, Admiral Spruance pinned Purple Heart medals on his shipmates of the Fifth Fleet flagship. When it was over, Admiral Spruance and members of his staff, Rear Admiral DeWitt C. Ramsey and Commodore H. D. Willicutts, drove over to Base Hospital No. 18 to complete the presentation to those still bedridden. At the field, Admiral Spruance had praised the men for their bravery during the terrible ordeal, and it was obvious that he was deeply moved. Here in the more intimate surroundings of the hospital, he moved slowly from bed to bed and spoke something personal to each man, many of whom he knew from past cruises.

When he got to Seaman First Class Edward J. ("Big Ed") Brown, one of those big, breezy sailors that every ship knows, Admiral Spruance said:

"You'll never know how happy I am to see that you made it, and I'm only sorry we had to lose so many men I had come to think of as my family."

"He was just as sincere as any father could have been," Big Ed told his wardmates later.

14

Within hours of hearing of the *Indianapolis* debacle, Fleet Admiral Nimitz ordered a court of inquiry to convene at Guam. This is required by Navy Regulations, and in this case was doubly urgent. The Navy had to find out quickly what had happened, and why, not only to prevent its recurring but also to be ready to present its case to a public which would certainly soon be asking questions.

Censorship was still on, so of course the world knew nothing about the sinking. The newsmen who interviewed Captain McVay at Peleliu, and spoke with survivors there and at Guam, had submitted their stories to the Navy, but nothing had come out the other end of the funnel. There was plenty of scuttlebutt around the Forward Area, but no two men heard the same story.

To get the facts, Nimitz named Vice Admiral Charles A. Lockwood, Jr., Commander Submarines Pacific, as president of the court, and as the other two members he chose Vice Admiral Murray, Commander Marianas, and Rear Admiral Francis E. M. Whiting. Captain William E. Hilbert of the ComMarianas staff was named judge advocate, a post combining the jobs of prosecutor, law officer, and clerk of the court. They were asked to convene on Thursday, August 9, or "as soon thereafter as practicable."

But the court could not convene on Thursday. The war was rushing to an end at a tremendous pace, and these men had vital work they had to dispose of first. The atom bomb had obliterated Hiroshima on Monday morning, changing the entire course of the world. Russia entered the war against Japan on Wednesday, and on Thursday the second atom bomb dropped on Nagasaki, the very day the court was to convene. And anyway, there weren't any witnesses.

The *Tranquility* had arrived from Peleliu only on Wednesday, with 166 survivors, of whom eighty were stretcher cases. They simply had to have a few days' rest. Witnesses had to be summoned from Guam, Leyte, Peleliu, and Samar. In the meantime, word came Friday morning that Japan was ready to accept the Potsdam Ultimatum. It was obvious that the war would soon be over.

In this atmosphere, the court finally convened at 10:00 A.M. on Monday, August 13, in secret, with "Uncle Charlie" Lockwood in the chair. Some of the Samar survivors had arrived the previous day in C-54 ambulance planes, and a few officers were available from Guam. The Leyte contingent was not on deck yet, because the dispatch to PSF had gone out only on Sunday. Its wording caused some head scratching at Tolosa, because it said:

> Judge advocate requests that officer acting as port director Leyte on July 31 and also your command responsible for keeping check movements of combatant ships be directed to report as witnesses court of inquiry *Indianapolis* case sitting Headquarters, Commander Marianas. Presence witnesses desired Monday, Aug. 13, if practicable. Request notification these officers.

The phrase that puzzled was "also your command responsible for keeping check movements of combatant ships." In the view of PSF there was no one so charged, and the question was, who to send?

It was finally decided that Commodore Gillette and his operations officer, Captain Granum, would go, along with Lieutenant William A. Green, the surface controller at PSF, and Lieutenant Edward B. Henslee, Jr., of the plotting section of the Surface Control Office. In addition, Commodore Jacobson, Commandant of NOB, Leyte Gulf, was ordered to Guam, along with an aide, Lieutenant James Donaldson Brown, and Lieutenant Commander

Sancho and Lieutenant Gibson from the port director's office. They scrambled over to Samar in light planes, singly and in groups, and there picked up big planes for Guam.

Rear Admiral McCormick was summoned from his battleship in Leyte Gulf, together with his aide, Commander Thomas D. F. Langen, Chief of Staff to Commander, Battleship Division 3.

The court met in a bare office room in one of the big buildings on Cincpac Hill overlooking Apra Harbor and spent the first few days groping in the dark. It was not even known what had sunk the *Indianapolis,* and for a time the possibility was entertained that she had struck a mine. But as more witnesses arrived and the story began to fall together, it was decided that an enemy submarine had been responsible. The court then named Captain McVay as an "interested party," along with Lieutenant Commander Sancho and Lieutenant Gibson. An "interested party" in Navy jurisprudence has a special status. He is a sort of quasi defendant and as such entitled to attend all court sessions and listen to all evidence. He is also entitled to counsel.

The procedure is similar to that of a grand jury in civil law. Witnesses filed in, were introduced all around, told what they knew, answered questions, and departed. They did not hear the testimony of other witnesses, and thus many were quite foggy as to what was going on. For example, Lieutenant Waldron, the routing officer at Guam, was an early witness. He had routed the *Indianapolis* out of Guam in a thoroughly routine manner, and had promptly forgotten it. Early in the week of August 13 he was ordered to appear before the court. He had heard, vaguely, a short time before, that the *Indianapolis* had been sunk. When he arrived outside the court, he was shocked to see bandaged and limping survivors in the corridor, awaiting their turn to testify.

Once in the courtroom, he was made at ease and recited what he recalled of the routing. He was not told what had happened, was asked only a few questions, and was out within an hour. He still did not know what had happened to the *Indianapolis* or where his testimony fitted in. This was true of many other witnesses, and there were some shocks in store for several of them, months later, when they learned they had been on trial, convicted, and reprimanded, without opportunity for defense or rebuttal.

There is no question that the court came at the worst possible time. Captain Hilbert testified later that he, the court, and Captain McVay all realized this. The witnesses were widely scattered, the war was coming to an end, "and the Russians were coming into the picture, complicating the duties of the members of the court of inquiry, especially the senior member, who was the commander of a submarine force—it was felt necessary to proceed with despatch . . ." Captain Hilbert said. But the court plodded on, with Admiral Lockwood presiding like the Virginia gentleman he was. The court stayed in session until August 20, and heard forty-three witnesses.

The testimony has never been made public and probably never will be. But the general outlines of the testimony are obvious. From the ship, Captain McVay and four other officers testified, along with fifteen enlisted men. This was not many, compared to fifteen officers and three hundred and one enlisted men surviving, but many were simply not physically able to talk. Besides McVay, the only other *Indianapolis* officers to appear were Lieutenant Redmayne, the engineering officer, Gunner Horner and two very junior ensigns, Twible and Blum. Those who did not testify included Lieutenant McKissick, senior surviving watch officer, the two doctors, Haynes and Modisher, Lieutenant Reid, the supply officer, and Ensign Woolston, senior surviving damage control officer.

The court's main concern was not the vessel but the operational aberration which left the vessel unsought for four days. From CINCPAC they summoned Commodore Carter, reportedly a chief author of the 10-CL-45 letter, which concluded with: "Arrival reports shall not be made for combatant ships." Commodore Carter testified that this was well-accepted practice in the Fleet, based on the thesis that combatant ships could take care of themselves. Also heard from CINCPAC were Captain Paul R. Anderson, assistant communications officer, Commander John Corry, assistant fleet aereologist and officer-in-charge of fleet weather control, and Lieutenant Gardner J. Roenke, of the CINCPAC staff.

From the headquarters of Commander Marianas, in whose area the vessel sank, the court heard Captain Archer M. R. Allen, shipping control officer of the Marianas Area (SCOMA), Captain Hilbert, doubling in brass as judge advocate of the court, Captain Oliver F. Naquin, surface operations officer, and Lieutenant Commander Moss W. Flannery, a pilot from Tinian. The headquarters people obviously were asked why the ship had not been escorted, how she had been plotted and "assumed" to have arrived, and allied questions.

These officers, together with the Leyte group and four officers from Peleliu who had a part in the rescue operations, completed the roster of witnesses.

Five days after the court adjourned, an interesting order went out from CINCPAC to no less than 24 commands. It said:

> All Naval vessels proceeding independently will be considered overdue when they fail to arrive at destination within 8 hours, merchant vessels within 24 hours, small craft and tows within 72 hours of original expected time of arrival (ETA). The port director at destination will report immediately all overdue vessels to his sea frontier or area commander, who will take appropriate steps to request a new ETA from the subject vessel, notify port director at port of origin, commanders of areas through which vessel was routed and arrange for necessary air and surface searches. Time and nature of measures taken will be understood to depend upon weather, evidence of enemy activity, and length of nature of voyage. Both CINCPAC headquarters (Guam and Pearl) will be kept informed. This does not modify Pacific Fleet Confidential Letter 10-CL-45. Pass to routing officers.

Here, at last, was closed the great operational gap through which the *Indianapolis* had sunk, unnoted by anyone. No clear-cut responsibility had existed before; now it did. It would not help the boys of the *Indianapolis*, but it might help others.

It should be noted, however, that even this was not the complete answer. Had someone at Leyte given the alarm at one minute past 11:00 A.M. on Tuesday, when the *Indianapolis* was one minute overdue, the men of the "Swayback Maru" would already have been floundering in the water thirty-five hours. The true operational problem—constant contact with combatant ships traveling alone—belonged directly to CINCPAC, and was never dealt with, so far as is publicly known. The same *Indianapolis* tragedy could have happened the day after this new order was issued, except that the survivors might have been found a few hours sooner.

As the court prepared for its third sitting on Wednesday, August 15, the war ended. It was Tuesday night in Washington, and President Harry S. Truman received the press in the White House, at 7:00 P.M. With Mrs. Truman and members of the cabinet around him, he stood behind his desk and read the great news to the reporters. When it was over, the newsmen rushed from the room to spread the word the world had been waiting for. A little later, around 8:00 P.M., President Truman strolled out on the north portico of the White House and spoke to happy throngs assembled outside the White House.

At just this time, the Navy released communique No. 622:

"The U.S.S. *Indianapolis* had been lost in the Philippine Sea as the result of enemy action. The next of kin of casualties have been notified."

Bound up in those twenty-five words was the greatest disaster at sea in the history of the United States Navy.

There had been other severe blows during the war, but none quite like this one. The *Essex* class carrier *Franklin* (CV 13) lost 772 men when a Jap suicide plane turned her into a pyre in March, 1945, only 55 miles off the coast of Japan, but the *Franklin* had been saved. The battle to quench her fires and get her clear of the fight was a glorious incident in naval history. There was no such redeeming achievement in the loss of the *Indianapolis*.

The cruiser *Juneau* (CL 52), torpedoed by the *I-26*, blew up in the wild night battle at Guadalcanal on November 13, 1942, with the loss of 676 men including the five Sullivan brothers. Only eleven of her crew survived as other U.S. ships scattered without waiting to pick up survivors. The third worst casualty after the *Indianapolis* was the carrier *Liscombe Bay*, torpedoed by the *I-175* on November 24, 1943, during the battle for Tarawa. Her magazines blew up in one terrific explosion, and 644 men were lost as the vessel disintegrated. Fragments of human flesh, steel, and clothing showered the battleship *New Mexico,* more than 1,500 yards away.

But all of these defeats had been sustained as part of large battle engagements in which the enemy had also been punished severely.

The circumstances could not be compared with those of the *Indianapolis.* Here the enemy had escaped unscathed, and the U.S. Navy had compounded the defeat through faults in organization. Only one-third of the *Indianapolis* casualties could be attributed to the Japanese submarine.

So on V-J night it was a very personal disaster which entered the homes of nearly 900 families across the nation.

Since Monday the grim telegrams had been going out from the Bureau of Naval Personnel, bearing those dread words "missing in action." In some homes, the doorbell rang even as the family was celebrating President Truman's dramatic announcement that the war was over.

For Mr. and Mrs. Philip Rhodes, the news that their son, Watertender Third Class Vernon Lee Rhodes, was missing reached them just an hour before the President held his victory news conference. Rhodes was twenty-six, married, father of two children, and had served on the *Indianapolis* exactly seven months.

Mr. and Mrs. Thomas D'Arcy Brophy were motoring in Canada. They heard the wonderful news of the end of the war on their car radio. They were thrilled, of course, but Mrs. Brophy remembered a friend whose son had been lost only a few weeks before. It never occurred to her that her only son, Ensign Brophy, had not come through. Then Mr. Brophy, a New York advertising executive, stopped to telephone his Montreal office on a routine matter. It took a rare sort of courage for him to return to the car, where Mrs. Brophy awaited him.

This personal tragedy, the circumstances varying only in detail, was enacted in hundreds of homes that night, the blow striking in the homes of rich and poor alike. In a way, it was worse than death itself, the uncertainty giving free rein to overwrought minds and promising only added hours of torture, to be ended perhaps by the worst.

To some 300-odd other homes went a different telegram. Over the signature of Vice Admiral Randall Jacobs, Chief of Naval Personnel, it said:

A report just received shows your son
————has been wounded in action 30 July
1945, diagnosis immersion (some said 'exhaustion from overexposure'), prognosis good. Your
anxiety is appreciated and you will be furnished
details when received. You are assured that he
is receiving the best possible medical care and I
join in the wish for his speedy recovery. Communications may be addressed to him care of
U.S. Base Hospital (Guam, Samar, or Peleliu).
To prevent possible aid to our enemies please do
not divulge the name of his ship or station unless the general circumstances are made public
in news stories.

Their grief was not long contained, for censorship
ended with the war and the papers of Wednesday morning, August 15, were full of the *Indianapolis* sinking.
It had to compete with tremendous news of course, but
many newspapers found room on page one for it despite
the stories of the end of the war, secrets of radar revealed,
manpower controls revoked, Marshal Pétain of France
sentenced to death, Russia and China signed treaty of
friendship and alliance, and the Japanese war minister had
committed hara-kiri.

In New York, stores and banks closed for a two-
day holiday, thousands streamed to churches to pray, four
dragons led a parade in Chinatown, and even Joe Louis
was heard from.

"We sure landed a knockout punch on Japan," he
said. "Looks like Japan might be on the canvas for quite
a spell."

But there was no happiness in many a home that day,
and the New York *Times* remembered the bereaved families with an editorial on Friday:

Only the heroism of a handful of wounded
survivors struggling for days to save their com-
rades in a cruel, sun-drenched sea relieves the
stark tragedy of the cruiser *Indianapolis*. Her
loss just a month before the dawn of peace,
with nearly nine hundred dead, marks one of the
darkest pages of our naval history. . . . The
grim story of the *Indianapolis* was the saddest

note in our day of victory. May it sound taps
for the last of our sailor dead.

Back at Guam, the court droned on through the week
in the blasting sun of summer and a plague of flies. As
the proceedings neared an end, Lieutenant Gibson moved
that he be exonerated as an "interested party," and in a
statement to the court summed up the case applicable
to both himself and Lieutenant Commander Sancho:

> The port director has no directives calling
> for the report of nonarrival of *any* type of ship
> —combatant or otherwise, except those in con-
> voy. In the absence of such a directive the port
> director has had to follow precedent which has
> never indicated it to be the duty or moral obliga-
> tion to report the nonarrival of any independent
> ship. It is a common, if not daily, occurrence for
> expected ships not to arrive—combatant or
> otherwise—and never within the interested
> party's experience has the port director been
> called upon to make such occurrence his concern
> or responsibility. . . . The method of reporting
> of vessels by a port director is concisely stated
> and is an hourly routine procedure which allows
> no room for making any decisions as to the
> policy or practice. The nonarrival of a ship being
> a common thing, it is not a matter of making
> a decision of what to do in each case, but of
> following an over-all rule, applicable to such
> cases as a whole. It would appear that the di-
> rect obligation rests with those issuing ship-re-
> porting directives to state specifically what
> should be done in the case of arrival or non-
> arrival of all types of vessels, and then to hold
> the port director or other activity reponsible
> for carrying out such directives.

The court rejected the motion, but it might be noted
that within three days of adjourning the new order went
out, setting forth the procedure suggested by Lieutenant
Gibson. Obviously, it would not have been issued had such
directive existed before the *Indianapolis* went down.

The court completed its hearings on August 20, and

recommended to Admiral Nimitz, the convening authority, that Letters of Reprimand be issued to Captain McVay, Lieutenant Commander Sancho, and Lieutenant Gibson. Letters of this kind were fairly common in the Navy during the war. Theye normally received no publicity and usually were quickly forgotten, particularly where reserve officers were involved. But for regulars, like Captain McKay, such a letter in the record could be damaging during consideration for promotion or new command.

Lieuetenant Commander Sancho received, within a few weeks, a Letter of Admonition, even less severe than a Letter of Reprimand, and appears to have shrugged it off.

Lieutenant Gibson, under date of September 6, received a Letter of Reprimand from Admiral Nimitz. Being of a serious and conscientious nature he was extremely upset at what he felt to be unwarranted punishment.

The letter said:

> . . . (he) incurred blame for failure to bring to the attention of the Port Director, Tacloban, the fact that the *Indianapolis* was overdue and that you had received no supplementary movement report setting a new ETA, or announcing a change of orders. Such failure resulted in several days' delay in inaugurating search for survivors which resulted in loss of many lives. . . . You are hereby reprimanded for the careless and inefficient manner in which you performed your duties in this instance.

Captain McVay's letter said:

> You erred in judgment when you failed to order zigzag courses steered on the night of the loss of the ship. The facts further indicate that you did not exert every effort at your command to cause a distress message to be sent out after the explosions and prior to the sinking. You are hereby reprimanded for the negligent manner in which you performed your duty in this instance.

As is customary, all three were advised that they had the right to make "such statement concerning this letter as you desire." Lieutenant Gibson did so almost immediately. He sent off, through proper channels, a 900-word letter to the Chief of Naval Personnel in which he disclaimed "any fault or blame for this tragic incident."

He declared:

> As no directive required the reporting of nonarrival of combatant ships prior to the loss of the *Indianapolis*, it is respectfully asked, 'How can I be guilty of failing to perform a duty which never existed?' I respectfully invite your attention to reference (d) and (e) (the orders issued after the fact by CINCPAC and PSF), which were promulgated after the *Indianapolis* was sunk, and indicate that higher authority realized that existing directives were inadequate. It will be noted that references (d) and (e) do not call for compliance with any prior directives, obviously because there were none.

Referring to the court record, he said:

> Each witness acquainted with shipping directives pertaining to port directors testified that there was no directive covering the reporting of the nonarrival of combatant ships. In short, no evidence could be produced in the inquiry showing it to be my duty to report the arrival or nonarrival of the *Indianapolis*.

He asked that the Letter of Reprimand be withdrawn, and concluded:

> I believe that I have been unjustly accused in this case and that my reputation as a naval officer has been greatly damaged by these accusations. It is respectfully requested that reference (a) (the reprimand) be removed from my jacket (service record). This entire case proved the inadequacy of provisions prior to 1 August 1945 for shipping control of combatant ships, and it is submitted that a junior officer, such as I was, should not be held responsible for duties which never existed.

Gibson's letter went forward under date of September 24 to begin its tortuous passage through Navy channels. Five months later, with no forewarning, the reprimand was to burst forth in a glare of national publicity that seared the life of Gibson and his family.

Captain McVay made no reply to his Letter of Reprimand; both his position and his temperament were different from Gibson's. He was a professional Navy man, and his career was at stake. Long naval experience had taught him that the matter would not end with the court of inquiry, and it may also have counseled him to patience and resignation to await the ultimate outcome.

When the court of inquiry was through with him and arrangements had been made for the care and homeward transportation of his men, Captain McVay flew off with Lieutenant McKissick and Yeoman Buckett for Honolulu. He reported to CINCPAC at Pearl Harbor, and the other two continued home by plane.

For most of the survivors, Guam was a pleasant interlude after their harrowing experience. They began to respond to treatment at the hospital, and burns, fractures, and shark bites began to heal. It was discovered that a large portion of the flesh on Coxswain Cozell L. Smith's hand had been torn away by a fish. Miraculously, no bones had been broken or severed. Other men had lost flesh on their buttocks, legs, backs, and arms from sharks or fish, and among the bodies recovered 88 had been mutilated.

The salt-water ulcers were slowest to heal. In some cases it took months and left permanent dents in the skin the size of a nickel or larger. Most of the men snapped back mentally with remarkable speed, but in some, trauma persists to this day. It is betrayed by a reluctance to talk of those terrible days, a bead of sweat on the brow, or a tremor of the hands. But there was comradeship of a common experience in the hospital, and there were lots of forms to fill out for lost clothing, survival allowance, and disability pensions. There was time for fun, too, particularly after they were well enough for transfer to the Submarine rest camp on the island. Schecterle the indestructible, victor over surgery, sea, sun, and sharks, borrowed ten dollars from his brother, a Seabee on Guam, and parlayed it into $2,000 in a nonstop poker game that lasted until the gang broke up in the States. They carried the game right aboard the escort carrier *Hollandia*, when most of the survivors were put aboard early in September, and kept it going all the long voyage home.

The carrier arrived in San Diego Wednesday afternoon, September 26, and the city turned out to celebrate the return of 311 survivors of the *Indianapolis*. Councilman Gerald C. Crary and dozens of WAVES greeted them at the dockside, and the band of the Naval Training Center blared "California Here We Come." Nineteen stretcher cases imparted a sobering touch to the festivities, and there was a hush as these men were transferred to ambulances and dispatched to the Naval Hospital. Then the able-bodied men were given a jeep parade up Broadway, with the Navy band and city officials leading the way. Lieutenant Redmayne, senior officer among them, was in the lead jeep, waving his cap to the cheering crowds. After the welcome, buses carried the men off to Camp Elliott, and in a few days they began dispersing to their homes. It was the last time these men were together.

Captain McVay reached Washington early in September, to be reunited with his wife and receive the counsel of his father, who had served forty-six years in the Navy. Dozens of letters were already waiting, some bitter, some accusing, some compassionate, but all wanting to know what had happened to loved ones. All the news stories had alluded to the delay in rescue, but none of them had explained it, and the Navy had said nothing. Indeed, many parents and wives were still suffering the terrible doubts raised by the first "missing" telegrams.

Captain McVay received a reporter at his home on September 18, and told him:

"I'd advise all those families who haven't heard that men reported as 'missing' have been found, to give up hope. No man can be out in that water for so long and still be alive."

It was forty-four days after the sinking, and still no final word was released.

The interviewer reported that McVay seemed a little distraught. Asked what he expected to happen, McVay replied: "I was in command of the ship and I am responsible for its fate. I hope they make their decisions soon and do what they want with me."

He did not assert, as he might have, that he had had

nothing to do with the delay in rescue. The whole matter was still before the court, so to speak, and the captain remained silent. He busied himself with answering the mail now pouring in. Lieutenant Erwin F. Hensch, the ship's electrical officer, came down from his home in Minnesota to help Captain McVay with the lugubrious task. For kin of those officers and men he had known well, Captain McVay had the sorrowful job of telling them what he knew of their final hours. For kin of those he knew only casually or not at all, there was the necessity of telling them something which might bring peace of mind.

Some bereaved called on him at the Navy Department or at his home, and not all the meetings were sympathetic. A few felt he was shallow, or callous, and some held him personally accountable for their loss. It was no doubt a trying time for all, and although the story had disappeared from view after a one-day sensation, the Navy Department and the captain were not allowed to forget it for a moment. Hundreds of saddened homes sought an answer to the question—how could this thing happen?

Edward Connelly, who lost his son, Ensign D. F. Connelly, met in San Francisco with other parents, widows, and sweethearts to exchange information and see what they could do to learn more. Letters went out to President Truman, Secretary Forrestal, senators and representatives. Some were bitter, others showed resignation or acceptance, but all sought more information. Dr. Haynes, still weak from his ordeal, invited widows and mothers of fellow officers and enlisted men to his home to help them as best he could. Everywhere there was the same need— to be told that those who had died had given their lives for something worthwhile. Death is infinitely more bearable if the cause seems noble. What hurt in so many hearts was the feeling that this tragedy could have been avoided.

A mother who had lost her son, an ensign, wrote to Bill Cunningham of the Boston *Herald:*

> They told us Bob was in the water from shortly after midnight Sunday night until 4:30 Thursday afternoon before he passed on. How can we draw any comfort from his sacrifice when we know that his life, and those of two hundred others immediately around him, could have been

saved if the Navy had been alert? I have tried hard not to shadow the sacrifices these boys made by bitterness and recriminations, but those agonizing hours my child suffered will not let me rest.

Here, eloquently set forth, was the heart of the problem, and the magnitude of the Navy's dilemma. How could it explain to thousands of grieving kin? Mistakes have been made in war since the beginning of time, mistakes that literally mean life and death for someone. But no one has yet devised an adequate means for the military to admit them. This case was no different from many others.

In the Navy Department the papers shuffled back and forth from one office to another, endorsement piled on endorsement, the files grew thicker and thicker. Meantime the pressure and clamor, far from declining, increased. Cunningham pounded away at it in his column and finally, in late November, the Navy announced that Captain McVay would be court-martialed. Cunningham, and many others, were not convinced. Speaking for this body of thought, he wrote in his column of November 29:

One now hopes they're entirely fair to Captain McVay. From the sidelines it would appear that, unless he simply took his ship and went sailing off out of contact on his own, they've got the wrong man. Whoever ordered him to go alone, and, principally, who failed to look for him quickly when he failed to show up, likewise belong in court. . . . The V-J Day timing was cute, but it was not cute enough.

The last sentence echoed a popular, though probably unjustified, feeling that the Navy had deliberately timed its disclosure of the tragedy so it would be lost in the wild exultation of the war's end. When the war ended, and censorship with it, the Navy could no longer conceal the loss.

The Navy announced the court-martial on Tuesday, November 27, and said it would begin the following Monday, December 3. It would be held at the Washington Navy Yard, and it would be public, a most unusual circumstance. The Navy had never disclosed who made the final decision to court-martial Captain McVay, but it is known that Admiral Nimitz opposed it. He had strong precedent for this. Nine cruisers had been lost in battle during the war, several under questionable circumstances, but not a single commanding officer had been court-martialed. In fact, for the 436 other combatant vessels lost during the war not a single court-martial resulted. One captain had been relieved of command of a cruiser, but in no case was there a trial. In those desperate days of the war, the Navy simply could not afford a court-martial. It seems clear that Captain McVay was unfortunate that this tragedy occurred so late in the war. The thinking in high Navy circles would unquestionably have been considerably different a few years earlier.

The Navy did say that events which followed the sinking of the *Indianapolis* did not come within the scope of the McVay court-martial. Here, for the discerning, was clear warning that the trial would be severely circumscribed, but the public, unfamiliar with Naval judicial procedure, could hardly be expected to grasp the full significance of the statement. In the minds of many was the belief that the full story was about to be unfolded.

When anyone inquired what was being done about the "events which followed the sinking," he was told that those matters were "still under investigation," or that "further action" was contemplated.

The New York *Times* asked Rear Admiral George L. Russell, Assistant Judge Advocate of the Navy, about this and quoted him as replying that "the investigation of the *Indianapolis* affair was continuing and that other courts-martial are possible."

It is true that investigation was continuing. The Naval Inspector General, Admiral Charles P. Snyder, was in charge of the task, aided by Commodore Thomas E. Van Metre and Captain Charles E. Coney. But for Captain McVay, the hour had struck.

15

Monday dawned wet and gray, with just a hint of snow in the air. It was a cheerless day, one that mirrored with remarkable validity the situation in which Captain McVay found himself.

It was December, life was at a low ebb, and the year was drawing to a close, even as was his career. Without being maudlin, for he was ever a realist, Captain McVay knew that it was over, and had known it ever since he saw his ship plunge beneath the sea with the death rattle only a ship can make.

Always careful of his appearance (some thought him vain), he dressed with extra care that morning and promptly at 9:30 left the apartment on upper Connecticut Avenue, his wife at his side. His father, Admiral Charles Butler McVay, Jr., stayed at home.

As the taxicab threaded downtown through commuter traffic and passed the White House, Captain McVay may well have reflected a moment on happier days, when he served there as senior naval aide in 1938. Another world it seemed now, with the country at peace and FDR, a true "Navy man," in office. In McVay's file was a letter commending him for service at the White House that was "satisfactory in every respect."

And as they passed Capitol Hill, he may have remembered the momentous business under way there—the Pearl Harbor investigation. But only for an instant. That was tragedy in the large, and he was faced with tragedy in the particular—his own.

The cab sped down New Jersey Avenue and turned into M Street. Only a few blocks to go now. At the Eighth Street gate, the driver turned his head for instructions, and Captain McVay motioned him to drive in. The cab passed through the gate, into Washington Navy Yard, and the show was on.

To the left stood the commandant's house, where his father had lived when he commanded this Yard and Naval Gun Factory. For the admiral, it had been but one episode in a brilliant career. For the son, likewise no stranger to the Yard, it meant the end to a career full of promise.

At the foot of a small park, lined with ceremonial and historic cannon, stood a square, three-story brick building, painted battleship gray. The only sign on it read, "Building 57."

McVay dismissed the cab, and with his wife walked down the park to the building. The Navy was ready for him. A large room on the top floor had been prepared for the trial.

Not many courts-martial are held in public, but this was no ordinary one. Carpenters, shipfitters, electricians, and other artisans had been at work, constructing nearly two hundred seats for spectators, a special section for the press, and installing microphones for the court. There hadn't been much time, for even as McVay, they had received only a few days' notice.

At one end of the bleak room was the judges' bench, arcing slightly away from the windows at the ends. In front of the dais, the prosecution table was at the left, and the defense table at the right, with the witness box in the center.

There were only forty spectators in the courtroom when the McVays entered, and there was little sense of repressed emotion present. The prevailing feeling was rather one of curiosity, of waiting to see what was going to happen to a high-ranking naval officer in a public drama without precedent.

But the court was now about to come to order. Mrs. McVay took a seat near the front, and Captain McVay passed inside the railing and went to the defense table. He was, as the papers said, "pale but composed." The only sign of nervousness was that he constantly twisted his class ring on his finger.

Waiting for him was an old-time acquaintance and

his chief defense counsel, Captain John P. Cady, a tall, ascetic-looking man with graying black hair. Captain Cady, two years McVay's junior, was graduated from the Academy in 1922 and had taken a law degree at George Washington University in 1932.

Captain McVay had asked him to take the defense and he had agreed. Also at the table were Lieutenant Ernest Volberg and Lieutenant William J. O'Donnell, assigned as assistant defense counsel. They scarcely knew McVay, each other, or Cady. Both had been in the lawyers' pool at the Pentagon, available for routine law work, and O'Donnell had actually been discharged a few weeks before and returned to his home in Baltimore. Then twenty-nine, he was preparing to open his own law practice when he was summoned back to duty, for this case only.

Across the room at the other table was the judge advocate, Captain Thomas J. Ryan, Jr., a dashing Irishman with a record few could match. At forty-four, he held the Medal of Honor, two Navy Crosses, and the Legion of Merit. He was a lawyer and at present head of the department of ordnance and gunnery at the Naval Academy.

The Medal of Honor episode typified the man. As a raw ensign, the Navy had sent him to Japan to learn the language. During the great earthquake of September 1, 1923, he ran into the burning Grand Hotel in Yokohama, extricated a young Japanese woman from her bath and carried her to safety. Thousands were killed and the city of half a million people was virtually destroyed that day. For the rest of his days Academy buddies gently kidded Ryan that among this chaos he had been called on to rescue a maiden in distress in her bath.

Ryan preceded Cady by a year in taking his Bachelor of Laws degree at George Washington University and won his two Navy Crosses as a destroyer squadron commander in the hot days of 1943 in the Russell and New Georgia Islands. Soon after this trial he, too, would become a cruiser skipper, taking command of the U.S.S. *Providence*.

Ryan's job was one peculiar to Navy jurisprudence in those days. As judge advocate he conducted the trial, acted as prosecutor, and interpreted the law. The court acted mainly as a sort of jury, although it was free to question witnesses and did so.

At exactly ten o'clock, the court filed in and took seats

along the dais, their backs to the windows. And a heavy load of brass it was—one rear admiral, two commodores, and four captains.

But the start was abortive. Nobody was ready. Newsmen quickly spotted the fact that one seat was vacant on the court. Captain Heman Judd Redfield, Jr., a battleship man, would come in the next day to explain that he had just received his orders.

The first day, however, court went on without him, and he didn't miss much. McVay arose and said he had received a copy of the charges and specifications on November 29—just four days before. Asked if he had any objections to the trial, he replied that he did. The first charge, he said, ". . . fails to state an offense, it merely sets forth a conclusion."

The court retired for ten minutes, returned and announced this thesis had been rejected. The charge stood.

The court then asked the judge advocate if he was ready to proceed. Captain Ryan replied that he was not. He said he had only heard of the charges four days previously and needed more time to prepare his case. Court adjourned until the following day.

Not a very auspicious beginning, but then the whole affair had been hurried. Acting Secretary of the Navy John L. Sullivan had not ordered the court-martial until November 21, and the charges and specifications delivered to Captain Ryan were dated November 29. That left just four days to prepare a case.

When Captain Ryan got a chance to read the file, he found the charges to be as follows:

CHARGE I

Through Negligence Suffering a Vessel of the Navy to be Hazarded

SPECIFICATION

In that Charles B. McVay 3rd, captain, U.S. Navy, while so serving in command of the U.S.S. *Indianapolis*, making passage singly, without escort, from Guam, Marianas Islands, to Leyte, Philippine Islands, through an area in which enemy submarines might be encountered, did, during good visibility after moonrise on 29

July 1945, at or about 10:30 P.M., minus nine and one-half zone time, neglect and fail to exercise proper care and attention to the safety of said vessel in that he neglected and failed, then and thereafter, to cause a zigzag course to be steered, and he, the said McVay, through said negligence, did suffer the said U.S.S. *Indianapolis* to be hazarded, the United States then being in a state of war.

CHARGE II

Culpable Inefficiency in the Performance of Duty

SPECIFICATION

In that Charles B. McVay 3rd, captain, U.S. Navy, while so serving in command of the U.S.S. *Indianapolis*, making passage from Guam, Marianas, to Leyte, Philippine Islands, having been informed at or about 12:10 A.M., minus nine and one-half zone time, on 30 July 1945, that said vessel was badly damaged and in sinking condition, did then and there fail to issue and see effected such timely orders as were necessary to cause said vessel to be abandoned, as it was his duty to do, by reason of which inefficiency many persons on board perished with the sinking of said vessel, the United States then being in a state of war.

/s/ James Forrestal.

Assembled to weigh the evidence was a seven-man court headed by Rear Admiral Wilder DuPuy Baker, at fifty-five an expert on escort and convoying and father of the Navy's modern antisubmarine warfare techniques. If anyone noticed a mild irony in the fact that the *Indianapolis* was neither escorted, nor carried antisubmarine devices, no mention was made of it.

Baker had commanded everything from submarines to battleships, and he knew all there was to know about cruisers, having been more than once a cruiser division commander in action against the enemy. A benign, soft-spoken man, he would nevertheless exhibit great keenness of mind and persistence in questioning witnesses.

Flanking him were a pair of commodores with distinguished records in amphibious warfare, Paul Seymour Theiss, 55, and William Sherbrooke Popham, 53.

A brace of captains, all just a bit senior to McVay, held down each end of the panel. Captain Redfield, the late arrival, and Captain Homer Louis Grosskopf had been classmates at the Academy (class of 1916), and both were just back from battleship service in the Pacific. Captain John Raymond Sullivan, also a few months back from the Pacific, had spent nearly three years fighting his way up the islands from Guadalcanal through Munda, Bougainville, the Palaus, Leyte, and Luzon.

Captain Charles Boardman Hunt, a year ahead of McVay in the Academy, won the Navy Cross for heroism while running supplies to Guadalcanal in August and September, 1942, when the Japanese were lashing back at the American invaders. Like McVay, he finally got his own cruiser, the brand-new *Oklahoma City*, which he had placed in commission just a year ago. Now he sat in judgment on a fellow cruiser commander.

The trial got under way on Tuesday morning, December 4, with all principals present. Summoned to the bench, Captain McVay was asked how he pleaded, and in a loud, firm voice replied, "Not guilty," in turn to the first charge, first specification, second charge, and second specification.

The first witness, Lieutenant Waldron, stepped from the witnesses' room at the right side of the court and took the stand. His deep tan, contrasting strangely with the cold gray weather of Washington, caused startled glances. The spectators did not know that four days ago he had been sweating out his points on Guam. Flying to Washington had been the farthest thing from his mind. But on Friday morning he had been summoned to the office of Commodore Roger E. Nelson, Commandant, NOB, Guam. In the commodore's hand was a dispatch from Washington—Waldron must be in Washington Monday morning with all records pertaining to routing the *Indianapolis*.

On Sunday afternoon, the lieutenant stepped off the NATS "Hot Shot Special" at Washington Airport, unshaven and exhausted from his 47-hour flight. There was snow on the ground, and the wind whistled through his summer khakis. In accordance with orders, he immediately telephoned Admiral Baker at the Navy Yard and was told to come right over. Lieutenant Waldron explained his fatigue and his need of a shower and shave, but the Admiral said heartily: "Come on over, Waldron. We're not going to take your picture, we want to talk to you." They did, for two hours.

Now on Tuesday morning he took the stand, rested, shaven, and immaculate in dress blues. (He had hurried up to his home in Trenton to get them.) He recounted the visits to his office by Captain McVay and Commander Janney, and told of fixing the route, speed, time of departure, and time of arrival.

Captain Cady asked if the question of escort had been brought up.

Lieutenant Waldron replied it had not, but "on my own, I checked with the area commander to see if one was available, and I was informed that an escort was not needed by the *Indianapolis* at that time."

He had not asked if one was needed, he had asked if one was available. He had received no reply.

As to the route, a straight line, Lieutenant Waldron said it was routine.

"There was no route in the Pacific that could be deemed perfectly safe," he said, "but it was a routine sailing as determined by higher authority at that time." There were other routes, he added, "but they were longer and not as direct, and generally were not used."

The second witness was something of a surprise.

Captain Ryan called to the stand Lieutenant Commander Alan R. McFarland, a destroyer skipper with experience at Bougainville, the Marianas, Palau, and the Iwo Jima and Okinawa campaigns. He said he did not know McVay.

Ryan undertook to qualify him as an expert ship commander, and McVay said he would accept him as an expert "within his experience."

McFarland was then given the circumstances of the *Indianapolis* route and the submarine reports and asked if this ". . . would take you through an area in which enemy submarines might be encountered?"

"In my opinion, I would say 'yes sir,'" McFarland replied.

McVay objected that he had not accepted the witness as "an expert cruiser captain," and on his motion the question and answer were stricken.

McFarland was then asked to plot the submarine reports and he did so on a plotting chart, placing them 72 and 105 miles south of the track, and 95 miles north. Under questioning, he then said that, assuming a speed of seven knots, one of the subs could have arrived at the sinking point on the 24th and the other two on the 27th.

The value of this, however, was demolished when Captain Cady asked him if the submarines ". . . could, likewise, have reached any other point on a circle of each same respective radius?"

McFarland gave the only possible answer: "Yes sir, that is correct."

(As a matter of fact, none of these submarines, if they were submarines, was Hashimoto's. He did not arrive in the area until July 27.)

Cruisers and destroyers are very different weapons, with separate uses and methods of operation. Why wasn't a cruiser captain called to the stand? It seems reasonable that none could be found who cared to testify what he would have done under the circumstances. It is most difficult in any profession to find one man willing to testify against a fellow professional.

Next up was Gerald Clemence, an astronomer and director of the Nautical Almanac Office at the U.S. Naval Observatory. He testified that at 10:30 P.M. on July 29, in the position of the *Indianapolis*, the moon would have been in the east, about 23 degrees above the horizon. It was two days before the last quarter, he said, and ". . . if the sky were perfectly clear, the moonlight would be approximately one-fourth that of the full moon."

The big weather question throughout the trial was, how clear was the sky? On that, opinions ranged from dark as a coal mine at midnight to bright enough to read a newspaper. The truth seems to be that visibility did range widely, depending upon how much the moon was obscured by clouds. Hashimoto would testify later, and also write in his memoirs, that almost immediately upon surfacing that night his lookout spotted a dark object on the horizon, silhouetted by the moon. By great good fortune (for him) he had surfaced during a light period.

Lieutenant Michael J. Barrett, of the Office of the

Chief of Naval Operations, was the next witness. He said he was in charge of secret and confidential mail for CNO and the Secretary of the Navy. Asked if his files contained a secret letter from McVay to Secretary Forrestal, dated August 12, on the loss of the *Indianapolis*, Barrett said he could not find the original, but did find a copy attached to the record of the court of inquiry.

This was received in evidence, with the stipulation by McVay that it was accepted ". . . on its face without admitting anything as to its accuracy."

The reason for this byplay became clear later when it turned out that McVay's letter, a customary report in the circumstances, contained the sentence: "There was intermittent moonlight, at which times the visibility was unlimited."

When McVay took the stand, he was asked if he saw any moonlight while he was on the bridge, after the explosion.

"No sir, I did not," he replied. "In fact, it was so dark on the bridge I couldn't recognize anybody."

Asked how this squared with the passage in his letter, McVay replied:

"At the time I made out that official report, the matter—the question of visibility—did not appear to me to be one of importance. I prepared the report under some duress. It had to be made in a hurry. In order to submit it, I said what the visibility was, as I remember it, after I got in the water."

Captain Ryan asked him to clarify the word "duress," and McVay said:

"I was in the hospital at the time. Some of my people were on Samar. I had a great many things to try to get ready for the court of inquiry. That was just one of the many things I had to do. They (unidentified) were in a hurry to get the court started, and that is what I meant by being pushed for time."

"Would it be more accurate to say that you were working under great pressure and hurried to get the report submitted, rather than you made the report under duress?" Ryan asked.

"Yes, I think I would prefer to change my statement to that," McVay replied. "Apparently my word was ill-chosen."

Asked if he had had an opportunity to correct the

letter later, McVay replied: "I never gave it a thought."

After the episode of the letter, there began a parade of survivors to the stand, each to tell his story of what had happened to him that night.

All witnesses called during the first two weeks of the trial were summoned by the judge advocate, Captain Ryan, and therefore called "prosecution witnesses," but this seems mostly to have been a formality. Many of them gave testimony favorable to Captain McVay, and some even volunteered statements in his behalf, an occurrence unlikely in civilian courts.

Lieutenant McKissick was first of the survivors to testify. McKissick said McVay gave the order to cease zigzagging at the end of the evening twilight, and he did not question it.

"I didn't feel it was anything unusual. We did it all during the war," said McKissick. He had served on the *Indianapolis* nearly two years and under two commanding officers.

McKissick told of the dispatch on the bridge regarding a possible submarine 75 to 100 miles south of them, and 200 to 250 miles ahead. This caused him no anxiety, he said, because "we received dispatches all through the war much to the same effect."

He said that if visibility had been good he would not have hesitated to continue zigzagging and notify the captain, "and I think that the captain would have been pleased at the action of any of his OODs had he taken such a measure in the event that he thought it necessary."

On the other question at issue, "timely orders" to abandon, McKissick said: "I think that at least 850 men, and possibly more, got off the ship.

"Any men that were not definitely in the explosion area, I think had ample opportunity to get off the ship, because there was no undue confusion at any time, as far as I know. When I reached topside the men were very calm, there was no undue confusion at this time and we were in the part of the ship which was in the worst condition, so I estimate that conditions were much the same in the afterpart of the ship, where most of the men lived. They had ample time to get topside and time to prepare to abandon the ship."

McKissick said he heard no order to abandon, but

". . . that order could very definitely have been given and I would not hear it. As I say, I was the furthest forward and was pretty busy doing what I was doing. I wasn't paying particular attention to any orders that I might receive from the bridge or hear from the bridge. It could have been given very easily, sir."

Not exactly a hostile witness. He stepped down, or, in the quaint language of the record, "the witness was duly warned and withdrew."

Wednesday's first witness was Lieutenant Redmayne, who was under instruction on the bridge that night. He had had a good teacher, Commander Lipski, who had served aboard since early 1943, under three skippers. Lipski wasn't there to testify himself, and Redmayne was not asked what Lipski had thought of conditions during the ship's last hours, but it seems reasonable to assume that he, Lipski, was completely satisfied. He could easily have given orders to resume zigzagging and he would not have hesitated to rouse McVay had he thought it necessary.

Though he was "under instruction," as the phrase went, Redmayne was no neophyte. He had been at sea constantly since joining the Navy in April, 1941, with duty in the Atlantic, Hawaiian area, and the Aleutians. And the OOD was Lieutenant MacFarland, with better than eighteen months on board.

Not a bad line-up for a routine night watch on any man's ship, and now Redmayne had to speak for them all. MacFarland was never seen again after he left the bridge at midnight, and Lipski, who had gone over the side badly injured, died in the water.

Redmayne said the weather was very poor until 11:00 P.M., very cloudy and no moon. After moonrise, things were different.

"It was intermittent moonlight with visibility good when the clouds weren't in front of the moon, and the visibility poor when they were in front of the moon," he said, in what appears to be a keen summary. His testimony was important, for he was the only surviving officer to observe the weather from the bridge up until a few moments before the sinking. Every other officer on his watch and the final bridge watch perished.

Redmayne told of Commander Janney, the navigator, coming on the bridge around 9:00 or 9:30 P.M. to report that a PBM and a DDE were searching for an enemy submarine in an area through which the ship would pass about eight o'clock the next morning.

Asked if any of the officers showed any concern, Redmayne said "Well, if they had paid particular attention to it or done anything I think I would have remembered." As for himself, "I wasn't particularly worried about it," Redmayne said. Asked if he thought the ship should have been zigzagging, he said, "No, sir." Nor would he have hesitated to bring up the matter of zigzagging if he had been worried about it, he added.

Redmayne estimated 800 men got off the ship. No one pursued this matter, because the question of why 500 men died in the water had been excluded from the court's purview.

The engineering officer said he got no orders from the bridge after the explosions. He explained that when he reached the after engine room all communications were out, except a few local sound-powered circuits, so he started for the bridge to find out what was going on. Halfway up the ladder the ship started to capsize, and he barely escaped. Redmayne was caught by surrpise; he had left his men on duty in the engine room.

"I didn't consider the conditions bad enough for the engine room to be abandoned," he explained. The list in the engine room was only 12 to 15 degrees, he said, but by the time he got to the main deck ". . . she was over more than ninety degrees to starboard and the water was up above the center line."

Lieutenant Commander Haynes, senior surviving officer next to McVay (rarely during the war had death cut such a wide swathe in the top echelons of command), took the stand.

The preliminaries over, Captain Ryan launched into some wildly irrelevant questioning with:

"You spoke of unloading some supplies at Tinian. Do you know the nature of those supplies?"

"I do now," he replied. "At the time, I had no knowledge of them. At Hunters Point, some Army officials brought some top-secret supplies aboard. Some of it was placed up in the captain's country, and a large box was in the hangar under heavy guard."

"Do you know now what the nature of those supplies was?" Ryan asked.

"Yes. From the newspaper reports and from being

told by one of the Army officials who later came to the hospital in Guam where we were patients, he told me that they were parts of the atomic bomb which had been dropped on Hiroshima."

Very interesting, but it had nothing to do with the questions at issue.

Lieutenant Commander Haynes then gave a dramatic account of the explosions, his escape from the burning wardroom, his attempts to aid the maimed, and the hurried abandonment as the ship rolled over. Once in the water, he said, there were 300 to 400 men in his group.

And how many of those were rescued? he was asked.

"I believe the *Cecil Doyle* picked up 93 out of that group," he answered, and you could feel the tension begin to rise. This was getting close to the nerve.

"What happened to the remainder?" was the next question.

"Well," the doctor began, "more than twenty died the first night from burns and injuries—"

He got no further. The accused objected. What happened in the water was in no way his responsibility.

Captain Ryan withdrew the question, and the court declared:

It had decided ". . . that it felt that any testimony regarding deaths in the water following the abandoning of the ship should have a proper foundation laid prior to being given. The court further advised that any testimony about deaths in the water should be connected up with any possible inefficiency of the accused that may have existed or occurred prior to the time of the death or deaths of said person or persons in the water."

And there it was. There was only one person on trial —Captain McVay. The court was not sitting to hear evidence bearing on the actions of others in this tragedy. This court could follow the men into the water, but no question concerning the next five days would be allowed.

Having quietly but firmly closed this door, the court settled back and the questioning resumed.

How many men did he think had escaped from the ship alive?

"When we abandoned ship, the side of the ship was black with men," Dr. Haynes said. "I would estimate that probably seven- or eight-hundred men did abandon ship, at least."

Earlier Captain Ryan had asked if Dr. Haynes had had any occasion to think submarines might be about, and this brought on the story of "Janney's joke."

"At the evening meal, on the night we were sunk," Haynes began, "the navigator, Commander Janney, jokingly remarked at the table that we were going to pass by a submarine during the night (Redmayne got it as 8:00 A.M.). I don't remember the details of the conversation. It was a—the usual jovial conversation around a wardroom table."

Returning to the subject later, Dr. Haynes continued:

"Yes, it was at the evening meal, and the conversation was in a joking vein. He remarked about it, but we thought nothing of it at the time. I didn't think so. I can't recall the exact conversation, but he remarked we were going to pass a submarine sometime during the night, and we joked back and forth for a few minutes about the situation and that was all. I immediately forgot the situation."

"What do you mean about 'jokingly'?" Ryan asked, and the doctor delivered some sound sea psychology.

"Aboard ship the only congenial time a group of officers have is during the meal hour, particularly in a forward area where your work is pressing, and as a result your congenial and happy hours are during meal hour. The *Indianapolis* was a very happy ship, and we had a congenial group in the wardroom, and we thought nothing of it at the time."

"Doctor, are you conversant with any orders that were in effect aboard ship not to discuss publicly any reports of enemy contacts?"

"Yes, the security regulations aboard the *Indianapolis* were always very strict, and, as a rule, we followed the Navy rule of discussions at the wardroom table, of never discussing ship's business, women, or politics at the table."

There being no further questions, Dr. Haynes made the following statement:

"I would like to say that under Captain McVay's command the *Indianapolis* was a very efficient, trim, fighting ship, and I would be honored and pleased to serve under him again."

With testimony like this, it was difficult at times to keep in mind just what the charges were. Certainly no

Caine Mutiny set-up, with a mad skipper leading his vessel to destruction.

Donald Mack, the bugler, was the first enlisted survivor to testify. Mack, in the Navy twenty-six months, better than half of that time on the *Indianapolis*, said he had the watch on the bridge that night and had his bugle with him, but nobody ordered him to blow it.

"I stood by on the bridge, to take any orders to sound 'Abandon ship,' which were none, and the next order I got was to go over the side, from Lieutenant Orr." It was a black night, he said, but he could see three or four miles to sea, and could recognize faces at six feet.

Nobody asked him where he might have been when McVay, as he testified later, gave Lieutenant Orr and the executive officer, Commander Flynn, the order to pass the word to abandon ship.

It might have been interesting to hear what the bugle call was for "Abandon ship," and speculate whether anybody would have known what he was blowing. It certainly wasn't as popular a tune as "mess call" or "pay call." And, since the sound power system was shot to pieces, would he have just stood there like Satchmo Armstrong and played to the breeze?

Then followed a truly remarkable witness. He testified at length, and throughout gave the kind of answers every man dreams he will give when he is grilled on the stand—quick, brilliantly clear, detailed to a fault. He testified to a lot of things he could not possibly have had any knowledge of, but then, he had just turned twenty-one.

It was Ensign Woolston, damage control officer. When the ship went down he was twenty years old and a veteran of two full weeks at sea.

But once on the stand he was the saltiest sea dog of them all.

After a few preliminary questions, Woolston started off in brisk fashion:

"At approximately five minutes after midnight, there was an explosion below and far forward. Flames came back along the main deck passageway through both forward doors of the wardroom, where I was sitting at the time."

He then told of his escape from the ship, and was asked:

"How many men lived through the night?"

"Yes, sir. On Monday morning there were approximately 740 men alive in the water. There were probably
fifty to a hundred men who had drowned during the night,
but probably could not have been saved even if rescue
had come Monday morning. The three forward living compartments, A309L, A312L, and A208L, were opened
to the sea by the second explosion. This meant probably
only half a dozen men were able to escape from these
compartments. A great many other men were probably
injured in abandoning ship or drowned immediately after
abandoning, due to the lack of life preservers."

In the first place, the survivors were already widely
scattered by dawn. No one could possibly have counted
them, with a twelve-foot swell running, let alone say how
many were alive or dead in their life jackets.

Who could possibly estimate how many died during a
dark night of choppy seas, debris, and heavy oil slick? The
compartments Woolston mentioned were all below him
and on the starboard side, where he never was. Very likely
they were opened to the sea, but he couldn't know it. Nor
could he know that "only half a dozen men were able to
escape," or even how many men were in the compartments.

And "the lack of life preservers." The court would
return to that later.

Woolston was asked if the explosions would have in-
terfered with the work of the repair parties, and he
launched into another long answer.

"Very definitely, sir. The after torpedo striking the
area of Central would immediately have flooded the internal communications room, which would mean that all
power communications would have been interrupted, and
all sound-power communications which entered the switch-
board would have been interrupted. This would leave the
only communications possible on the antiaircraft circuits
and on the forward circuit on the bridge. The No. 1 fire
room being open meant the complete loss of steam to
No. 1 engine room.

"The explosion apparently also ruptured the fire
mains, because the pressure in the mains forward dropped
to zero, and the pressure in the after engine room went
down to ten pounds per square inch. No. 1 repair party
was used only for darkened ship. No. 2 repair party was
wiped out. Central station was wiped out.

"Oil on the water was floating in the passageway on the second deck and in the main deck, and was soon ignited. Repair parties from aft attempted to fight fire forward and recover some of our watertight integrity but their efforts were not of much value due to the flames, because the fire-main pressure dropping gave them no water to fight fire with. Doors were closed and the fire was fought from the topside, but it was of very little value."

He was obviously speaking the recollections of others, since he had not been in the fire rooms, engine rooms, central station, or much of anywhere except topside after the explosions.

Woolston was asked what Condition Yoke Modified was and again he was off and running:

"Yes, sir. Normally a ship is supposed to be able to cruise in wartime in Condition Yoke. However, this ship had not been reclassified during the last—probably ten—years; the fittings had not been reclassified, and Condition Yoke was much too tight to allow the ship to cruise comfortably. Condition Yoke on the ship as it stood at the time would have meant that most of the ventilation would be cut off—the doors and hatches were occasionally classified X-ray or Yoke when they were necessary for the running of the ship. Condition Yoke Modified had been used on the ship apparently since the beginning of the war. There were no definite doors to be opened for ventilation during this condition. It was more habit than anything else.

"The damage-control book was not up to date, and the plates were not up to date. We on the ship were bringing it up at the time. We had finished most of the important bills so that the ship could cruise under Condition Yoke comfortably. However, they had not been printed and distributed so that we still had to cruise under the old condition. This meant, actually, that the entire main deck was open, all the doors in the second deck were open, and the doors leading from central station into the internal communications room, the thyratron room, the battery room and the plotting room were open.

"And the hatches were open from the second deck to the living spaces below the second deck. Aft, only scuttles were open to the living compartments on the first platform deck from the second deck. The main deck hatches

forward and aft were shut, but amidships were not. One
hatch was left open into each engineering space. Hatches
were left open into the trunks leading to central station,
to the evaporator rooms and to steering aft and aft gyro
(compass).

"Also, scuttles were occasionally left open to other
compartments on the second deck which were used by
personnel as sleeping compartments. These were mainly
the two after store rooms in the forward section of the
ship 307A and 308A.

"There was a habit among certain of the engineering
crew, who went to the forward diesel generator room, to
leave the hatches open down to that room, which was on
the second platform deck. This was discouraged, but they
may have been opened. All ventilation was open to living
spaces and was closed to dead storerooms. The ventilation, was I believe, in accord with FTP 170 Baker."

When Ryan could get a word in, he asked about the
open hatches, saying, "Do you mean to infer that the damage-control discipline was not proper?"

"Damage-control discipline was not proper with regards to men outside the damage-control departments,
unfortunately," Woolston replied. "This was, I believe, due
to the fact that Condition Yoke Modified was not definitely settled."

Returning to the question of life jackets, Ryan asked:
"You said certain people died during the night for
lack of life jackets, is that correct?"

"Partially, yes," Woolston replied. "There was sufficient lifesaving gear available on the ship, but it was not
cleared from the ship. The life rafts were fastened with
toggle ropes to the ship, and when the ship listed it put
such a strain on them that the men were unable to release
the rafts by pulling the toggle pin, as is usual, so the men
had to cut the rafts loose.

"Many of these were to the starboard side of the
ship and were lost. The life-jacket bags, which had not
been cut loose, floated to the surface, or at least several of
them did for they were found the next morning, but the
rafts apparently were held—fastened securely enough to
the ship that they were not released by the sinking."

Woolston estimated a dozen life rafts and six floater
nets got off.

This was reasonably accurate. The *Indianapolis* car-

ried two twenty-six-foot motor whaleboats, thirty-five
rafts, and twenty-four floater nets. The boats, being securely chocked, never cleared the ship. When survivors
were rounded up, they were found on twelve rafts and
eight floater nets, and days later other rafts and nets were
found containing bodies or nothing. No one can say for sure
how many cleared the ship, although some very likely did
not.

Ryan wound up his questioning with an exchange that
spoke eloquently of the magnitude of the tragedy:

"Q. Are you the senior surviving officer in damage
control?"

"A. Yes, sir. I am the *only* surviving officer."

Captain Cady's cross-examination was brief:

"Was this Condition Yoke situation known to the
skipper and were steps being taken to correct it?"

"I believe the commanding officer knew about the
condition, and steps were being taken, yes, sir."

"Do you know, or did you know then, of any better
way of securing life rafts?"

"Yes, sir. There is a hydrostatic release which the
Bureau of Ships has worked out which is, I believe, supposed to be on all ships in the fleet. However, there had
not been sufficient of them available to the fleet so that
they had not been placed on this ship."

There was a "yes" answer that meant "no."

Joseph John Moran, radioman, first class, took the
stand and the first question put to him again outlined the
stark tragedy of the affair:

"Q. Are there any surviving officer personnel of the
communications department of the *Indianapolis?*"

"A. No, sir, there are none."

(Moran himself was electrocuted seven months later
in an accident aboard the U.S.S. *Albemarle* at Bikini, July
4, 1946.)

Moran, a level-headed boy of twenty-three, had his
"submarine story," too. Off duty, he was batting the breeze
in the radio room on Sunday when a high priority message
came through and was decoded immediately. Moran testified that the officer on watch had said that "it was just
another report of a merchant ship having two torpedoes
fired at her in position about 300 miles from us." He
added, "I believe the position was due south."

This was very likely another version of the same

story already told by Redmayne and Haynes. The phrasing "just another report" indicates how common these merchant ship "contacts" were and how much weight was given them by the fighting Navy.

He told of the scenes in Radio I as they attempted to get off an SOS. They had to quit, he said, because receivers, typewriters, desks, and other heavy equipment were beginning to crash down from the high side all around them.

That concluded the second day of testimony, and the court recessed at 3:15 until 10:00 A.M. the next day.

Lieutenant Reid, the supply officer, was the next witness. Reid estimated "at least 800 men" were on the fantail when he got there, and they began going over the side as soon as the ship began to list. He said he believed he was the senior officer there, and he tried to keep the men on board, but as the list increased "it seemed impossible to do anything but go over the side so the men did, and I was—I fell back against the turret and finally the ship just went down from under me."

He estimated 500 men got off the ship alive, and was not questioned as to what might have happened to the others of the "at least 800" he thought were on the fantail.

He volunteered the following statement as he left the stand:

"I have nothing further to say, except the fact that I don't see how word to abandon ship could have been received on the fantail without communications of some sort. I don't see how it could have been passed through the hangar or over the hangar."

Coxswain Keyes then told of being sent below to order all men topside. There weren't many men down there, he said, because they "were all going topside" when he went below. When he got back to the bridge, he said, Captain McVay was there, and in about five minutes he gave the order to abandon ship. How?

"He hollered down from the bridge to the men that were standing on the—that were getting ready to abandon ship."

Keyes recalled there were thirteen men on watch on the bridge, including himself. Asked how many of them survived, he replied "King and Mack."

Seaman Second Class Sinclair, just out of boot camp, had the lookout watch on the starboard quarter, where the enemy sub lay. He said he saw no wake, no periscope, only the horizon, which was clear in his binoculars. Sinclair said he heard no order to abandon ship, although he was on the bridge.

Ensign Rogers set the time of sinking at 12:10.

"My watch stopped at 12:40, and it was 30 minutes fast," he said.

Rogers said he could not estimate how many men escaped from the ship, "but I found people that came from such surprising parts of the ship—I believe it was a very high percentage. They seemed to get out of the lower berthing places, the—some of the engine rooms, and other places that I wouldn't have expected them to get out of."

Seaman First Class Jurkiewicz, a veteran of two years on the ship, told of being in CIC with two officers and two other enlisted men.

"How many of that number, three enlisted men and two officer personnel, survived?" he was asked.

"I did," he replied.

"Will you repeat that, please?"

"Just me, just myself."

"Did all of the officers and men in CIC get out?"

"Yes sir, all of them died in the water."

Seaman Second Class Jacquemot, lookout on the forecastle, was asked what he observed after the torpedoes hit.

"That the men were running around—officers—and going over the side," he said. He was not pressed on this point, and the rest of his testimony was routine.

Gunner Harrison, an old-timer on board, made several points. He had fifty to sixty men around him on the boat deck, and all got off safely. Asked how many men he thought got off the ship, Harrison replied:

"I could only give an estimate that we got together in Guam when we figured between eight and nine hundred were in the water by asking the various people what groups they were in and how many in the group they were in."

The floater nets, he pointed out, were lying free in net baskets, so they would float to the surface in just such an emergency. As to life jackets:

"There were so many kapok life jackets aboard the ship that they were issued on all topside stations, and these kapok life jackets were hung in bags around the ship. We

—they were excess jackets that we had no place to put. We had, I believe I heard one damage-control officer say, something like 2,500 kapok life jackets, due to duplication of our order, and they were in our way, and that was the answer to getting them out of the way."

At the end of his testimony he volunteered the following:

"I do not believe it was possible that anyone could have known the ship was going to sink until it took the last list and started to roll."

Radioman Sturtevant said he was on watch in Radio I.

"If anything unusual occurred, please state what it was."

"The ship sank about midnight," he replied.

Gunner Horner testified he did not believe the magazines exploded. He was well qualified to state this because he visited the area of the magazines after the torpedo hits and actually turned on the magazine sprinklers.

Horner said he saw no disorders among the men.

"I thought everyone was very cool and collected under the circumstances."

Again there was a welcome touch of humor. Ensign Blum was asked:

"Did anything unusual occur during the night of 29-30 July? If so, state what it was."

"The ship sank," he replied.

The court adjourned until Friday morning, but when it convened no further witnesses were available and further adjournment was taken until Tuesday morning.

16

During the long weekend a witness did arrive in town, and one who lifted the trial right back on to page one. It was Commander Hashimoto. (He had been promoted just before the Imperial Navy disintegrated.)

The Navy set off the bombshell on Saturday, December 8, by announcing the enemy officer was en route to Washington to testify. The Navy has never disclosed who decided to bring Hashimoto to Washington. Recalling the temper of the times, it was an explosive move. The Pearl Harbor investigation was in full swing in Washington, the War Crimes Trials were on in Nürnberg, and the papers were daily disclosing new atrocities perpetrated by the Japanese in Malaya, the Philippines, and in Japanese prison camps. The war and its horrors were fresh in everyone's mind, and the bringing of an enemy officer— a defeated enemy—to testify against an American officer was in the nature of a national affront.

The New York *Times* carried a box, high on page one in the Sunday paper, telling of the Navy's action, and many other Sunday papers around the country gave it similar prominence. The move was, at best, fantastically ill-timed. Said the *Times* on Monday, ". . . officials could recall no precedent for the appearance of an enemy officer at the court-martial of an American officer in connection with an act of warfare."

Hashimoto arrived in Oakland, California, by NATS plane on Sunday, December 9, and the next day he stepped off the plane in Washington, in the custody of Lieutenant (j.g.) Allan Smith. Photographers swarmed around, taking pictures of this strange little man in wrinkled civilian clothing, a slouch hat pulled down over his eyes. Smith explained patiently to the reporters that his charge spoke little English, and in a short time Hashimoto was whisked off to the Roosevelt Hotel, where he was kept under guard.

It was a strange position for the Japanese officer. He knew of the atrocities and indignities committed by some Japanese officers. As for himself, he was proud of the professional correctness of his own war record. Before he left Tokyo he was assured that he would be treated as a naval officer, not as a prisoner or a war criminal, and of course he did not come of his own accord; he had no choice in the matter. Now that he was in Washington, however, things were not quite as he had been led to expect. After one night in the hotel, he found himself at the Navy Yard, a virtual prisoner. He was not allowed a step outside, and though the Navy assured him the men assigned to him were not guards, it certainly seemed that way to the Japanese. The Navy said the men were to protect him from harm, and this was true. Feeling was running high.

On the whole, the officers and men he came in contact with treated him decently. Many of the "guards" joked and laughed with him but a couple glared at him and refused to talk with him. And though he could not read English (he understood it a little), he sensed that some of the newspapers were insulting him. He was short, by American standards, and a little bowlegged—perhaps from long hours in the cramped quarters of Japanese submarines. The badly fitting clothes, the constant bowing (perfectly natural to him, of course), and the inability to talk with Americans, all added up to a picture bound to generate derision. Add to this the high emotion stirred up by the war and it is not hard to see the difficult position in which he found himself.

But he handled himself with dignity, even through such uncomfortable scenes as when a guard shoved under his nose a newspaper containing revelations of Japanese cruelty to Allied prisoners. Hashimoto, himself a father and devoted family man, innocent of any such conduct himself, could only mumble in confusion and embarrassment.

The press and the public were off in full cry over the arrival of Hashimoto. Mrs. Evalyn Walsh McLean fired off a telegram to Navy Secretary Forrestal, saying she was "shocked and horrified" to hear that Hashimoto would be allowed to testify. Representative Robert L. Doughton, North Carolina Democrat then in his 81st year, declared "It is the most contemptible thing I ever heard of to summon a Jap officer to testify against one of our own officers. I made my living practicing law before Navy courts and boards for twenty-five years and this reaches an all-time low in courts, board, or Congressional investigations."

Nationally syndicated columnist Robert Ruark sounded off with a column headed: "Was Jap Commander Brought to 'Hype Up' Sagging Court-Martial?"

Ruark said the trial ". . . is beginning to take on some aspects of a sideshow. All along it has departed from standard Navy procedure by being well press-agented, but the importation of Hashimoto is unprecedented in the annals of anything, and is causing much talk among Navy men. Just why the submarine commander is here is unclear, and the Judge Advocate's office won't talk."

Ruark said Hashimoto's evidence could have been taken by deposition in Japan. Why wasn't this done? "The answer, some Navy men speculate, is that Hashimoto was flown over to enliven a court-martial which was beginning to sag in reader appeal," Ruark said.

The Washington *Post* asked in an editorial:

> We wonder how many readers shared our shock when they read of the arrival of Commander Hashimoto? . . . What we are doing in this case is putting an enemy in the position of determining the justice we mete out among ourselves. It was a perverted sense of values that produced this course of action.

Recalling the wartime propaganda that the Japanese were congenital liars, the *Post* said:

> It will be a debasing spectacle when Hashimoto takes the witness stand, and the danger of making our own people cynical and of undermining the morale of our Navy is involved in it.

Alan Stevenson, past commandant of the Marine Corps League, asserted that bringing Hashimoto here warranted "the strongest possible protest" by all veterans organizations and all American citizens. He urged national veterans' leaders to complain to the Navy.

But the court-martial went right on. First witness Tuesday morning was Commander DeGrave, who had been forced to leave the *Indianapolis* ten days before the sinking. He now had shore duty, and was called out of turn as a defense witness because he had to get back to his post. His principal contribution was his estimate of officers he had served with as chief engineer.

"I would consider Commander Lipski the most capable head of department in the *Indianapolis*," DeGrave said. "He had several years of experience. The other officers were considered experienced officers, having served as OOD and head of a department. I don't know how long they had served, but I do know they had served for some time.

"Mr. Moore had been standing supervisory watches since January of last year, or December of last year, I should say. Orr came on the ship as an experienced officer and he had been standing OOD watches since he reported aboard. Mr. MacFarland was a qualified deck officer."

When he was finished, the prosecution asked Commander DeGrave only one question—did all the testimony he had given relate to time before July 19, the date he left the ship? It did. Still, that would not change the fact that he considered all those who held the bridge that night to have been among the ship's best officers. All were dead now, but Commander Lipski had the bridge when the ship ceased zigzagging, Lieutenant Commander Moore had it when the torpedoes hit, and MacFarland and Orr were their aides, respectively. Had conditions warranted, in their estimation, either Lipski or Moore could have ordered zigzagging resumed, or have notified McVay. Lipski was in command when the moon rose and had the bridge when the enemy sub spotted the ship. Certainly he was not the type to hesitate to take either action if he had felt the ship endangered.

Quartermaster Allard, who had the watch ending at midnight, testified he had kept the deck log on weather, and recalled the wind was moderate, barometer normal. Asked what he had entered under the heading "Clouds: low, medium, high," he replied:

"Well, there would be no entry in the 'low'; there would probably be an entry in the 'medium' clouds and 'high' clouds. That is I would say, an alto-stratus entry, in medium, and cirrus clouds, or cirro-stratus, for high clouds." The ceiling was four or five thousand feet, he said, and stars were dimly visible through the overcast. Where the log said "Total amount of sky covered, in tenths," he had entered "six."

In other words, the weather was clearing, and the lower one-third of the sky was free of clouds. Taken with the evidence of Clemence, the astronomer, the moon would have been almost directly behind the vessel, twenty-three degrees above the horizon. Any enemy vessel lurking ahead of the *Indianapolis* at midnight would have found it clearly silhouetted by the low moon. That is exactly the situation in which Hashimoto found himself. No attacking commander could have asked for a more perfect set of circumstances.

Allard went on to tell how he had escaped from the ship, happened on the raft carrying McVay, and helped rescue two buddies. He was already well into the second day on the raft when Captain Ryan interrupted.

"If the court please. I'm sorry, Allard, but we don't want to go beyond the immediate time of the sinking," said the judge advocate.

There it was again, he brass curtain, stopping any evidence except that bearing on the two narrow charges against McVay.

When the questioning was over, Allard offered this statement:

"There is nothing that I would know that would pertain to these charges, but under the circumstances, I do not believe that we would have been zigzagging or zigzagging was necessary. In fact, when I came on watch (8:00 P.M.) the helmsman that was steering was wondering why we were zigzagging, and I also did. But I checked the night orders and knew that we were going to cease zigzagging, and that is all. I don't believe that there was any reason to have been zigzagging.

"I would like to say that in my service aboard the ship with Captain McVay there was—we had better—training and more precautions taken with regards to life jackets and so forth than at any other time aboard ship." He had served three-and-a-half years in this ship, under five different captains.

Several other enlisted men told their stories, and the

final witness of the day was Seabert, Seaman Second Class, who had the bridge lookout watch in the very sector where the sub lay. What was the weather?

"Well, the only thing I can remember right now is the glow of the moon on the water, because I remember saying to Sinclair, who had the watch with me, that it was a pretty nice night out," Seabert said.

Wednesday's only witness, Chief Benton, made a dramatic appearance, limping into court on crutches. But he was off the stand in less than an hour, and the court adjourned until Thursday. Benton's main testimony, for which he was well-qualified both by his long service aboard (nearly three-and-a-half years) and the nature of his rating, was that communications on the *Indianapolis* were dangerously antiquated. They were all concentrated in the center of the ship. If that area was damaged, everything went out. That was precisely the area that was damaged. When the second torpedo hit, it cut the ship's spinal cord.

Captain Ryan had his first interview with Hashimoto on Tuesday afternoon, after the court session. He talked with the Japanese officer four hours, trying to establish his "credibility and competence" as a witness. At the end of this time, Ryan said he was not satisfied and was still in doubt as to whether the Japanese officer would be called to the stand.

Captain Cady got his turn on Wednesday. Chain smoking as usual, rolling his cigarettes back and forth across his lips until they were wet halfway down, Cady questioned the Japanese a good part of the afternoon.

Some of the answers given by Hashimoto this day were interesting, compared to answers he gave next day on the stand.

Q. What was the visibility then (at time of sighting)?

A. In the direction of the moon it was relatively good.

Q. About how many meters?

A. More than 10,000 meters in the direction of the moon. In any other direction it was not impressed on me, and I don't remember, but it was not very good.

In other words, surfacing as he did, he could see six miles or more in the direction from which the *Indianapolis* was approaching. Had he surfaced a short time sooner, or later, he might have seen nothing. He did not pick up the ship at any time on his radar—it was a completely visual sighting. His sound-detector gear was not working too well, he said, but he did use it to compute the speed of the target, *after* the sighting.

Q. Was the target zigzagging?

A. I am not clear about that.

Q. Would it have made any difference to you whether the ship was zigzagging or not?

A. It would not have made any difference.

At another point there was this exchange:

Q. During this twenty-seven minutes (between sighting and firing), what was the visibility?

A. In the path of the moon I could see as far as the horizon. In areas other than that it was poorer; I could hardly discern the horizon.

Q. What was the phase of the moon?

A. That particular night it was 20.6, computed on a scale from 0 to 30, with the brightest being 15. It was five days after full moon.

Q. What was the actual aspect of the moon?

A. A little more than half, and it was hidden by clouds.

Q. The whole time or just part of the time?

A. I was not looking at the moon; I was looking at the target. Judging from the relative consistency that I saw it, I would say the moon was not hidden any of the time.

Q. Were there any other Jap submarines in the area?

A. None nearby.

Q. Did you report this attack to your superiors?

A. Yes.

By late Wednesday the Navy had made up its mind. It announced to the press that Commander Hashimoto would be called to the stand the next day. At ten o'clock the next morning the court was crowded, over 150 spectators in the gallery, the best attendance yet. Everyone wanted a look at this man, a genuine enemy Naval officer, one who had inflicted a disastrous defeat on the United States Navy and escaped unscathed.

But they had to be patient. The first witness that day was Captain Hilbert, who had been judge advocate of the court of inquiry. Under questioning, he recited at length the circumstances at the time of that court—the war ending, atom bombs dropping, Russia coming into the war against Japan, witnesses hospitalized or scattered far and wide, court members anxious to get off to their war-end assignments, the knowledge by everyone that matters were being rushed, but the directive that the inquiry must be held quickly. Finally the court intervened and "directed that the accused confine his questions only to those bearing on the charges and specifications in this case."

Captain Ryan said the reason for calling Captain Hilbert was to further establish the authenticity of exhibit 6. This was Captain McVay's report to Forrestal on the loss of his ship, and in particular the sentence that said: "There was intermittent moonlight, at which times the visibility was unlimited."

Hilbert identified the document, and said it was revised several times, as new facts came in, and Captain McVay was given permission by the court of inquiry to update it so the final repot to Forrestal would be correct. Hilbert was dismissed, but McVay would be asked about this later.

Boatswain's Mate Second Class James Edgar Reid was on the stand briefly, and then the moment arrived: Captain Ryan announced that his next witness would be Commander Hashimoto, and that he understood the defense would object. He was quite right. Captain Cady had written and rewritten his speech several times, toning it down. He arose and advanced toward the bench. He was a tall man, and he could look stern, almost schoolmasterish, when he wished, as he did now.

"If the court please," he began, "I wish to make formal objection to the idea of calling one of the officers of the defeated enemy who, as a nation, have been proven guilty of every despicable treachery, of the most infamous cruelties, and of the most barbarous practices in violation of all of the laws of civilized warfare, to testify against one of our own commanding officers on a matter affecting his professional ability and judgment. I am sure I express the feeling of every American citizen, especially those who so recently fought against the Japanese, in protesting at this spectacle. (The adjectives "repellent and nausating" preceding "spectacle" had been stricken from an earlier draft of the speech.) This objection is not, and cannot, be based on any legalistic grounds, since our lawmakers have never imagined through the centuries of Anglo-Saxon law any such grotesque proceedings."

In the context of the times, these were powerful but, on the whole, restrained words. Fresh in the minds of Americans were the bloody and maniacal campaigns through the islands of the vast Pacific, starvation of American prisoners of war in Japan and China, beheading of American prisoners in the Philippines, and atrocities throughout Malaya, the Dutch East Indies, and Indo-China. The horrors of the "Death March" for the survivors of Corregidor, and Santo Tomas prison in the Philippines, and the picture of an emaciated General Wainwright staggering out of a Japanese prison into the arms of rescuers were now known to all Americans.

When Captain Ryan arose to reply, a rustle swept over the spectators, as a light breeze over a wheat field, and then the courtroom settled into deadly silence.

"If the court please," he said, "the judge advocate regrets exceedingly that emotional aspects to the introduction of this witness are being stressed in this court. It is not the intention of the judge advocate, and he would resent, asking this witness—anybody's asking this witness—to give any opinions as to the honor or the actions of the accused in this case. This witness is being called to testify as to the facts, within his knowledge, which, I believe, are necessary to a decision in these proceedings. I have no intention to ask the witness other than, in effect, where and when he was at or about the time of this incident, what he saw, what he did, and how he did it."

Captain Ryan then proposed that Commander Hashimoto take two oaths, American and Japanese, so that he could be prosecuted if he lied. In both the Navy and War Departments, he said, "there are many cases of members of our armed forces having been tried by courts-martial, and in the proceedings of these courts-martial enemy aliens testified before the court."

He was not asked to substantiate this statement, but as a matter of fact no commanding officer of the United States Navy had ever been tried in connection with the loss of his vessel in wartime. During the American Revolution, commanding officers of two Continental ships were tried and acquitted (Captain John Manley of the *Hancock* and Captain Elisha Hinman of the *Alfred*). Therefore it is certain that never before had an enemy officer testified against an officer of the United States Navy in a circumstance such as this.

Captain Ryan continued: "The witness Hashimoto is not being called to testify against the accused; he is being called in an effort to establish just what caused the explosions which led to the sinking of the *Indianapolis*." This was a point well taken in semantics, but nevertheless could not overcome the popular feeling that the Japanese was, indeed, testifying "against" Captain McVay.

The accused, who obviously felt that Hashimoto was certainly not *for* him, told the court: "If the proposed witness Hashimoto is going to be called, I will also make legal objection on the grounds of competency, since his nation is not of Christian belief, thus affecting ability to take the oath as a witness to tell the truth."

Captain McVay, noting that the oath says testimony is given "under the pains and penalties of perjury," told the court: "However, I submit to the court how, under the circumstances, can there be any pains or penalties of perjury upon such a witness, an enemy alien of a defeated nation, who has no standing in this country at all. There are numerous questions as to the veracity of the Japanese as a race, and it is a question for the court to determine how he may be placed upon oath or affirmation to tell the truth."

Captain Ryan replied that he had no doubt that if it appeared that Hashimoto was lying "the naval authorities will turn this witness over to the proper civilian authorities, and he can then suffer such pains as the court would adjudge in this country, and then he could get it again in his own.

"Furthermore," he said, "this oath with the alternative provisions also applies, by our own statutes, federal statutes, for people who are heretics or atheists, those who have no religion, and I think there have been many cases in which such people have testified in our courts."

McVay then said, "It appears that the proper procedure would be to bring in the proposed witness and to examine him as to his understanding of truth and falsehood, the meaning of perjury, and his belief in punishment following upon falsehood."

Captain Ryan agreed, and the court concurred. Then entered Francis Royal Eastlake, of the Office of Naval Intelligence, who would be translator for the Japanese. Eastlake, who had already interpreted at length for both prosecution and defense in the pre-trial interrogation of

Hashimoto, was born in Japan of American parents, and had lived there eighteen years.

Eastlake outlined his qualifications and produced oaths he said were used in both naval and civil courts of Japan. Asked if he had any objection to this oath, Captain McVay replied:

"The witness (Eastlake) says that he has been informed that that is the civil oath. He personally does not know it of his own knowledge, and as far as any Japanese naval oath, I think the Japanese Navy has been demilitarized, or destroyed, and I don't see that it has any bearing."

After further wrangling, Admiral Baker announced that the court was of the opinion that it was proper to give Hashimoto the Japanese civil oath, plus the "pains and penalties" oath contained in Naval Courts and Boards. The Japanese oath was entered in the record in both languages, being translated in English as, "I swear to tell the truth, neither adding thereto nor concealing any matter whatsoever."

Eastlake was accepted as interpreter, along with Commander John R. Bromley, USN, on McVay's behalf, and Captain D. C. White was seated as assistant counsel and technical adviser to Captain McVay. The stage was set.

The door from the witness room opened, and Hashimoto walked in. After all the haggling, it was a sort of anticlimax. In his ill-fitting civilian clothes, a white shirt and blue-black suit, with the coat collar turned up, he hardly looked like a man who could have sunk the mighty *Indianapolis*, Flagship of the Fifth Fleet. Hashimoto advanced a few steps, bowed from the waist to the court, then to counsel, and took the witness stand. He was completely impassive, and despite the setting and his incongruous garb managed to give an impression of dignity and competence.

Captain McVay began to question him:

Q. What is your religious belief?

A. He is a Shintoist, (the translator replied).

Throughout his testimony, Hashimoto spoke in a soft voice which nevertheless carried authority. It was clear that he was a man used to command.

Q. What do you know of the meaning of truth and falsehood?

A. He says he is fully aware of the difference between truth and falsehood.

Q. What happens to you in your religion if you tell a falsehood?

A. Should he happen to utter a falsehood, he will have to pay for it; that is to say, he will be punished for it.

Q. Does your religion include a belief in the life hereafter?

A. He believes the soul exists after death.

Q. And that this punishment for falsehood will be in the hereafter?

A. He believes that the punishment, under his religion—that is, according to his religion, he believes that he will be punished during his life for any falsehoods, or wrongdoing that he may utter, or wrongdoing that he may do, but that upon his death here will be forgiveness.

Q. Do you know what perjury means?

A. He has full knowledge of it.

Q. Is there punishment in Japanese law for perjury?

A. He says he doesn't know all the details, but he does know that he is of the opinion that they are punished.

Q. Are you listed on any of the lists of war criminals of any of the Allied powers,

A. His name is not, to his—to his knowledge, his name is not on any list of war criminals.

At this point, the court was satisfied and ruled that Hashimoto was competent to testify. He was given the U.S. Navy oath of "pains and penalties," and his own Japanese civil oath, the latter in both English and Japanese. With a pen he scratched his name in English and Japanese under the respective oaths. Hashimoto then said that he had received no threats or promises to influence his testimony, and that he fully understood the implications of his oaths.

After this lengthy preparation, his testimony proved extremely limited as to the points at issue. He could not testify at all as to the second charge—failure to give timely warning to abandon ship—as he knew nothing whatever of conditions on the *Indianapolis*. On the first charge, the only things he could testify to concerned the weather (the charge said "in good visibility") and failure to zigzag.

In describing the attack, he declared, as he had from

the first, that he scored three hits. He said that the center hit produced a flame which showed another column of water on either side. After the luncheon recess, Hashimoto was questioned at length about his cruise, from the time he left Japan until the attack. He stepped down from the stand and sketched his course on a Japanese chart, then drew a sketch of the attack maneuver. He said his target was blurred at first sighting and he could not say if it was zigzagging.

Q. Was it zigzagging later?

A. There is no question of the fact that it made no radical changes in course. It is faintly possible that there was a minor change in course between the time of sighting and the time of attack.

Q. Would it have made any difference to you if the target had been zigzagging on this attack?

A. It would have involved no change in method of firing the torpedoes, but some changes in maneuvering.

A few more questions by the court and Hashimoto was allowed to step down. After fifty minutes on the stand, suddenly it was all over, and the episode was surprising for the questions not asked. Not once was he asked specifically about the weather, a vital point of the charge, yet he had discussed the weather at length in pre-trial questioning. As the attacker and as an experienced submarine officer, he was probably the best qualified man alive to discuss the weather conditions of that night.

As to zigzagging, his answer at pre-trail was much less equivocal. He simply said: "It would not have made any difference."

In sum, his testimony made clear a nearly miraculous combination of circumstances—from an attacker's standpoint. By sheer chance, he surfaced at the perfect time and place for an attack. Had he surfaced a half hour later, he might never have seen the *Indianapolis*. He was not using his radar, and his sound gear was not functioning well. Had he surfaced ten miles east, he, and not the *Indianapolis,* would have had the moon behind him. Had he surfaced ten miles north or south, he might never have gotten in firing position, even if he had sighted the vessel. Had the *Indianapolis* been escorted by vessels with sound gear (she had none of her own), the tables might have been turned. Had the moon not risen at that particular time and position, and had the clouds near the horizon not parted at that particular time, the vessel might have been spared. In short, had any one or two fortuitous circumstances out of the half dozen been changed, the thing might never have happened. For Hashimoto, it was his one big break in nearly four years of hunting. For the *Indianapolis,* it meant immediate death for 300 crewmen and their ship. For 500 others, it meant horrible and torturous death in the water, but that had nothing to do with Hashimoto, with McVay, or this court.

Hashimoto gave a final bow as he left the stand, and his Marine guard, Captain George Correa, of Akron, Ohio, again took him by the arm. As they entered the witness room, the six-foot-three Guadalcanal veteran said, "I gotta take this monkey back to Japan." Like most Japanese officers, Hasimoto understood English fairly well.

But it would be some time before Commander Hashimoto was back in Japan. After his brief appearance on the stand, he disappeared from public view, but he remained in custody in Washington through the Christmas holidays. His guards, on the whole, were friendly, though one of them told him some of the American officers were "boiling mad" at him for testifying that the *Indianapolis* steered a straight course. By Christmas Eve, however, the guards produced a bottle and offered Hashimoto a drink. After a struggle, his good sense overcame his desire, and he declined. The guards, after a few more drinks, thought it would be a good idea to take Hashimoto out on the town. He vetoed that suggestion, too, although he appreciated the Christmas spirit in which it was offered. Following the holidays, Hashimoto was taken to San Francisco, and sailed home on the APA *Effingham,* still under guard.

While Hashimoto himself was secluded directly after his testimony, a storm continued to rage around his head. The Chicago *Sun* reckoned it would have cost $1,820 at regular fares, not to mention food, lodging, and guards, to bring Hashimoto over for the trial, and questioned why this money had been spent.

On Monday, Representative Edith Nourse Rogers, of Massachusetts, introduced House Concurrent Resolution 116, to expunge from the records testimony given by Hashimoto. Three days later she expressed profound shock in a House speech at the Navy having allowed Hashimoto to testify. She said she had not "found a person yet who does not deplore it."

Her resolution was simple:

> Whereas, the Japanese concepts are contrary to our own, and
> Whereas, the testimony of an enemy Japanese submarine commander during the war as a witness is entirely incompetent: Therefore be it
> Resolved by the House of Representatives (the Senate concurring) that it is the sense of the Congress of the United States that in the trial of Captain Charles B. McVay the testimony of the enemy alien officer, Captain Hashimoto, be expunged from the records of the court in order that the ends of justice may not be prejudiced.

House Concurrent Resolution No. 116 was referred to the Committee on Naval Affairs and there died with the 79th Congress.

Representative Henry D. Larcade, Jr., of Louisiana, took the floor of the House in anger. While he did not know Captain McVay, he said, he felt a great injustice was being done, and he told the House:

"Mr. Speaker, the Navy court-martial of Captain Charles B. McVay 3d, held here in Washington, in my opinion leaves a blot on the Navy that will never be erased." Noting that the court apparently had convicted McVay of failure to zigzag, Representative Larcade said ". . . and the most reprehensible fact of the trial was that this officer, the scion of an illustrious Navy family, was convicted of that charge upon the testimony of an enemy officer, Commander Iko Hashimoto, a despicable Japanese commander of the submarine which sent his ship to the bottom." ("Iko" is a nickname in Japanese meaning "companion" or "pal," and some newspapers mistakenly believed it was his first name.)

Warmed by the fires of his own oratory, Representative Larcade continued:

"Mr. Speaker, I am advised that never before in the annals of our country has a court-martial called an enemy to testify against a brother officer. In view of the brilliant record of Captain McVay, it is difficult to understand the action of the men who constituted this naval court-martial. Mr. Speaker, I have followed this case from the beginning of the court-martial, and it seems to me that instead of Captain McVay being brought to trial, that those responsible for the loss of the 860 men of the complement of 1,160 for not sending rescue craft until five days after the disaster should have been the ones to summon for court-martial.

"Mr. Speaker, I hope that the Secretary of the Navy or the President will reverse the findings of this scandalous and undeserved action of the court-martial in this instance. However, even this action will never remove the stain from the court-martial and Navy in summoning a prejudiced enemy officer to testify against a brother officer with a record such as that of Captain McVay."

There is no doubt that these were sentiments held by many. They simply could not understand why it was necessary to bring the Japanese here, in an atmosphere of great hostility, to establish facts that were not even contested. If necessary at all, his testimony could have been taken by deposition, leaving him in Japan and avoiding the expense and spectacle caused by his appearance. There is no similar case on record, before or since.

Representative Larcade also spoke for many when he suggested the wrong man was on trial, or at least should have some company in the dock. Though the Navy did not mention it, letters were beginning to arrive in increasing number, questioning the limited nature of the proceedings and asking when the full story was to be brought out.

But the day after Hashimoto testified, the court plodded on through the prosecution's last day. Ensign Woolston, he of the remarkable memory, was recalled to the stand on Friday morning, and under questioning again rattled off a long report of dozens of hatches, doors, and scuttles open inside the ship. When the prosecution finished, Captain Cady for the defense asked him:

Q. Mr. Woolston, this long list of hatches and doors which you testified were open—do you mean that you are actually testifying that they were open that night, or that they should have been open?

A. They should have been open, and they were open.

An incredible statement. It can only be supposed that it went unchallenged because the subject had nothing to do with either of the charges. The court did, however, pick him up on one point. The court was curious to know how he could have seen holes in the starboard side of the ship, when he was on the port side.

"Well, I believe the court misunderstood my statement," he replied. "I quoted Dr. Haynes as having seen the hole in the ship below the wardroom." He then went on quickly to describe cracks he had seen in the deck and wound up by estimating that possibly 330 men failed to get off the ship alive. This was slightly lower than his first estimate, and would have meant that 866 men escaped from the ship.

Commander Albert K. Romberg (Annapolis 1931) was called to the stand as a stability expert. He had studied naval architecture at MIT for three years, and throughout the war was in charge of the stability section of Bureau of Ships. The plans of the *Indianapolis* were placed in the record, and Commander Romberg was asked to assume that heavy underwater explosions had occurred at Frames 7 and 50.

Assuming also an eighteen degree list, and every door on the second deck in every watertight bulkhead open, ". . . would there be any doubt in your mind that the ship would sink?"

"There would not," he replied, estimating that sinking would occur in thirty minutes or the ship would capsize sooner. This was based, he said, on "the large area of the openings in the second deck through which subsequent spaces could fill up from the flooding."

On the plans he outlined the position of the hits in relation to the probable waterline, and added:

"It was obvious, then, that the water was free to flow down the second deck into the engineering spaces, so that the ship, for all practical purposes, was wide open."

Commander Romberg said he could not know if the *Indianapolis* was conforming to current regulations for this type of cruiser, but ". . . the Bureau also realizes that there are very practical causes which may govern the extent to which doors can be kept closed. Living conditions may be so bad with certain watertight doors closed that they become intolerable."

Radioman Moran returned to the stand briefly to testify that all radio equipment was in good order aboard the ship, and the proper frequencies were being monitored.

These were two standard channels, NPM HOW and JUMP FOX; the 500- and 3000-kilocycle bands and the forward TBS, 72.1 megacycles.

Lieutenant Clayton T. Piercy, of CNO, who kept records on loss and damage to ships, testified three ships were lost in the Pacific between July 26-August 5: the U.S.S. *Callaghan* off Okinawa July 28, the *Indianapolis*, July 29, and submarine *Bullhead*, missing from Freemantle, sailing July 31. When McVay got his turn, he asked if Piercy had any record of a tanker being attacked about July 28, at 13N, 137-3OE? This obviously referred to Hashimoto's testimony that he had attacked a tanker near that spot with human torpedoes.

Lieutenant Piercy said he had no such card with him, and Captain McVay asked that he be instructed to search his records and return. Captain Ryan objected, saying that this ". . . exceeded the scope of direct examination" and further that it was "apparently an attempt to attack the credibility of a witness (Hashimoto) who had previously testified in this case." His objection was sustained.

Captain Ryan then took the stand and read the *Wild Hunter* dispatches into the record, describing the sub sighting in the *Indianapolis*'s path. He stepped down at 3:30 and the prosecution rested, after hearing thirty-nine witnesses in twenty-one hours, thirty-six minutes of testimony.

17

The defense opened Saturday morning, December 15, and the same day the Army & Navy *Bulletin* came out with a story headlined: "Vice Admiral May be Tried in Indianapolis Debacle."

The story started right off:

> What must have been apparent from the outset to all impartial observers seems now to have become the conviction of the Navy high command—that responsibility for the debacle with its needlessly high toll of American lives must be fixed several echelons higher than a lone commanding officer. For if 800 to 900 men escaped from the sinking ship, as has been testified repeatedly in the proceedings of the court-martial, then the commanding officer of the *I-58* accounted for less American lives than did the negligence of the high command. The Navy is instituting preliminary investigations toward fixing responsibility where it properly belongs and if the Navy continues belatedly this forthright approach the public may witness the unusual spectacle of disciplinary action being directed against a three-star naval commander.

Since several vice admirals had some part in the case, it is not known who was meant.

In quick succession, Captain Cady called to the stand six enlisted men, who testified they had received orders to abandon ship, either from the bridge or through another officer. Bosun DeBernardi testified there were plenty of life jackets aboard, and estimated 900 men got off the ship. Almost all of the ninety-three men in his division got off the ship, he said, and he saw them standing by abandon-ship stations so ". . . they must have gotten the word from below deck to stand by their abandon-ship stations."

The record appends: "The court took notice of the fact that this man was a leading petty officer for about five years and had considerable knowledge of the ship and its habits over that period."

Seaman First Class King told his story and then said: "I was on the ship a year, and during that time I never heard any complaints against the captain, and—anyone I talked with about the captain thought he was a good captain and, in general, the ship was run better, so they told me, than it had been previously."

Machinist Harley C. Hanson and Ensign Howison told of getting off the ship, and the latter added: "Well, just that I believe that the 'abandon ship' was given early enough for most men to get life jackets and to be prepared to leave the ship."

Dr. Modisher said he believed an additional reason why it was difficult to pass the word to abandon ship was that the foreward decks were covered with oil. "It was hard to get from one place to another. We did have a lot of slipping around, most of us were in our bare feet," he said.

Lieutenant Hensch testified he heard the order to abandon ship, and Ensign Twible said he did not, because he was up in Sky Amidships, but he ordered his men to abandon on his own initiative. No more witnesses were ready, so court adjourned for the weekend at 11:48 A.M. Thus far Captain McVay had received strong support on general conditions on the ship, availability of life jackets, and orders to abandon ship.

On Monday morning the defense plunged into the matter of hazarding the ship by failure to zigzag, and the opening witness on that subject was a man who had once been something of a national figure. He was Captain Naquin, surface operations officer in the Marianas. As

Lieutenant Naquin, he had been in command of the submarine *Squalus* when it sank on May 23, 1939, off Portsmouth, New Hampshire. As the nation waited tensely, all but twenty-six men were saved from the vessel in a dramatic rescue using a diving bell. Now, as a fellow professional (Annapolis 1925), he was testifying as to matters within his competence in the Marianas.

Captain Cady started by asking Captain Naquin why the *Indianapolis* sailed without escort, but Captain Ryan bobbed up to object that such testimony was "incompetent, irrelevant, immaterial and not germane to the issues in this case."

Captain Cady replied that it was relevant to the part of the first charge reading ". . . through an area in which enemy submarines might be encountered." He pointed out that the language used did not state that enemy submarines were known to be present, and contended this was a material element in the charge. But the prosecution's objection was sustained, so Captain Cady had to go at it from another tack.

Q. What is your estimate of the risk of enemy-submarine activity at that time, at the end of July, along the route the *Indianapolis* was to proceed?

A. I would say it was a low order.

Upon questioning by the court, Captain Naquin clarified that to say, "My estimate is that the risk was very slight."

He was asked who would have diverted the *Indianapolis* if anything had arisen after her departure, and he said it would be the area commander, in this case the Commander Marianas, Vice Admiral Murray, who had been a member of the court of inquiry. Asked if there was any question of diverting her after she sailed, he said, "There was not."

The court intervened again, to inquire why he considered the danger slight, had not submarines been reported in the area?

"Yes, we had had reports of submarines," Captain Naquin said. "At the investigation in Guam in this case I furnished a chart showing the recent submarine reports. These, of course, were not borne out by sinkings; they were graded very low. In other words, the actual number of sinkings in the area were extremely slight, and as a result such reports were downgraded."

"Then you did not have confidence in the reports that had been broadcast of probable submarine positions?"

"That is correct. A great many of these reports were made by merchant skippers, and they were never borne out by actual attacks against any of our ships. There were literally dozens of them, but the actual submarine activity against us was at a very low ebb," Captain Naquin replied.

Next witness was Captain Granum. As operations officer of the Philippine Sea Frontier, his duties included plotting reports of enemy submarine activity in his area. Captain Granum said he recalled the dispatch telling of the departure of the *Indianapolis* from Guam.

Q. Was there any enemy activity at that time within the Philippine Sea Frontier which caused you to have any concern over vessels which might be approaching from Guam?

A. No more than a normal hazard that could be expected in wartime.

Q. Did you ever receive reports of enemy submarine contacts in the area?

A. There were frequent reports of submarine contacts throughout the area which were continuously being investigated.

Q. Was there ever any actual confirmation of the presence of an enemy submarine in the Philippine Sea Frontier at about this time along the route in question?

A. In this area, no.

He was then shown Exhibit 2, the plot of the three submarine contact reports given to Captain McVay before he sailed. Captain Granum merely confirmed that they were all outside his area, therefore he had no direct responsibility for knowing about them. They were all well within the area of Commander Marianas.

Next witness was a truly extraordinary fellow, Captain Glynn R. Donaho, a peppery little Texan whose submarine exploits in the war earned him no less than the Navy Cross, four times, Silver Star, twice, and Bronze Star, twice. He and a brother, Doyle George Donaho, both graduated from the Academy in 1927. Glynn went into subs in 1930, and during the war he made seven patrols as commander of the *Flying Fish* and the *Barracuda*, commanded a wolf-pack operation, made 234 successful consecutive attacks, and sank or damaged twenty-eight vessels, totalling 200,000 tons. Both sides accepted him as an expert on submarine operations, and he testified that every vessel he ever fired on was zigzagging, and one was unescorted.

The defense took him first, and the questioning was brief:

Q. Based on your experience as outlined above, what is your opinion of the value of zigzagging of a target as affecting the accuracy of torpedo fire?

A. With our modern submarines, fire-control equipment, high-speed torpedoes, a well-trained fire-control party, and with torpedo spreads, I didn't find that zigzagging affected the results.

Q. As commanding officer of a modern submarine, if you found yourself on the base course ten thousand yards ahead of a target whose normal speed—whose speed you estimated would be about 12 knots, would the normal zigzagging of this target affect the accuracy of your attack?

A. Not with a normal zigzag plan. By normal zigzag plan, I mean plans encountered during the war.

Here was unquestionably the toughest adversary the prosecution had yet met, and when Captain Ryan took over on cross-examination he set about trying to overcome the impact of this testimony.

Q. Under the conditions stated in that question by the accused, would it have been more or less difficult for you to attain the proper firing position if the target had been zigzagging at the time you picked it up and until the moment you would have fired torpedoes?

A. No, not as long as I could see the target.

Q. Do you mean, if the target was zigzagging, no more calculation would be required?

A. No, sir. If the target had been zigzagging, I would have had to change my setup in my torpedo-data computer (TDC) to meet the new course, or the new speed, from my sound gear.

Q. Assuming you were set to fire, and thirty seconds before the target makes a radical change, say forty-five degrees.

A. I would put the setup in my TDC and fire on the next leg.

Q. Assuming the target was making 17 knots, when would you have had another chance to fire?

A. It takes five seconds to make an observation,

and about five seconds for the integration to take effect, and I could have fired within ten seconds.

Q. Assuming it turned forty-five degrees away, would your spread have been as likely to hit as if it had not turned?

A. Yes, sir.

Q. Then do you mean to say that there is no merit whatever in combing torpedo wakes, or the tracks of torpedoes, by surface ships?

A. It depends upon whether you are turning into the track, how wide your torpedoes are spread, what kind of wake has been thrown up, the speed of your torpedo, the speed of the ship, the setup.

Q. Let us assume concretely that you were somewhere on the bow of this target at this point—here is the target and you are on the bow (indicates on rough pencil sketch)—maybe not as good as that, but you are forward of the beam, and she turns forty-five degrees, are you telling the court—forty-five degrees away from you, are you telling the court that your spread would have as good a chance of hitting as if she maintained a steady course.

A. Yes.

(This was getting tougher all the time.)

Q. Is it a reasonable inference from what you have just said, that zigzagging as an antisubmarine measure is of no value to surface ships?

A. On the contrary, you always expect a target to zig, and you anticipate what is going to happen on the next leg. I have personally found that a target not zigzagging would have confused me.

Q. Will you please repeat the question to the witness, and I ask the witness, please, to be attentive to the question, and to respond to the question, rather than state his experiences.

A. I am sorry sir.

The question was read again.

A. Yes. (Zigzagging is of no value to surface ships.)

Becoming a little nettled, Captain Ryan pressed him on this point.

Q. You have answered the last question 'yes'?

A. I have answered 'yes,' speaking for myself.

Q. And that is perhaps, Commander (*sic*) Donaho, because you have had success in attacking surface ships

which have zigzagged: is that correct—*Captain* Donaho,
I beg your pardon.

A. That—will you ask that question again?

The question was repeated, and Captain Donaho replied:

A. I maintain a qualified submarine captain does not
have to have a target steer a straight course, to get his
torpedoes to hit. You make this hard for me. I can't give
you a yes-or-no answer because there are too many things
that enter into it. The statements I have given you yes or
no to, I am positive of, but someone else may not be able
to say that.

The enormity of Captain Donaho's statements began
to sink home. Here was one of the Navy's most decorated
heroes, questioning basic doctrine by saying that zigzagging was useless. This was a view widely held, but seldom
expressed, at least in high circles.

Captains Donaho and Ryan fell into a wrangle on
the general subject of why, if zigzagging was useless, the
regulations books were full of instructions and admonitions
on the subject.

Emerging finally on firmer ground, Donaho said zigzagging had some value after torpedoes had been fired,
but ". . . if my torpedoes haven't been fired, it just means
that I delay my firing."

Captain Ryan, by now in quite bad humor, then
slipped in an assertion hardly expected in a setting of this
kind. After all, this was not a public courtroom, but a discussion among members of the same club.

Q. I mean no discourtesy, Captain Donaho, but I
should remind you that in your capacity here as a witness
you have been accepted as a submarine expert, and that
you are a professional Naval officer, is that correct?

A. I think so, sir.

It is true that Donaho did not have the Medal of
Honor, as Ryan did, but he wore at least eight medals,
and had a record matched by few in the Navy.

Q. And the way the question was put to you was to
obtain your understanding as such a professional Naval
officer of the value or lack of value of zigzagging as an
antisubmarine measure.

A. I don't understand your question.

The question was repeated.

A. I understand what you have stated, but what you are trying to get me to answer, I am at a loss. I am not hedging; I don't understand how you want me to answer.

The question was read a third time, and Donaho repeated that zigzagging was effective only after torpedoes had been fired. Ryan retired.

McVay then took over his own questioning, and asked:

Q. Assuming, Captain, that original setup that we first put to you, where you found yourself about 10,000 yards ahead and on the base course, and that you had contact by periscope for about twenty-seven minutes, would a zigzag of the target have made any difference to your ability to make a successful attack?

Here was the *Indianapolis* case stated precisely, and Captain Ryan was on his feet objecting. McVay insisted the question was proper, and Ryan's objection was denied.

A. Not as long as I could see the target for twenty-seven minutes.

Ryan had one more question. He showed Donaho a secret zigzag plan of the U.S. Navy, and asked him if that would have made any difference. Donaho replied it would not.

McVay then asked one final question, a rather stupid one.

Q. Is it disconcerting to you as a submarine commander to have a ship, a target, zigzag?

A. Yes, because you may be—just before firing, a zigzag throws your calculations off, and you have to get a new setup.

In other words, had the *Indianapolis* been zigzagging, a change of course at the last minute might have disconcerted Hashimoto. In his answer, Donaho not only contradicted part of his previous testimony, but left the impression it might have been better had the *Indianapolis* been zigzagging. With testimony clearly in his favor up to this point, it is incomprehensible why the defense asked this last question. It is even more amazing that the prosecution failed to make anything of it.

McVay then entered into the record certain sections of the publication FTP-170-B, Damage Control Instructions of 1944. These said, in general, that if a ship does not sink immediately, there is a good chance of saving her if progressive flooding is prevented. The sections were summarized in the statement: "The extremely important lesson from this experience is that no matter what the list or trim, every possible step must be taken to save the ship, because the chances are good."

The inference here was clear. The history of the war was replete with examples of vessels abandoned too hastily, and thus lost unnecessarily to the enemy. A classic example was the carrier *Yorktown* at the Battle of Midway.

The document McVay was now introducing was based on this and similar war experience, and so there could be no misunderstanding, the title page bore the motto, "Don't Give Up the Ship." Having received the document, court adjourned for the day at 11:47 A.M.

On Tuesday, December 18, the final day of testimony, Captain McVay had the witness stand all to himself with the exception of brief testimony from Seaman First Class Chester O. B. Reeves, now a farmer in Paris, Texas. Reeves's only important statement was that he was on lookout watch far aft and received word there to abandon ship. The word came "from below on the port side," he said.

Then in the words of the record, "the accused was, at his own request, duly sworn as a witness in his own behalf."

As in a civilian court, McVay did not have to take the stand. A fairly good case had been presented on his behalf, and he could have stood on that. But right from the start he had wanted to tell his version of the events. Tension ran high as he began his story, because it was always possible that he might drop a bombshell. There was always the chance that he would make, or attempt to make, statements outside the narrow scope of the charges against him. But those who expected anything of this nature simply didn't know their man. McVay was prepared to defend his competence and his honor, insofar as the charges against him reflected on them, but he was far too Navy to go beyond that. He could have blown the thing wide open, and many fellow officers hoped he would, but his testimony was a model of correctness.

He began with his arrival at Guam, his talks there with Admiral Spruance, and the routing of the vessel to Leyte. Then his counsel asked:

Q. Had you made inquiry about an escort?

A. Yes, I had the usual conversation with the routing officer about an escort, and he said, "I will ask for one for you, but I do not believe there is one available." I didn't give it another thought, because I had traveled many times without an escort.

It has never been disclosed officially whether one was "available." The matter is of some interest because one of the sailors who helped in the rescue wrote in a letter published in the Boston *Herald*:

"There were many destroyer escorts tied up with nothing to do, and, from experience, an escort should always be sent with another ship without sound gear when there is any hazard of submarine activity at all."

McVay continued his story up to the hours preceding the attack:

Q. What was the visibility at about 2200? (10:00 P.M.)

A. As was my custom, I made frequent trips to the bridge to check the weather conditions and alertness of the lookouts, through the officer of the deck, supervisor of the watch, and so on. The visibility at that time was poor; we remarked on it.

Q. Were you on the bridge at the time of the moonrise?

A. I was. I made a trip out on the bridge at that approximate time (10:30 P.M.) and did not see the moon rise.

McVay said he signed his night orders about 10:30 P.M., then retired to his emergency cabin, behind the bridge. He said the night orders were the usual thing about course and speed and:

"We also had in there that any submarines which were encountered should be considered enemy. I always put in the night-order book to carry out the standing night orders. I also put in there to notify me of any change in the weather, and to call me if anything appeared on the radarscope. I had a voice tube from the forward part of the bridge direct to my bunk in the emergency cabin, right by my ear, and I had told the OODs not to hesitate to call me under any conditions, and written in the order book was, 'call me in case of doubt.' "

Q. Did you give any instructions regarding zigzagging to the OOD before turning in?

A. I did not. The conditions were such that I did not

believe zigzagging was necessary. Visibility was poor. There was no moon. I saw no necessity for it.

Q. Were any reports made to you after you turned in?

A. No report was made to me from the time I turned in, about 11:00 P.M., until the first explosion.

He then ticked off the names of the officers who had the last two watches, indicating he was completely satisfied with their ability and judgment.

Q. Do you still have confidence in the judgment of these officers? (Only one of the seven survived.)

A. I do indeed. I consider that those officers in the *Indianapolis* were better qualified than could be expected of wartime conditions. In fact, I had asked for one or two other officers when I had been in the States and they laughed at me and said that I had better qualified officers than on any cruiser they knew of. I admitted I thought they were good, but I was always reaching out for something better if I could get it.

He then described the sinking and Captain Cady brought him back to the question of visibility.

Q. Did you see any moonlight after the explosion?

A. No sir, I did not. In fact, it was so dark on the bridge I couldn't recognize anybody.

Q. When did you see the moon?

A. Some time later on that morning, after I had been in the water for an hour or so. The moon apparently came out behind the clouds.

Q. In view of your testimony, given here, regarding the visibility prior to and after the explosion, why did you make the statement regarding visibility which is contained in your official report of the loss?

(His report of August 12, 1945, paragraph 4, said: "The sea was confused and choppy with long ground swells moving from the northeast. The wind was from the southwest, force about three. There was intermittent moonlight, at which times the visibility was unlimited.")

A. At the time I made out that official report the matter—the question of visibility did not appear to me to be one of importance. I prepared the report under some duress. It had to be made in a hurry. In order to submit it, I said what the visibility was, as I remembered it, after I got in the water.

In other words, when he retired at 11:00 P.M. it

was a dark night, when he rushed to the bridge shortly
after midnight it was still a dark night, and the moon
came out only about 1:15 A.M. or later.

Testimony of his own officers and men on visibility
was mixed, ranging from poor to good, but the implications of Hashimoto's testimony were clear. If he were able
to sight an object on the horizon at 10,000 meters, the
light was good enough, regardless of how individuals
classed it. The charge said McVay failed to zigzag "during good visibility after moonrise." Months later, in its
final summation of the case, the Navy stated flatly that
the attack occurred "under good conditions of visibility."
Since there is no absolute scale of visibility, any words
used to describe it are necessarily subjective. But it was
impossible to gainsay the fact that an enemy did sight the
target, fire on it, and sink it. Whether zigzagging would
have made the slightest bit of difference is also a subjective matter: the court found that it did.

When Captain Ryan took over the witness, he asked:

Q. Did you tell the OOD, Lieutenant McKissick, to
cease zigzagging during the second dog watch on 29 July?

A. I told him he could cease zigzagging when it became dark. That was routine. I told him that.

Q. Did you know that in Condition Yoke Modified
on the *Indianapolis* all the watertight doors on the second
deck were open?

A. I not only knew it, but was quite perturbed about
it. It was an accepted risk that the Bureau of Ships was
also upset about.

Q. Did you personally order the word passed, 'All
hands abandon ship.'

A. I told the OOD to pass the word, 'All hands
abandon ship.' I personally told him that, when the executive officer was standing alongside me.

Q. Do you know what means he utilized to carry out
your orders?

A. He had no means other than messenger.

The court intervened to inquire:-

Q. In your recollection, had the OOD on the *Indianapolis* ever started zigzagging when the need for that
became apparent and then notified you of it?

A. Yes, not once but several times. They were
brought up to do that.

Q. Then your doctrine as laid out in your standing night orders had been demonstrated effective, is that correct?

A. That is correct.

There were no more questions, but Captain McVay asked permission to make a statement.

"I only want to re-emphasize the fact that I considered the supervisor and the OOD on the eight to twelve, and on the midwatch that night, competent officers, and I believe that if conditions had been such as to require them to zigzag they would have done so and informed me—that is, in their opinion if conditions were such as to warrant it, they would not have hesitated to notify me that they considered that they should."

Captain McVay stepped down, after some ninety minutes on the stand, and Captain Ryan said he had more witnesses but he felt they could not add anything. The court announced it felt the case had been well and fully presented, it desired no further testimony and adjourned at 11:43 A.M.

It was all in now, with only summations remaining. First thing Wednesday morning, Captain Ryan took the floor for his "opening argument," to be followed by the defense summation and, finally, the "closing argument," by Ryan. Under the system then in use, the judge advocate got in two shots to the defense's one, and also carried with him the additional authority of being law officer of the court. Captain Ryan summarized the evidence given in support of each phrase of each specification, even down to the point of saying McVay "admitted" he was McVay. When the defense took over, Captain Cady asserted that each part of each charge had been "disproved, without even the necessity of giving the benefit of reasonable doubt to the accused."

Naturally, each side made as strong an argument as it could. Captain Ryan's summary leaned heavily on citations of Navy Regulations and references to testimony by page and number. Captain Cady's left out such detail, but did take the opportunity to stick the knife in the Navy's corporate hide. At one point he said:

"The captain's first reaction was to save his ship (in contrast to some other cases which are known of)."

At another point he said:

"It is clear that the tragic and regrettable loss of life, reaching upwards to 900 (*sic*) souls, did not occur upon the sinking of the *Indianapolis*."

This was pretty strong language for club members in a professional society.

Captain Ryan, in his closing argument, dwelt mainly on the question: "Did the accused, through negligence, suffer the ship to be hazarded?"

He defined negligence in the usual terms—failure to do something a reasonable man would have done, or doing something a prudent and reasonable man would not do. His closing words were:

"And the negligence in this case, as we see it, is that the accused failed in his general overall responsibility to cause a zigzag course to be steered under the conditions proved, together with the fact that he failed to incorporate in his night orders, or by issuing definite instructions to commence zigzagging if and when the moon rose. He failed to issue these instructions to the officers of the deck."

"The trial was finished, the court was cleared," stated the record. Now began the time of waiting. Many newsmen covering the trial were sure Captain McVay would be acquitted on both counts. Captain McVay sweated it out nearly two hours. Though he did not know it, during the intervening time the court summoned Captain Ryan and directed him to record the following findings:

"The specification of the first charge proved. And that the accused, Charles B. McVay 3rd, captain, U.S. Navy, is of the first charge guilty.

"The specifications of the second charge not proved. And that the accused, Charles B. McVay 3rd, captain, U.S. Navy, is of the second charge not guilty; and the court does therefore acquit the said Charles B. McVay 3rd, captain, U.S. Navy, of the second charge."

Court reopened, everyone assembled, and Captain McVay stood before the court. He was informed that he had been acquitted of the second charge. Nothing was said about the first charge; the Navy does not announce convictions until the case has passed through all reviewing authorities. Captain McVay knew precisely what this silence meant. It meant he was guilty of negligence, the only thing to be decided was his punishment.

He also knew, in that moment, the end of a career. He did not expect death or dismissal from the service (both possible under the charge), but he did know that whatever the penalty was, he was through. If not dismissed from the service, a man with that kind of conviction on his record could hardly hope again for advancement, for a sea command, for any form of recognition of value to a professional career. Suddenly, at forty-seven, in the full vigor of life, his profession was, in effect, taken from him. Ever since the war started, he had written in his quarterly fitness report, in the space provided for "duty desired," that he would like to command a cruiser. He got his wish on November 18, 1944, when he took command of the *Indianapolis*. Now, exactly one year, one month, and one day later, it was all over.

As he continued to stand there, he probably didn't even hear Captain Ryan enter his fitness report record in evidence and declare:

"This record contains only one unfavorable entry, a Letter of Reprimand concerning the loss of the U.S.A. *Indianapolis*, but otherwise this record of the accused deserves the rating of outstanding during his entire commissioned service."

Twenty-six years and the Silver Star "for conspicuous gallantry and intrepidity" in the Solomon Islands campaign, the Bronze Star with combat V for the Okinawa assault, the Purple Heart and the Asiatic-Pacific Campaign Medal with four bronze stars. His commendations and his awards were read into the record, but what did it matter now?

Captain Cady told the court he had no further evidence to offer in mitigation. The court adjourned, and all departed except the court and Captain Ryan.

As Captain McVay left the room, Captain Ryan crossed and said to him, "Charlie, I want you to know there was nothing personal in this and I wish it had come out the other way." They had been friends for twenty-five years, and Captain Ryan had found his assignment as prosecutor in this case most distasteful.

Captain McVay's reply epitomized the man:

"Whatever the verdict, it is for the good of the service," he said in a firm voice.

After he had left the court, Captain Ryan was directed to record the following sentence:

"The court therefore sentences him, Charles B. Mc-Vay 3rd, captain, U.S. Navy, to lose one hundred (100) numbers in his temporary grade of captain and to lose one hundred (100) numbers in his permanent grade of commander."

The seven members of the court and Captain Ryan signed the record in turn, and then appended a most unusual paragraph:

"In consideration of the outstanding previous record of the accused, and our belief that no other commanding officer who lost his ship as a result of enemy action has been subjected to a court-martial, we strongly recommend Charles B. McVay 3rd, captain, U.S. Navy, to the clemency of the reviewing authority."

All seven members of the court signed below. The case was out of their hands.

Back at home waiting for McVay was the old gentleman, Admiral McVay, and the captain's own sons by a previous marriage, Charles B. McVay IV, and James Wilder McVay, aged 20 and 17, respectively. Charles had served in the Navy as a seaman and had recently been medically discharged after losing the sight of an eye through an accident. From the McVay enclave there issued no statements, no protests, only silence. Navy discipline held firm.

Looking over Captain McVay's record, dating back to 1919, it was full of commendations from senior officers, capped by one dated May 3, 1945, less than three months before the sinking of the *Indianapolis*. Admiral Spruance, scarcely the effusive type, wrote to the Chief of Naval Personnel, following carrier strikes on Toyko, bombardment of Iwo Jima, carrier strikes on Kyushu, and bombardment of Okinawa:

> At all times during the period covered by this report, Captain McVay handled his ship in a skillful manner. His performance of duty as commanding officer of my flagship (*Indianapolis*) was highly satisfactory. I would be pleased to have Captain McVay in command of my flagship during future operations.

The court's verdict was not well received by the public. Paul B. McGee of the Chicago *Sun's* Washington bureau echoed the immediate reaction and wrote the day the trial ended:

> The verdict came as a complete surprise. The evidence in the case was believed by most to have indicated that instead of McVay's being negligent, his ship was an efficiently run vessel. No evidence was introduced at the trial with respect to possible culpability ashore for the lack of a search for the overdue cruiser at the time it was sunk.

Leo Cullinane wrote in the New York *Herald Tribune* the next day:

> The verdict caught the defendant, his counsel, spectators, and newspapermen by surprise. Some reporters were so sure that the court would dismiss both charges against Captain McVay that they had stories announcing his acquittal prepared before court convened for announcement of the verdict.

Columnist Ernest Lindley wrote that the trial "has left a bad impression in Washington" for a number of reasons. He said it was felt that Hashimoto never should have been called, there was grave doubt that zigzagging would have made any difference, there was doubt as to McVay's culpability, as he was sleeping at the time, and then the one that many people had a hard time swallowing:

> . . . the fact that the greater part of the loss of life in the disaster was due to a failure on the part of others to notice that the *Indianapolis* was overdue at Leyte and to begin a search. The Navy has not brought before a court-martial anybody responsible for this costly piece of negligence. Suspicion that Captain McVay was being "railroaded" or chosen as a "goat" are the inevitable consequences.

The New York *World-Telegram* said in its "Heard in Washington" column:

Ranking Navy officers say full blame for the U.S.S. *Indianapolis* tragedy will never be fixed, though Captain McVay has been court-martialed and soon will be sentenced. Sentence is expected to be light because Captain McVay, either willingly or unwillingly, was fall guy for higher-ups, officers say.

Alternatives were to bring an admiral to trial for lapses of his subordinates, or to hang blame on an enlisted man or low-ranking reservist. Fact that Navy is fighting desperately against unification with Army would make court-martial of brass undesirable, and court-martial of a reservist is considered out of question for political reasons.

The *World-Telegram* was right on at least one score —McVay's sentence—and maybe more.

The McVay case went the full rounds of the Navy Department, and finally on February 20, 1946, Secretary Forrestal signed this statement:

The proceedings, findings, and sentence are approved. In view, however, of the recommendations of the Chief of Naval Personnel and Fleet Admiral E. J. King, based upon the outstanding record of Captain McVay, which clearly evidences his long and honorable service, performance of duty of the highest order, including combat service in World War II, numerous commendations, and the award of the Expeditionary, China Service, Silver Star and Purple Heart Medals, and further, in view of the unanimous recommendation to clemency signed by all members of the court, the sentence is remitted in its entirety. Captain McVay will be released from arrest and restored to duty.

Two months later, Captain McVay departed Washington for the last time. He went to New Orleans to become chief of staff and aide to the commandant of the Eighth Naval District, his old mentor Rear Admiral A. S. (Tip) Merrill, Class of 1912. He had been serving under

Merrill at one of the high points of his career, the night of March 5, 1943, when he earned the Silver Star for an engagement in which Merrill's task force sank two Japanese destroyers.

McVay was happy in his new assignment, but his experiences had left a scar on his soul, as well as a nearly invisible, but nonetheless real, mark on his record. He retired from the Navy on June 30, 1949, just short of his fifty-first birthday, and was given the usual "graveyard promotion" to Rear Admiral.

While the court-martial held the headlines, and inspired polemics in press and Congress, another crisis was building up behind the scenes in the Navy Department. It was obvious to everyone that the court-martial of Captain McVay had not been the complete answer to the *Indianapolis* tragedy.

Letters were still coming in asking when the "real" culprits would be named. Malcolm Johnson, one of the newsmen who had interviewed Captain McVay on that August Sunday on Peleliu soon after he reached dry land, wrote a hard-hitting story distributed in late December by NANA (North American Newspaper Alliance), in which he started out:

> Is the Navy trying to hide something? Is it trying to make a scapegoat of Captain McVay . . . ? Is the Navy making a studied attempt to distract attention from some embarrassing questions which might point to derelictions elsewhere in connection with the sinking of the warship?

These were questions in many minds, and the Navy was, indeed, in a difficult position. As if the *Indianapolis* case were not enough, the Congressional Pearl Harbor Investigating Committee, which has been in session since November 15, extended its hearings indefinitely. The Senate Committee on Military Affairs had opened hearings on unification of the Armed Forces and the Navy felt it was in a death struggle to prevent being swallowed up by the Army and Air Force. Veterans' groups were kicking up a storm over the Army's Rapido River debacle in Italy during the war. Powerful forces were demanding a Congressional investigation. First thing you know, someone might demand an investigation of the *Indianapolis* case. Some Navy men muttered to themselves: Did we win this war or did we lose it?

But the wheels were turning inside the Navy, though not a single mimeograph hummed in the press section where the *Indianapolis* was concerned. The public did not know it, but even as the court-martial droned on, the inspector general's office was busy. Lieutenant Waldron stepped down from the witness stand at the court-martial on Tuesday, and on Wednesday morning he was summoned to the inspector general's office. Commodore Van Metre and Captain Coney greeted him warmly and said they would like to ask a few informal questions. The lieutenant said he would be happy to answer, but was puzzled to see a stenotypist prepared to take down his "off-the-record" remarks.

The Commodore said the record would be just for the use of the inspector general's department. Lieutenant Waldron was not inclined to make an issue of it, and for the next hour and a half the talk ranged freely and widely over the whole case. Toward the end, the lieutenant, soon to be a civilian again, was asked: Who do you think was responsible for what happened? Without hesitation, Lieutenant Waldron replied he believed CINCPAC on Guam, or CNO, Washington, was at fault, since there was no overall directive to prevent just such a thing as had occurred. To savor the full meaning of this reply, it should be remembered that Lieutenant Waldron was a port director officer of considerable experience. He was not at fault in any way, he knew none of the persons involved in the affair; he could speak honestly and from experience. The interrogators thanked him and dismissed him, and he disappeared into the happy oblivion of private life.

Did the question to Lieutenant Waldron mean that the Navy did not know who was to blame or had not decided yet? Quite right. This was mid-December, and the hot potato was still bouncing around the Pentagon.

Many other officers were questioned by the inspector general's agents in December and January, in the same private and informal atmosphere. There was no question of anyone being a defendant, or being represented by counsel; it was all very friendly and "in the family." So much greater was the shock, therefore, a few weeks later when several of those questioned found themselves publicly branded, without prior notification or opportunity for defense, as responsible for some of the larger proportions of the tragedy.

By early January the report of Commodore Van Metre and Captain Coney began to take shape, and one day it wound up on the desk of the inspector general, Admiral Snyder. The admiral's final report gave the first full picture of the affair that had yet been compiled. Here, for the first time, it became clear that, as in most human matters, there was very little black and white. It was mostly gray, and it was going to be extremely difficult to allocate the "blame." And it seemed necessary to the higher review echelons that "blame" be placed. Many hundreds of persons were vitally concerned and they sought an explanation, a placing of responsibility. Some, in the bitterness of personal loss, demanded punishment; others wished only peace of mind and assurance that the same thing could not happen again.

The inspector general's report circulated through the highest echelons of the Navy, in great secrecy, and endorsements and recommendations piled one on top of another. Opinions began to crystallize, and by early February certain courses of action became clear. In the first place, it seemed that Captain McVay's punishment should be remitted. It seemed inequitable to do otherwise: No other commanding officer had been court-martialed under similar circumstances, the court had unanimously recommended clemency, and there was considerable doubt that the action for which he was convicted (failure to zigzag) would have made any difference in the only part of the tragedy for which he was accountable—loss of the vessel. So that much was agreed upon.

That left an even larger problem: Where was blame, or responsibility, to be placed for the real tragedy—loss of contact with an operational vessel, with the consequent disaster? Here was the heart of the problem, and in dealing with it two courses of action were open: the blame could be placed on the system, or it could be placed on persons. To place the fault with the system would be to admit serious administrative errors, an action virtually unknown in military history. To admit that individuals err is one thing, to admit that the system errs is quite another. It is not possible to know how the argument went, or who was ranged on either side, but the outcome was certain: Individual heads must roll.

But whose heads? Only two heads were on the block at the moment. Lieutenant Commander Sancho, the acting port director at Leyte, had been admonished, and Lieutenant Gibson, his operations officer, had been reprimanded. Not a word of refutation had been heard from Sancho, but Gibson had reacted vigorously. His three-page letter of September 24 had been working its way up the chain of command ever since, gathering endorsements like barnacles on the hull of a ship. His immediate superior had forwarded it "recommending favorable consideration"; his next superior, Commodore Jacobson, had merely said "for consideration," but when it reached Vice Admiral Kauffman in October there was more solid support. The admiral, now back on duty as commandant, Philippine Sea Frontier, wrote:

"Since there was no directive assigning the responsibility to this command, or activities under this command, for checking and reporting the movements of combatant ships, it is considered that this responsibility did not rest with any person under the commander, Philippine Sea Frontier."

The file moved on, and came next to Admiral Charles H. McMorris, chief of staff to Fleet Admiral Nimitz. "Soc" McMorris was in no mood for overruling the action already taken by his command in issuing the reprimand in the first place.

He wrote that Nimitz "does not concur" with the view expressed by Vice Admiral Kauffman.

"It is true," he wrote, "as stated in the basic letter, that there was no directive which required a report of arrival or nonarrival of combatant ships. However, the port director has a responsibility for keeping himself informed as to all ships arriving and departing from his port. Having been officially informed that the U.S.S. *Indianapolis* was expected to arrive on a certain date, it should have been a matter of interest to him that the ship failed to arrive as scheduled.

"Alertness to the situation on the part of the reporting officer or port director would normally have led to inquiry as to the ship's location. This, in turn, might have brought about earlier discovery of the sinking and rescue of survivors."

Admiral McMorris recommended that the reprimand "be not withdrawn."

This letter is interesting on several grounds, particularly since it came to represent the final thinking of the Navy. In the first place, it admitted at the outset that port directors had no responsibility to report "arrival or nonarrival of combatant ships." It also overlooked entirely the deeper question of operational control—CINCPAC, sending out a warship and losing contact with it. Even had Sancho and Gibson acted instantly, the ship would already have been sunk thirty-six hours. Suppose its journey had been three days longer, would it then have been sunk four and one-half days before an arrival report was expected? If the *Indianapolis* had been sunk one day out of Pearl Harbor she would have been six days overdue at Tinian before anyone raised the alarm, even conceding that the Tinian port director had performed a duty admittedly not required and reported the nonarrival. Here was the fatal fault in the organization, and it had lain there undetected throughout the war. How inestimably tragic that it should have been exposed in the closing moments of a glorious war effort.

Admiral McMorris's letter made no mention of Rear Admiral McCormick's command, then at Leyte, or the Marianas Command at Guam, both of whom had been action addressees on the departure dispatch, equally with the port director, Tacloban.

But by February all of this was useless talk; the matter had been decided and the day of accounting was approaching. The public may have forgotten the case, temporarily, but newsmen assigned to the Pentagon kept close check on their sources, waiting for the final announcement on the McVay case. And with it, they suspected, must come some final declaration on the whole affair.

They were right. The Navy had decided to wrap the whole package up in one big news conference, and even now Rear Admiral Harold B. Miller, chief of information, was preparing for it. His staff was putting together a 4,500-word document entitled "Narrative of the Circumstances of the Loss of the U.S.S. *Indianapolis*." Since this was to be the Navy's final public word on the affair,

great care was taken in its preparation, as much on what
not to say as on what to say.

The draft made the rounds of the highest levels, with
here a deletion, there an addition, here a change in phrasing, there a change in emphasis. At length it was ready,
with only one step remaining—a pre-press conference, or
"dress rehearsal" as it came to be known. This was set for
Saturday morning, February 15, one week in advance of
the public press conference. The site would be Secretary
Forrestal's office, with the secretary, himself, in the chair.

It was decided to invite Lieutenant Gibson to the
"dress rehearsal." He was no longer Lieutenant Gibson, of
course; just plain Mr. Gibson, back at his old job in the
bank in Richmond, Virginia. He had decided it was futile
to continue the battle to clear his name, and of course the
Letter of Reprimand still reposing in his file was not
public knowledge. He had resolved to forget the matter
as best he could, though in no way retreating one step
from his denial of responsibility.

He was surprised, therefore, when he received a telephone call at the bank on Friday afternoon from Rear
Admiral Miller. Could he come to Washington the next
morning for a talk? A plane would be sent specially to
Richmond for him and would take him back. After a few
moments of conversation, Gibson agreed to make the
trip, still with no clear idea of what it was all about. Consequently, at 7:30 the next morning the plane set down at
Richmond, picked him up and whisked him to Washington, where a car awaited. In no time, he found himself
seated in front of Secretary Forrestal, and surrounded by
more admirals than he had ever seen. After a few preliminary remarks, it developed that there was to be a
public press conference a week hence.

The secretary, puffing vigorously on his pipe, brought
up the question of CINCPAC's 10-CL-45 letter, the one
that concluded with the sentence: "Arrival reports shall
not be made for combatant ships."

Gibson replied that it was the only directive port
directors had concerning combatant ships, and that port
directors had never considered it their duty, nor was it
the practice in general, to report the nonarrival of any
type ship.

The next question was, "Well, Mr. Gibson, what shall
we tell the press?"

Gibson was bowled over. He had lost touch with the case, and until this moment had not realized that the press must be told anything, except that Captain McVay's punishment was being remitted. He finally stammered something to the effect that this was a highly technical matter which could never be clearly understood by the public. Perhaps it would be better to say nothing.

Someone in that room crowded with brass threw in the suggestion that the press be told exactly what disciplinary action had been taken. A welter of discussion followed, but shortly Gibson found himself on the plane back to Richmond. He never realized for a moment that within a week his name would blare from radio and press across the nation.

There were shocks in store for others. Commodore Gillette, on duty in the commandant's office at Terminal Island, San Pedro, California, received a telephone call from Washington on Friday afternoon, February 22. It was Vice Admiral Ramsey, advising him that he was being given a Letter of Reprimand and this would be announced at a press conference the next morning. Gillette was thunderstruck. He had not been an "interested party" at the court of inquiry, and the report of that body had said no further proceedings against him were warranted. He, too, had been interrogated in December by the inspector general's agents, and there had been no hint of any action against him. In both instances he had testified without counsel and answered questions freely, with no feeling that he was, or might ever be, a "defendant." His name had not been mentioned at the "dress rehearsal" the previous Saturday. Shorty Gillette was enraged, and he set about preparing a statement for the reporters.

Captain Granum got one of those phone calls, too, the same afternoon, and he, too, was stunned. Like Gillette, he was not an "interested party" at the Guam inquiry, and the final report had recommended that no action be taken against him. He had sat through the "dress rehearsal" and heard not a word about himself or anyone else being publicly disciplined. He was right in Washington but received no copy of his Letter of Reprimand until after it had been given to the press.

18

Saturday morning the newsmen gathered at the Pentagon and were taken into the presence of Fleet Admiral Nimitz, now Chief of Naval Operations. He was flanked by his deputy, Vice Admiral Forrest P. Sherman, and the Chief of Naval Personnel, Vice Admiral Louis E. Denfeld, plus various other admirals and captains. Copies of the Narrative were distributed, and Admiral Nimitz opened the press conference by declaring that "we have no desire or intention to deny any of our mistakes." He then read a short statement disclosing the final action in the case of Captain McVay. This had been the ostensible purpose of the press conference, and the result announced was as most of the reporters had expected.

The statement said Captain McVay's conviction on one charge had been reviewed all the way up the line, and concluded with this sentence: "Secretary of the Navy James Forrestal has approved these recommendations (for clemency) and has remitted the sentence of Captain McVay in its entirety, releasing him from arrest and restoring him to duty." In answer to a question, Admiral Nimitz confirmed, for the first time publicly, that he had opposed a court-martial for Captain McVay. He said he had recommended merely a Letter of Reprimand, but "the (Navy) Department in Washington saw fit to disregard my recommendation." Admiral Denfeld put in that despite the clearing of McVay, "I question that McVay will ever again get a command of great responsibility . . . or ever become an admiral."

Then, also for the first time publicly, Admiral Nimitz disclosed the fact that angered or sorrowing kin of the dead men had been bombarding the Navy for redress or explanation. As a "sample" of the type of letters that poured in, the white-haired and fatherly-looking Nimitz picked up and read a letter from Edward Connelly, who had been a leader on the West Coast in efforts to secure some explanation from the Navy. Connelly, shocked and deeply grieved by the loss of his son, Ensign D. F. Connelly, wrote forthrightly to Nimitz. He said he had "searched the press and other publications diligently for acknowledgment by you, for your part in the mistake and inefficiency connected with the sinking of the U.S.S. *Indianapolis.*" Up to the present, he said, he had seen nothing.

"On behalf of the 1,023 (*sic*) bereaved families you owe to us, and yourself, to make a public statement," Connelly said. "We hold the Navy responsible for the loss of our son, which they refuse, so far, to do. When does the admiral and officers at Guam and Leyte go on trial, or is this being whitewashed?"

Admiral Nimitz said he had replied to this letter, expressing sorrow, and adding:

As commander in chief of the Pacific Fleet and the Pacific Ocean Areas I carried the broad responsibility for all operations of the Pacific Fleet in the areas under my command. This included, of course, responsibility for both successes and failures. To the extent that a commander in chief should be held responsible for failures or errors of judgment on the part of subordinates, I must bear my share of responsibility for the loss of the *Indianapolis.*

There is no thought of exonerating anyone in the Navy who should be punished for his performance of duty in connection with the sinking of the *Indianapolis* and the attending loss of life."

The admiral said that an understanding of the Pacific situation at the same time was necessary to a full understanding of the tragedy and to prevent the judgment of "hindsight."

But the big news of the press conference was the Narrative, with the Navy's account of how and why the tragedy had occurred, plus the news that four officers had been disciplined. Here were four names the public had never heard before—Gillette, Granum, Sancho, and Gibson. Captain McVay had been cleared of all blame, these four men had been disciplined—it was not difficult to see how the public would put those two facts together. One was innocent, the others must be guilty. The reporters, rushing for the phones to dictate their stories, tried to digest the 4,500-word Narrative. Their dilemma illustrates vividly the problems of a newsman in dealing with the military. Whatever the military chooses to announce, he must take as fact. He cannot check public records, as he does in the case of courts and governments, because there are none. In this case the Narrative had to be accepted for what it said, with no opportunity to know what it had left unsaid.

The story, as it had been timed to do, hit the Sunday papers with considerable impact. The New York *Times* printed the Narrative in full. Radios and newspapers blared forth the story, and in the public mind it was quickly synthesized into a few words—four officers on Leyte sat around twiddling their thumbs while 500 men slowly and horribly perished. The impact on the four men so named was shattering.

Gillette and Granum had had a few hours' warning; Sancho and Gibson had none. Gibson was puttering around his house on Saturday, the radio playing in the background, when suddenly he was astounded to hear his name over the air waves. The voice said that Lieutenant Gibson had been reprimanded in connection with the *Indianapolis* tragedy. Quoting the Narrative, it said he "was the officer who was immediately concerned with the movements of the *Indianapolis*. The nonarrival of that vessel on schedule was known at once to Lieutenant Gibson, who not only failed to investigate the matter but made no immediate report of the fact to his superiors."

For a moment Gibson was speechless. The enormity of the misstatement was staggering. He had been reprimanded five months before, he had vehemently denied the charge, and had been strongly supported by Vice Admiral Kauffman. Suddenly his name, the name of a little private man, working around his home, leaped to prominence in every section of the nation, in words hard to misunderstand—he knew the vessel was coming, he knew it didn't arrive, and he did nothing. He trembled in agitation. What could he do? Could he rush to a microphone and shout, "Stop, that's not so. Here's the real story." Thoughts of a libel suit ran through his head, he briefly weighed the possibility of a Congressional investigation. He had to think fast, because he knew the press would be after him in a short time. What should he do?

As he talked it over with his wife, his normal calm gradually returned, and when within the hour the wire services began calling he was ready. "No comment." He had made his decision. In his own mind he was completely free of guilt, but how could he ever explain the whole complex story to millions of people who had heard his name, put him down as guilty, and forgotten the matter? How could he, an ordinary civilian without influence, fight the Navy, either in the courts or in Congress? It would mean months, maybe years, of hard fighting, not to mention the money. It might warp and twist his own life, and expose his wife and children to public glare, and for what? Would the same millions of people who heard him condemned today still be listening months or years later to hear him exonerated? Of course not. The main thing was his own conscience, and it was clear. He would stand on that.

Sancho could not be found. The Navy said he had left the service and it did not know where he was. Captain Granum had no comment. He had not even seen the Letter of Reprimand, and furthermore he was a regular Navy man and would fight this thing out in private.

But Shorty Gillette was a fighter. When newsmen reached him on Saturday, he was ready. He gave out a statement declaring he felt no fault or blame whatsoever in the *Indianapolis* matter. In this he could have been speaking for all four of the disciplined men.

I base this statement upon directives and orders existing at that time. My contention is supported by a recommended citation from my immediate superior officer for a period of time which includes the *Indianapolis* incident.

He referred to a letter from Vice Admiral Kauffman dated December 15, 1945, when the commodore left the PSF. The vice admiral had said, "The initiative, tireless effort and administrative ability demonstrated by Commodore Gillette was a great contribution toward the execution of the mission of the Philippine Sea Frontier."

Commodore Gillette's statement appeared in some papers, usually in brief at the end of the Navy's account, but there can be no question of the general impression left in the public mind. *Newsweek* magazine capsulized it the following week:

> Concurrent with the announcement (of Mc-Vay's exoneration), Admiral Nimitz issued a nine-page narrative which disclosed four land-based Naval Officers in the Philippines—Commodore N. C. Gillette, Captain A. N. Granum, Lieutenant Commander Jules C. Sancho and Lieutenant Stuart B. Gibson—failed to take prompt action when the cruiser became overdue. As a result, about 500 of the 800 men lost were drowned while waiting five days on rafts for rescue ships.

In fairness to the Navy, the Narrative said no such thing and neither did the Letters issued to the four. The Letters had never been made public, but they can be summarized quickly: Lieutenant Gibson was reprimanded for failure to report the nonarrival of the ship. "Such failure resulted in several days' delay in inaugurating search for survivors which resulted in loss of many lives," the Navy said. Sancho was admonished for not checking up on Gibson and the nonarrival of the ship. Captain Granum and Commodore Gillette were reprimanded for "administrative laxities within your command, which contributed to heightening the tragic consequences of this Naval disaster. . . ." It was acknowledged that word of the nonarrival reached PSF only early Wednesday morning, and that Granum and Gillette had not been notified until Thursday morning, a few hours before the chance discovery of survivors.

This is what the Narrative says regarding the delay in search:

The *Indianapolis* was scheduled to have arrived at Leyte at 11:00 A.M., July 31. It is probable that under normal conditions, no concern as to her nonarrival would have been felt until she was eight or nine hours overdue. Several additional hours would have elapsed incident to the despatch traffic necessary to check her movements so that, in all probability, search for her would normally not have commenced until she would have been approximately twenty-four hours overdue. That would have been some time in the forenoon of August 1. The survivors of the *Indianapolis* were actually sighted at about 10:25 A.M., Leyte time, on August 2, by a plane on routine patrol.

In other words: The vessel was due Tuesday morning, no concern would have been felt until Wednesday morning, and the survivors were discovered Thursday morning. So the sum total of Leyte's responsibility, granting "normal conditions" and many alleged duties which PSF would never admit, was for the twenty-four hours from Wednesday morning to Thursday morning. Assuming that search "would normally not have commenced" until Wednesday noon, there is no assurance that the survivors would have been discovered before darkness Wednesday. With the greatest good fortune under the system the Navy said should have been used, the survivors would have been sighted something less than twenty-four hours sooner than they were. They would have been in the water two and a half instead of three and a half days. A system which would allow that seems somewhat less than perfect.

The public of course did not absorb this part of the Narrative, and in fact very few newspapers even drew attention to it. The overriding impression gathered from the news stories was that the whole *Indianapolis* tragedy could have been prevented if the Leyte crowd had just done its duty. It must be supposed that the Navy did not intend to create that impression, but nonetheless it flashed across the front pages of the nation in that context and was retained as such in the average mind.

The Narrative said many other things which the man

in the street never knew about nor scrutinized carefully. One was the plotting of the vessel's course. The Narrative said a plot was kept at both Guam and Leyte, and the vessel's "estimated position was plotted on each board daily." At the proper time the vessel was "assumed to have arrived" and both plots were erased.

"However, since the *Indianapolis* did not arrive, the responsible officers at the office of the port director, Leyte, who knew of her non-arrival, should have instituted action to determine the reason," says the Narrative. But these officers did not consider that they were "responsible," and the Navy admitted they were not, since no such directive existed. And even if they were, "no concern . . . would have been felt" for eight or nine hours and "in all probability" no search would "normally" have been started before Wednesday noon.

It is a good system that allows an "assumption" that a vessel has arrived at a destination for which it departed? It is a good system which allows another twenty-four hours delay before any concern is felt? That was the system in effect.

Then there was Commander Hashimoto's radio report on the sinking. Three hours after the sinking, he radioed Japan that he had definitely sunk a "battleship of *Idaho* type," half knowing that the Americans would intercept the message and be able to decode it. They did intercept it, and they did decode it, and they sent it to Intelligence for evaluation. Here is what the Narrative says:

> Within 16 hours of the actual sinking of the *Indianapolis*, there was in the Advance Headquarters of the Commander in Chief, Pacific Fleet (in other words, in Nimitz's headquarters on Guam), an indication, from a single enemy source, to the effect that the Japanese had sunk something, the nature of which was unknown, in a position which was approximately the predicted position of the *Indianapolis* at the time. Had this information been evaluated as authentic, it is possible that the survivors of the *Indianapolis* might have been located within twenty-four hours of the time of the sinking of the ship and many additional lives might have been saved.

Nothing further has ever been said on this subject, but to reconstruct the circumstances: The intercepted message said a battleship of the *Idaho* class had definitely been sunk in the position of the *Indianapolis*. Was it the *Idaho?* It might have been. She was operating out of Leyte on training cruises in this area. Was it the *Indianapolis?* It might have been, because the position given was right. Shall we query to see if these vessels are okay?

No check was made, and the Narrative devotes two long paragraphs to saying why not. A particularly poignant sentence reads:

> Regrettable though it was, failure to evaluate accurately a report made by a Japanese submarine did not necessarily have a bearing on the prosecution of the war as a whole and was actually of only local significance.

Did the parents of 500 men lost in the debacle consider it "of only local significance?"

Perhaps in mitigation, perhaps not, the Narrative adds:

> This intelligence was also in the hands of the Commander in Chief, United States Fleet, in Washington at about the same time, and was passed by him to the Commander, Seventh Fleet, in Manila. No impression was created in the Headquarters of Commander, Seventh Fleet, that this intelligence involved the *Indianapolis.*

Leaving out Washington, the reference to the Seventh Fleet is mystifying. The *Indianapolis* belonged to the Fifth Fleet (the Nimitz Navy). The Seventh Fleet (MacArthur's Navy) had no knowledge of her whatever. The Seventh Fleet was not an addressee of any kind, action or information, on either dispatch having to do with the *Indianapolis*'s fatal voyage. The first CINCPAC dispatch of July 26 was addressed to *no* command in the Seventh Fleet. The departure dispatch of July 28 named PSF as one of seven information addressees. In no case would this have been passed on to the Seventh Fleet in Manila. Having received intelligence from Washington that a battleship of the *Idaho* type had been sunk within the Nimitz command, what was the Seventh Fleet supposed to have done about it? Told Guam, "Don't look now, but one of your battleships may be missing"?

In excusing the failure of the Combat Intelligence Section at Guam to do anything, the Narrative said: "Evaluating intelligence is not an exact science. It is at best an estimate; frequently it is only an intelligent assumption." It went on to say that the work of this Section "has been outstanding" and had "made possible the successful execution of several operations which were of such significance and importance at the time as to have changed the entire course of the war against Japan." It said the failure to act was attributable "in part" to the fact that Japan had made many false claims during the war. True, but how unfortunate that a routine query could not have been dispatched to the *Indianapolis*, the *Idaho*, or both. This was Monday, the men were in their first day in the water, and they might have been found that day.

And what about Rear Admiral McCormick and TG 95.7? He was an action addressee of the departure dispatch, which said the *Indianapolis* would arrive at Leyte, Tuesday noon. Put together with the earlier dispatch of July 26, on which he was an information addressee, the picture was: *Indianapolis* reaches Leyte and "on arrival report to CTF 95 by despatch for duty. CTG 95.7 directed to arrange 17 days' training for *Indianapolis* in Leyte area." But what a shambles this was in fact. CTF 95, Vice Admiral Oldendorf, received the July 26 dispatch but not the July 28 dispatch. CTG 95.7, Rear Admiral McCormick, received the July 28 dispatch but not the July 26 dispatch. Result, nobody did anything. Admiral McCormick sailed right by the spot where he would have encountered the *Indianapolis,* and no one raised a murmur. What does the Narrative say about this? It says nothing.

The Narrative, excusing all others, concentrated its fire principally on Lieutenant Gibson. It said Sancho "was not aware" that the *Indianapolis* was overdue but "it, however, was his duty in his capacity as acting port director to keep himself informed of such matters."

When it came to Gibson, the Narrative said he was the officer "immediately concerned with the movements of the *Indianapolis*." One would have to search a long time for any port director officer, or officer of any service organization, who would admit that he was "concerned with the movements" of any combatant vessel. Service organizations simply had nothing to do with the fighting fleet, except to render service upon request. As to the "movements" of fighting ships, CINCPAC would have been the first to slap down any service command that presumed to interfere in operational matters. More than one port director knows what happened when he wandered into operational matters.

The Narrative continues: "The nonarrival of that vessel on schedule was known at once to Lieutenant Gibson, who not only failed to investigate the matter but made no immediate report of the fact to his superiors." Taking the sentence phrase by phrase: Nonarrival "known at once." The ship might have been in that vast harbor hours before he knew it. "Failed to investigate." No port director would presume to inquire the position of a fighting ship. That was precisely the kind of message CINCPAC wanted to keep off the air. Not only would it clutter up the radio channels but it might give the enemy valuable intelligence.

"Made no immediate report." As conceded by the Navy, no report was required, in this case or any similar one, by Gibson or by any port director officer. This position was supported by each one of Gibson's superiors right up to the top of the PSF. It was admitted by Admiral Nimitz's chief of staff, Admiral McMorris, when he wrote: "It is true . . . there was no directive which required a report of arrival or nonarrival of combatant ships." He had gone on to say that, however, since he knew the vessel was coming, ". . . it should have been a matter of interest to him that the ship failed to arrive as scheduled." This seems to say that while it was not his duty, it would have been welcomed if he had assumed a responsibility he did not have. In this case, the Navy would certainly have preferred such an assumption of duty, but unfortunately experience had shown minor officers that it was unwise to assume anything beyond what was set forth in directives.

The Narrative went on to explain CINCPAC's 10-CL-45:

Although these directives were prepared with thought and care, that they were subject to misinterpretation is shown by the inference

drawn by Lieutenant Gibson. It was not the intention to <u>prohibit</u> (Navy's underlining) in these
directives the reporting of the <u>non-arrival</u> (also
Navy) of combatant ships. Nonarrivals were expected to be reported. However, no mention of
this was made in the letter and the inference
was drawn by this officer that since arrival reports were not to be made for combatant ships,
by the same token neither were reports of nonarrivals to be made. This matter has since been
clarified in terms which cannot be misinterpreted.

A more accurate summary might have said: The
original order neglected to mention nonarrivals, we have
now covered that oversight by the supplementary order of
August 26, sent out after the court of inquiry recessed. It
is difficult to find any basis for the statement "Nonarrivals
were expected to be reported." Time and again Gillette,
Granum, and Gibson asked to be shown some authority
for this statement; it was never forthcoming.

Passing on to Gillette and Granum, the Narrative
conceded that the PSF was an extremely busy command,
with typhoons and heavy ship traffic, but added:

> These facts do not, however, relieve these
> senior officers of their responsibility connected
> with the failure of their subordinates to take ap-
> propriate action to ascertain the whereabouts of
> the overdue *Indianapolis.* The junior officers
> who were directly concerned with this failure
> were members of the organization which was
> being administered by these senior officers. For
> this demonstrated weakness in the organization
> under their control, brought on largely through
> their failure to give closer personal attention to
> the work of these inexperienced juniors, Com-
> modore Gillette and Captain Granum have been
> held responsible.

This turgid wording is assumed to refer to junior
officers in the operations, surface control and plotting
sections at PSF. Several junior officers from PSF had been

called to testify at the court of inquiry, and the reprimand to Gillette said:

"Although notice of nonarrival was received in the Operations Office, Philippine Sea Frontier, as early as 0400-0500 on 1 August, cognizant superiors were not notified, and no action was taken by that Office prior to 0800 on 2 August, shortly after which the first reports of sighting survivors were received." The letter said that the ". . . failure to institute timely search . . . with consequent increase in suffering and loss of life, was largely due to a loose state of organization within the Philippine Sea Frontier Command. The inexperience of junior officers within that Command only made it all the more incumbent upon you to exercise rigid personal supervision over various command activities." This may be contrasted with Vice Admiral Kauffman's commendation of Gillette for his "initiative, tireless effort and administrative ability." Again the Navy places heavy emphasis on what was not done Wednesday and Thursday, when the vessel had been destroyed since midnight Sunday. Had the system of control prescribed by the Navy worked perfectly (an unlikely assumption), search would not have been started until the men of the *Indianapolis* had already been sixty hours in the water.

The general public, however, had neither the time nor the facts for such an analysis. Forced to rely on what the Navy chose to disclose, the press and radio, in both news stories and editorials, could only present a most superficial picture of what had actually happened. While the public quickly dismissed the matter as closed, it was the erroneous impression left in the public mind that deeply wounded the four men disciplined. Cruelly exposed by the fanfare of the full-dress press conference, the role of these men in the tragedy had been magnified out of all proportion to their actual participation in it. A Letter of Reprimand, normally a private and relatively minor form of punishment, had been waved in public as a badge of dishonor.

They left it keenly, and while Sancho and Gibson resolved not to contest it, Commodore Gillette refused to concede for a moment and was joined in battle by Captain Granum. It was a private struggle, of course, for no further word on the *Indianaoplis* case ever came from the

Navy. With legal counsel from an old friend in private practice in Chicago, Commodore Gillette prepared his reply and forwarded it to the Chief of Naval Personnel, as was his right, on March 16.

In it, he denied that he was guilty of "administrative laxities," "loose state of organization," and "lack of rigid supervision." He pointed out that the Philippine Sea Frontier Command had been built up by Vice Admiral Kauffman over a period of ten months, and said: "I have seldom been associated with an organization that attained as high a state of efficiency as the Philippine Sea Frontier, or one in which so much personal supervision by senior officers was exercised." He said Admiral Kinkaid, Commander Seventh Fleet, ". . . was well informed as to the workings of the Philippine Sea Frontier and he never intimated that he thought there was any lack of efficiency in our organization, but on the contrary he commended us on several occasions."

The commodore said Vice Admiral Kauffman would never have gone on leave ". . . if he had thought that there were inefficiencies in the organization or that I was not capable of acting during his absence. Furthermore, he would not have retained me, or anyone else, on his staff upon his return from leave had he thought us blameworthy in the tragedy that occurred."

Contending that the PSF had no responsibility for the movement of combatant vessels, he said: "For an organization to take upon itself responsibilities not assigned to it, and properly assumed to rest with the other organizations, would create confusion and court disaster."

Commodore Gillette said he had continued the routine set up by Vice Admiral Kauffman, and told of frequent plane trips around his big command and daily conferences with department heads when he was present at headquarters. The charges against him, therefore, ". . . are not based on facts and do not constitute a justifiable basis for a reprimand," he said.

He then recounted the case point by point, as based on the records of the court of inquiry, the court-martial and the inspector general's investigation, and declared:

The court of inquiry stated that the instructions in letters 10-CL-45 and 2-CL-45 (identical letters, the former for the "Nimitz Navy" and the latter for the "MacArthur Navy"), which contained the provision that, 'Arrival Reports shall not be made for combatant ships,' were the primary causes of the failure of any Naval activity to inquire into the reason for the nonarrival of the *Indianapolis* at its estimated time of arrival. The subsequent change in this provision to require such reports indicates that it was considered to be a serious omission in the instructions existing at the time of the loss of the *Indianapolis*. Since the directive was not explicit, it led to misunderstanding and misinterpretation.

In closing, I wish to submit that it is only by a very tenuous thread that I can be connected with the *Indianapolis* disaster and certainly not to the extent of a reprimand which fact unfortunately became public beyond any I have ever known the Navy Department to issue; one which to the general public, as expressed by many newspapers, radio broadcasts, and weekly news magazines, charges me with delaying rescue for five days and brands me as being criminally responsible for the loss of 500 lives. Such an interpretation was, of course, not intended nor anticipated by the Navy Department, but the fact that such an interpretation was nationwide is attested by many articles. . . .

The nation should not be permitted to retain such an impression. It is my earnest plea that the Navy Department take steps to correct such an inadvertent injury to me as a citizen, and as a Naval Officer.

The Commodore concluded his seven-page letter with a summary of the *Indianapolis* case that might well stand for history.

I have made it clear in this letter that I do not blame anyone. There is no definite clear-cut fact that points in one direction. The investigations disclosed many interrelated circumstances, unknowns, incompletely defined or misunderstood responsibilities, matters subject to more than one interpretation, assumptions, opinions, incomplete data, and the activities of many organizations and persons. It was the almost impossible that happened. It was the unbelievable coincidence of many circumstances that combined in an unbelievable manner to produce delay in the rescue. I therefore contend there exists a real doubt as to my deserving a reprimand and consequently a basis for withdrawing the reprimand and removing it from my record.

Captain Granum's reply, dated April 3, covered much the same ground. After a reasonable waiting period, with no results, Vice Admiral Kauffman went in to see Secretary Forrestal, and repeated personally what he had maintained all along—the Philippine Sea Frontier had no responsibility for combatant ships. Commodore Gillette, now commanding officer of the Naval Ammunition Depot at Hawthorne, Nevada, went to Washington and saw Forrestal. When still nothing happened, Gillette wrote directly to the secretary, a bold move in the Navy, where channels are rigid. Under date of July 26, he recalled their interview and said the secretary had ". . . informed me that you would review the evidence and that you were determined to leave office with the conviction that you had not been unjust to anyone."

The commodore requested considerations of two points:

> I was never permitted to defend myself against any charge. You agreed with me during our meeting that that was an injustice.
>
> The Philippine Sea Frontier was not charged with the security of combatant ships. . . . If there was a directive assigning responsibility for combatant ships to the Philippine Sea Frontier it is requested that I be furnished a copy of it.

Finally, perseverance was rewarded. On December 9, 1946, four letters went out from Secretary Forrestal. They were identical in wording, and went to Gillette, Granum, Sancho, and Gibson. They said:

1. Careful reconsideration of all facts and circumstances in connection with the loss at sea of the U.S.S. *Indianapolis* (CA 35) on 30 July 1945 focussed upon your individual performance of duty as (title inserted) convinces me that the disciplinary action heretofore taken in your case was more severe than the circumstances warranted.

2. Consequently, reference (a) (the disciplinary letter) is hereby withdrawn. The Chief of Naval Personnel is directed to attach copies of this letter to all copies of reference (a) appearing in your official record.

There was no press conference this time, and these letters were not made public. Few people, inside the Navy or out, know that they exist. To the recipients, however, they were welcome as a final admission, even if belated and somewhat grudging, that the manner in which they had been pilloried was unjust.

The strange case of the *Indianapolis* was closed.

EPILOGUE

When all the bickering was over, it had nearly obscured the only bright page in the whole story—the courage and sacrifice of the men in the water. These men, cast by ill fortune into a hostile sea, were forced to battle for their lives in circumstances perhaps never paralleled. When the sun rose Monday morning, it turned out to be an enemy, and when it set, night proved even more malevolent. The sea, far from being impersonal, became alive with dangers, not only in itself but because of the marauders within it. The menacing dorsal fin, spiraling ever closer, the flashing teeth of the striking fish were added terrors in the already unequal battle. Alone and helpless, burned by day and chilled by night, the men struggled on. That any survived was a miracle. That some found the strength to offer, and in some cases give, their lives for their shipmates was proof once again of man's divine heritage.

When the *Indianapolis* is remembered, let it bring to mind not alone the imperfections of human-ordered events but also the heroism of those who battled the sea.

GLOSSARY

APA—Auxiliary, Personnel Attack. A transport designed to carry troops and their arms directly to an invasion beachhead.

APD—Destroyer-Transport. Destroyers fitted to carry 150 or so troops for fast delivery to trouble spots.

ASN—Army Serial Number.

ATC—Air Transport Command.

Can—Destroyer, slang.

CA—Heavy cruiser.

CE—Corps of Engineers, U. S. Army.

CIC—Combat Intelligence Center on a ship, where all battle information is correlated and action decided.

CINCPAC—Pronounced "Sink-Pack." Commander-in-Chief, Pacific, the person and the headquarters in overall command of the United States Pacific Fleet.

CNO—Chief of Naval Operations, the person and headquarters in Washington responsible for operational control of combatant vessels and strategy around the world.

CPO—Chief Petty Officer.

CTF—Commander, Task Force, the person in command of a task force. Task Forces were designated by a double whole number, such as TF 95 or 77.

CTG—Commander, Task Group, the person in command of a Task group. Task Groups were subdivisions of task forces, and designated by the whole number plus one decimal, as TG 95.7.

CTU—Commander, Task Unit, the person in command of a task unit. Task Units were still smaller subdivisions of

253

task forces, desginated by the whole number and two decimals, as TU 94.6.2.

DD—Destroyer.

DDE—Destroyer escort.

ETA—Expected time of arrival.

Fantail—The part of the deck farthest aft.

Fish—Torpedo, slang.

Gedunk—The soda fountain on shipboard, and what it dispenses.

Hedgehog—A concentrated rocket barrage laid down ahead of a vessel by launchers on the bow.

LCT and LCVP—Landing Craft, Tanks and Landing Craft, Vehicles and Personnel, small craft designed to carry the indicated cargo but often used for myriad tasks.

Midwatch—The watch from midnight to 4 A.M.

NATS—Naval Air Transport Service.

NOB—Naval Operating Base.

Oil King—The rating on shipboard who has charge of the fuel.

OOD—Officer of the deck, the one in charge, or the one who "has the deck."

PBM and PBY—Patrol planes.

PO—Petty Officer.

PSF—Philippine Sea Frontier. A sea frontier had overall administrative and defense control over wide areas, taking in many local commands.

SCOMA—Shipping Control Officer, Marianas Area.

Scuttlebut—Drinking fountain on shipboard; also gossip.

SOA—Speed overall, or net-forward speed allowing for zig-zagging, drift, etc.

SOPA—Senior officer present afloat, who normally took command of forces present.

Striker—An unrated seaman bucking for a particular rating, such as quartermaster-striker, yeoman-striker, etc.

TBS—Talk between ships, a short-range radio for voice communication among vessels in company.

VPB—Patrol plane squadron, followed by designating number.

SURVIVORS

Adams, Leo H.	Seaman First Class	Atlantic City, N.J.
Akines, William R.	Seaman Second Class	Chattanooga, Tenn.
Allard, Vincent J.	Quartermaster Third Class	Omak, Wash.
Altschuler, Allan H.	Seaman Second Class (Radioman)	Los Angeles, Calif.
Anderson, Eric T.	Seaman Second Class	Vallejo, Calif.
Andrews, William R.	Seaman Second Class	Munhall, Pa.
Anunti, John M.	Metalsmith Second Class	Duluth, Minn.
Armistead, John H.	Seaman Second Class	Memphis, Tenn.
Ashford, John T. Jr.	Aviation Radio Technician Third Class	Lubbock, Texas
Ault, William F.	Seaman Second Class (Radioman)	Louisville, Ohio
Baldridge, Clovis R.	Electrician's Mate Third Class	Waco, Tex.
Barto, Lloyd P.	Seaman First Class	Gile, Wis.
Bateman, Bernard B.	Fireman Second Class (Watertender)	Cleveland, Ohio
Beane, James A.	Fireman Second Class	Eatonville, Wash.
Beaty, Donald L.	Seaman First Class (Radioman)	Fort Wayne, Ind.
Belcher, James R.	Seaman First Class (Radioman)	Abbeville, Ala.
Bell, Maurice G.	Seaman First Class	Bellwood, Ill.
Benton, Clarence U.	Chief Firecontrolman	Cloudcroft, N.M.
Bernacil, Concepcion P.	Firecontrolman Third Class	Oakland, Calif.
Bitonti, Louis P.	Seaman First Class	Detroit, Mich.
Blanthorn, Bryan	Seaman First Class (Gunner's Mate)	Grouse Creek, Utah

255

Blum, Donald J.	Ensign	Hartsdale, N.Y.
Booth, Sherman C.	Seaman First Class	Avondale, Ariz.
Brandt, Russell L.	Fireman Second Class	Clifton, Ill.
Bray, Harold J. Jr.	Seaman Second Class	Ramsay, Mich.
Brown, Ed J.	Seaman First Class	Inglewood, Calif.
Brundige, Robert H.	Seaman First Class (Gunner's Mate)	Des Moines, Iowa
Buckett, Victor R.	Yeoman Second Class	Rye, N.Y.
Bullard, John K.	Seaman First Class (Shipfitter)	Chicago, Ill.
Bunai, Robert P.	Signalman First Class	West Roxbury, Mass.
Burdorf, Wilbert J.	Coxswain	Gibban, Minn.
Burton, Curtis H.	Seaman First Class	Kewanee, Ill.
Campbell, Homer E. Jr.	Gunner's Mate Third Class	Wilmington, Ohio
Campbell, Louis D.	Aviation Ordnanceman Third Class	Richmond, Calif.
Carter, Grover C.	Seaman Second Class	Rotan, Tex.
Carter, Lindsey L.	Seaman Second Class	Pinsonfork, Ky.
Carter, Lloyd G.	Coxswain	Holdenville, Okla.
Carver, Grover C.	Seaman First Class	Simpson, La.
Cassidy, John C.	Seaman First Class (Radioman)	West Springfield, Mass.
Celaya, Adolfo V.	Fireman First Class	Tuscon, Ariz.
Centazzo, Frank J.	Signalman Third Class	Bristol, R.I.
Chamness, John D.	Seaman Second Class	Malvern, Ark.
Clark, Orsen	Seaman Second Class	Philipsburg, Kan.
Clinton, George W.	Seaman First Class	Rosedale, Miss.
Coleman, Robert E.	Fireman Second Class	West Monroe, La.
Collier, Charles R.	Radioman Second Class	Fayetteville, Tenn.
Costner, Homer J.	Coxswain	Tecumseh, Okla.
Cowen, Donald R.	Firecontrolman Third Class	Boise, Idaho
Cox, Loel D.	Seaman Second Class	Sidney, Tex.
Crane, Granville S. Jr.	Machinist's Mate Second Class	Galveston, Tex.
Daniel, Harold W.	Chief Boatswain's Mate	Des Moines, Iowa
DeBernardi, Louie	Boatswain's Mate First Class	Sacramento, Calif.
Dewing, Ralph C.	Firecontrolman Third Class	Columbus, N.D.
Dizelske, William B.	Machinist's Mate Second Class	Coleraine, Minn.
Douglas, Gene D.	Fireman Second Class	Bucyrus, Miss.
Drayton, William H.	Electrician's Mate Second Class	Philadelphia, Pa.

Dronet, Joseph E. J.	Seaman Second Class	Cameron, La.
Dryden, William H.	Machinist's Mate First Class	Edwardsville, Ala.
Eck, Harold A.	Seaman Second Class	New Orleans, La.
Erickson, Theo M.	Seaman Second Class	New Canada, Minn.
Erwin, Louis H.	Coxswain	Chattanooga, Tenn.
Ethier, Eugene E.	Electrician's Mate Third Class	S. Minneapolis, Minn.
Evans, Claudus	Gunner's Mate Third Class	Henrietta, Tex.
Farmer, Archie C.	Coxswain	Houston, Tex.
Farris, Eugene F.	Seaman First Class (Radioman)	Bethlehem, Pa.
Feakes, Fred A.	Aviation Ordnanceman First Class	Santa Cruz, Calif.
Fedorski, Nicholas W.	Seaman First Class	Milwaukee, Wis.
Felts, Donald J.	Boatswain's Mate First Class	Artesia, Calif.
Ferguson, Albert E.	Chief Machinist's Mate	Coeur D'Alene, Idaho
Fitting, Johnny W.	Gunner's Mate First Class	Kooskia, Iowa
Flaten, Harold J.	Watertender Second Class	Snohomish, Wash.
Fortin, Verlin L.	Watertender Third Class	Burbank, Calif.
Foster, Verne E.	Fireman First Class	Detroit, Mich.
Fox, William H. Jr.	Fireman Second Class	Perth Amboy, N.J.
Francois, Norbert E.	Fireman First Class (Machinist's Mate)	Green Bay, Wis.
Funkhouse, Robert M.	Aviation Radio Technician Second Class	Waveson, Ohio
Gabrillo, Juan	Seaman Second Class	Laredo, Tex.
Galante, Angelo	Seaman Second Class	Detroit, Mich.
Galbraith, Norman S.	Machinist's Mate Second Class	Chicago, Ill.
Gardner, Roscoe W.	Fireman First Class	Bolivar, Mo.
Gause, Robert P.	Quartermaster First Class	Miami, Fla.
Gemza, Rudolph A.	Firecontrolman Third Class	Detroit, Mich.
George, Gabriel V.	Machinist's Mate Third Class	North Canton, Ohio
Gettleman, Robert A.	Seaman Second Class (Radarman)	Los Angeles, Calif.
Gibson, Buck W.	Gunner's Mate Third Class	Mart, Tex.
Gilcrease, James	Seaman Second Class	Baskin, La.

Gladd, Millard Jr.	Machinist's Mate Second Class	Ogdensburg, Ky.
Glenn, Jay R.	Aviation Machinist's Mate Second Class	Van Nuys, Calif.
Goff, Thomas G.	Shipfitter Third Class	Homerville, Ohio
Gooch, William L.	Fireman Second Class	Martinsville, Ind.
Gray, Willis L.	Seaman First Class	Ferndale, Mich.
Green, Tolbert Jr.	Seaman First Class	Yale, Okla.
Greenlee, Charles I.	Storekeeper Third Class	Waynesburg, Pa.
Greenwald, Jacob H.	First Sergeant, USMC	Santa Ana, Calif.
Griffith, Robert L.	Seaman First Class	Pottsboro, Tex.
Hanson, Harley C.	Machinist	FPO, New York, N.Y.
Harrell, Edgar A.	Corporal, USMC	Rock Island, Ill.
Harrison, Cecil M.	Chief Gunner	FPO, New York, N.Y.
Hart, Fred J.	Radio Technician Second Class	San Bruno, Calif.
Hatfield, Willie N.	Seaman Second Class	Salt Lick, Ky.
Havener, Harlan C.	Fireman Second Class	Decatur, Ill.
Havins, Otha A.	Yeoman Second Class	Shafter, Calif.
Haynes, Lewis L.	Lieutenant Commander	Chelsea, Mass.
Heller, John	Seaman Second Class	Detroit, Mich.
Hensch, Erwin F.	Lieutenant	Fergus Falls, Minn.
Hershberger, Clarence L.	Seaman First Class (Firecontrolman)	Elkhart, Ind.
Hind, Lyle L.	Seaman Second Class	Jasper, Minn.
Hinken, John R. Jr.	Fireman Second Class	Norfolk, Neb.
Hodge, Howard H.	Radioman Second Class	Lyndhurst, N.J.
Hoopes, Gordon H.	Seaman Second Class	Yankton, S.D.
Horner, Durward R.	Gunner	Vallejo, Calif.
Horvath, George J.	Fireman First Class (Motor Machinist's Mate)	Cuyahoga Falls, Ohio
Hoskins, William O.	Yeoman Third Class	Neosho, Mo.
Houck, Richard E.	Electrician's Mate Third Class	Columbus, Ohio
Howison, John D.	Ensign	Richmond, Calif.
Hubeli, Joseph F.	Seaman Second Class	Chicago, Ill.
Hughes, Max M.	Private First Class, USMC	Wilderville, Ore.
Hupka, Clarence E.	Baker First Class	St. Mary, Neb.
Hurley, Woodrow	Gunner's Mate Second Class	McCrory, Ark.
Jacob, Melvin C.	Private First Class, USMC	Detroit, Mich.
Jacquemot, Joseph A.	Seaman Second Class	Neptune, N. J.
James, Woodie B.	Coxswain	Mobile, Ala.

Jarvis, James K.	Aviation Metalsmith Third Class	Weston, W. Va.
Jensen, Eugene W.	Seaman Second Class	St. Paul, Minn.
Johnson, William A.	Seaman First Class	Midway, Tex.
Jones, Clinton L.	Coxswain	Boise, Idaho
Jones, Sidney	Storekeeper Third Class	Danville, Ky.
Jurkiewicz, Raymond S.	Seaman First Class	Hamtranck, Mich.
Justice, Robert E.	Seaman Second Class	Left Hand, W. Va.
Katsikas, Gust C.	Seaman First Class	Chicago, Ill.
Kazmierski, Walter	Seaman First Class	Kewanee, Ill.
Kees, Shalous E.	Electrician's Mate Second Class	Montgomery, W. Va.
Kemp, David P. Jr.	Ship's Cook Third Class	Sporta, Wis.
Kenly, Oliver W.	Radarman Third Class	Chicago, Ill.
Kerby, Doe E.	Gunner's Mate Third Class	Mt. Zion, W. Va.
Keyes, Edward H.	Coxswain	Antigo, Wis.
King. A. C.	Seaman First Class (Yeoman)	Murray, Ky.
Kinzle, Raymond A.	Baker Second Class	Chicago, Ill.
Kirkland, Marvin F.	Seaman First Class	Tampa, Fla.
Kiselica, Joseph A.	Aviation Machinist's Mate Second Class	Forest City, Pa.
Kittoe, James W.	Fireman Second Class	Cuba City, Wis.
Klappa, Ralph D.	Seaman Second Class	Milwaukee, Wis.
Klaus, Joseph F.	Seaman First Class	Cleveland, Ohio
Koch, Edward C.	Electrician's Mate Third Class	Denison, Iowa
Koziara, George	Seaman Second Class	Oil City, Pa.
Kreis, Clifford E.	Seaman First Class	Kalamazoo, Mich.
Krueger, Dale F.	Fireman Second Class	Winside, Neb.
Krueger, Norman F.	Seaman Second Class	Poynette, Wis.
Kurlick, George R.	Firecontrolman Third Class	Akron, Ohio
Kuryla, Michael N. Jr.	Coxswain	Chicago, Ill.
Lane, Ralph	Chief Machinist's Mate	Fairfield, Ill.
Lanter, Kenley M.	Signalman Third Class	Thomasville, Ga.
LaPaglia, Carlos	Gunner's Mate Second Class	Tempe, Ariz.
Laws, George E.	Seaman First Class	Springfield, Ill.
Lebow, Cleatus A.	Firecontrolman Third Class	Abernathy, Tex.
Leenerman, Arthur L.	Radioman Third Class	Sibley, Ill.
Lockwood, Thomas H.	Seaman Second Class	Columbia, Mo.
Loftis, James B. Jr.	Seaman First Class	Alton, Va.

Lopetz, Sam	Seaman First Class	Shinnston, W. Va.
Lopez, Daniel B.	Fireman Second Class	Sacramento, Calif.
Lucas, Robert A.	Seaman Second Class	Streator, Ill.
Lucca, Frank J.	Fireman Second Class	Cleveland, Ohio
McCall, Donald C.	Seaman Second Class	Champaign, Ill.
McClain, Raymond B.	Boatswain's Mate Second Class	LaRue, Tex.
McCoy, Giles G.	Private First Class, USMC	St. Louis, Mo.
McCrory, Millard V. Jr.	Watertender Third Class	Ponchatoula, La.
McElroy, Clarence E.	Seaman First Class (Gunner's Mate)	Baldwin Park, Calif.
McFall, Walter E.	Seaman Second Class	Cloquet, Minn.
McGinnis, Paul W.	Signalman Third Class	Elm Grove, W. Va.
McGuiggan, Robert M.	Seaman First Class	Chicago, Ill.
McHenry, Loren C. Jr.	Seaman First Class (Radioman)	Rivermines, Mo.
McKenzie, Ernest E.	Seaman First Class	Columbia, Mo.
McKissick, Charles B.	Lieutenant, junior grade	McKinney, Tex.
McKlin, Henry T.	Seaman First Class	Madison Heights, Mich.
McLain, Patrick J.	Seaman Second Class	Detroit, Mich.
McVay, Charles B. 3rd	Captain	New Orleans, La.
McVay, Richard C.	Yeoman Third Class	Logansport, Ind.
Mass, Melvin A.	Seaman First Class (Shipfitter)	Los Angeles, Calif.
Mace, Harold N.	Seaman Second Class	Lansing, Mich.
Mack, Donald F.	Bugler First Class	Easton, Pa.
Maday, Anthony F.	Aviation Machinist's Mate First Class	Chicago, Ill.
Makaroff, Chester J.	Gunner's Mate Third Class	Chicago, Ill.
Maldonado, Salvador	Baker Third Class	Los Angeles, Calif.
Malena, Joseph J. Jr.	Gunner's Mate Second Class	Dayton, Ohio
Malski, Joseph J. Jr.	Seaman First Class	Grand Rapids, Mich.
Matrulla, John	Seaman First Class (Firecontrolman)	Bloomsburg, Pa.
Maxwell, Farrell J.	Seaman First Class	Peoria, Ill.
Meredith, Charles E.	Seaman First Class	Sylvania, Ohio
Mestas, Nestor A.	Watertender Third Class	Walsenburg, Colo.
Meyer, Charles T.	Seaman Second Class	Houston, Tex.

Mikolayek, Joseph	Coxswain	Detroit, Mich.
Milbrodt, Glen	Seaman Second Class	Akron, Iowa
Miner, Herbert J. 2nd	Radio Technician Second Class	Northbrook, Ill.
Mitchell, James E.	Seaman Second Class	Savannah, Ga.
Mitchell, Kenneth E.	Seaman First Class	Mishawaka, Ind.
Mitchell, Norval J.	Seaman Second Class	Lansing, Mich.
Mlady, Clarence C.	Seaman First Class	Cleveland, Ohio
Modesitt, Carl E.	Seaman Second Class	Galloway, W. Va.
Modisher, Melvin W.	Lieutenant, junior grade	Erie, Pa.
Moran, Joseph J.	Radioman First Class	Johnstown, Pa.
Moran, Eugene S.	Boatswain's Mate Second Class	Seattle, Wash.
Morgan, Glenn G.	Buglemaster Third Class	Delaware, Okla.
Morris, Albert O.	Seaman First Class	Akron, Ohio
Moseley, Morgan M.	Ship's Cook First Class	Opp, Ala.
Mowrey, Ted E.	Storekeeper Third Class	Long Beach, Calif.
Muldoon, John J.	Machinist's Mate First Class	New Bedford, Mass.
Mulvey, William R.	Boatswain's Mate First Class	Gand Rapids, Mich.
Murphy, Paul J.	Firecontrolman Third Class	Chillicothe, Mo.
Myers, H. B.	Fireman Second Class	Harden City, Okla.
Naspini, Joseph A.	Fireman First Class	Cudahy, Wis.
Nelsen, Edward J.	Gunner's Mate First Class	Omaha, Neb.
Nelson, Frank H.	Seaman Second Class	Greenville, Mich.
Newhall, James F.	Seaman First Class (Gunner's Mate)	Phoenix, Ariz.
Nichols, James C.	Seaman Second Class	Hornbeak, Tenn.
Nightingale, William O.	Machinist's Mate First Class	Deer Island, Ore.
Nixon, Daniel M.	Seaman Second Class	Robinson, Pa.
Norberg, James A.	Chief Boatswain's Mate	Duluth, Minn.
Nunley, Troy A.	Seaman Second Class	Bellwood, Ill.
Nuttall, Alex C.	Seaman First Class	Cordova, N.C.
Obledo, Mike G.	Seaman First Class	San Antonio. Tex.
O'Donnell, James E.	Watertender Third Class	Indianapolis, Ind.
Olijar, John	Seaman First Class	Chicago, Ill.
Orsburn, Frank H.	Ship Serviceman (Laundry) Second Class	Manila, Ark.
Outland, Felton J.	Seaman First Class	Sunbury, N.C.
Overman, Thurman D.	Seaman Second Class	Canton, N.C.
Owen, Keith N.	Ship's Cook Third Class	Chula Vista, Calif

Pace, Curtis	Seaman Second Class	Ashland, Ala.
Pacheco, Jose	Seaman First Class	Wagon Mound, N.M.
Palmiter, Adelore A.	Seaman Second Class	Monroe, Mich.
Paroubek, Richard A.	Yeoman First Class	Skokie, Ill.
Pasket, Lyle M.	Seaman Second Class	St. Paul, Minn.
Paulk, Luther D.	Seaman Second Class	Dothan, Ala.
Payne, Edward G.	Seaman Second Class	Berkeley Springs, W. Va.
Pena, Santos A.	Seaman First Class	Tucson, Ariz.
Perez, Basilio	Seaman Second Class	Pearsall, Tex.
Perkins, Edward C.	Fireman Second Class	Steubenville, Ohio
Peterson, Avery C.	Seaman Second Class (Firecontrolman)	Waupun, Wis.
Phillips, Huie H.	Seaman First Class	Dothan, Ala.
Podish, Paul	Seaman Second Class	Eighty-Four, Pa.
Podschun, Clifford A.	Seaman First Class	Wichita, Kans.
Pogue, Herman C.	Seaman Second Class	Roff, Okla.
Poor, Gerald M.	Seaman Second Class	Vienna, Mo.
Potts, Dale F.	Seaman Second Class	St. Paul, Minn.
Price, James D.	Seaman First Class	Ravenna, Tex.
Quealy, William C. Jr.	Parachute Rigger Second Class	Santa Monica, Calif.
Ramirez, Richard	Seaman First Class	El Paso, Tex.
Rathbone, Wilson	Seaman Second Class	Waynesville, N.C.
Rawdon, John H.	Electrician's Mate Third Class	Obion, Tenn.
Redmayne, Richard B.	Lieutenant Commander	FPO, New York, N.Y.
Reeves, Chester O. B.	Seaman First Class	Paris, Tex.
Rehner, Herbert A.	Seaman First Class (Signalman)	Chicago, Ill.
Reid, Curtis F.	Seaman Second Class	Trafford, Ala.
Reid, James E.	Boatswain's Mate Second Class	Middletown, Ohio
Reid, John	Lieutenant Commander	Eccleston, Md.
Reid, Tommy L.	Radarman Second Class	Bell, Calif.
Reynolds, Alford	Gunner's Mate Second Class	Wanette, Okla.
Rich, Raymond A.	Private First Class, USMC	Mansfield, Ohio
Riggins, Earl	Private First Class, USMC	Champaign, Ill.
Rineay, Francis H. Jr.	Seaman Second Class	New Orleans, La.

Roberts, Norman H.	Mechanist's Mate First Class	New Boston, Ohio
Robison, John D.	Coxswain	Tulsa, Okla.
Rogers, Ralph G.	Radarman Third Class	Stout, Ohio
Rogers, Ross Jr.	Ensign	Garden City, N.Y.
Russell, Virgil M.	Coxswain	San Benito, Tex.
Saathoff, Don W.	Seaman Second Class	Los Angeles, Calif.
Sanchez, Fernando S.	Ship's Cook Third Class	Tucson, Ariz.
Scanlan, Osceola C.	Seaman First Class	New Orleans, La.
Schecterle, Harold J.	Radarman Third Class	Shattuckville, Mass.
Schmueck, John A.	Chief Pharmacist's Mate	Steger, Ill.
Seabert, Clarke W.	Seaman Second Class	Dearborn, Mich.
Setchfield, Arthur L.	Coxswain	St. Louis, Mo.
Shaffer, Robert P.	Gunner's Mate Third Class	Ontario, Calif.
Sharp, William H.	Seaman Second Class	Decatur, Ala.
Shearer, Harold J.	Seaman Second Class	Canton, Ohio
Shown, Donald H.	Chief Firecontrolman	Olympia, Wash.
Shows, Audie B.	Coxswair	Odessa, Tex.
Simpson, William E.	Boatswain's Mate Second Class	Oquawka, Ill.
Sinclair, J. Ray	Seaman First Class	Detroit, Mich.
Sitek, Henry J.	Seaman First Class	Detroit, Mich.
Sladek, Wayne L.	Boatswain's Mate First Class	Cleveland, Ohio
Slankard, Jack C.	Coxswain	Bakersfield, Calif.
Smeltzer, Charles H.	Seaman Second Class	Comstock, Mich.
Smith, Cozell L. Jr.	Coxswain	Eufaula, Okla.
Smith, Frederick C.	Fireman Second Class	Gorham, Kans.
Smith, James W.	Seaman Second Class	Pontotoc, Miss.
Sospizio, Andre	Electrician's Mate Third Class	Chicago, Ill.
Spencer, Daniel F.	Seaman First Class	Morris, Ill.
Spencer, Roger	Seaman First Class (Radioman)	Baltimore, Md.
Spinelli, John A.	Ship's Cook Second Class	Gallup, N.M.
Spooner, Miles L.	Private First Class, USMC	Bayard, Fla.
Stamm, Florian M.	Seaman Second Class	Strongs Prairie, Wis.
Stephens, Richard P.	Seaman Second Class	Birmingham, Ala.
Stevens, George G.	Watertender Second Class	Humphrey, Idaho
Stewart, Glenn W.	Chief Firecontrolman	Fort Worth, Tex.
Sturtevant, Elwyn L.	Radioman Second Class	Los Angeles, Calif.
Suter, Frank E.	Storekeeper Third Class	Hartshorne, Okla.

Tawater, Charles H.	Fireman First Class	Chickaska, Okla.
Thelen, Richard P.	Seaman Second Class	Lansing, Mich.
Thomas, Ivan M.	Seaman First Class	Boise, Idaho
Thompson, David A.	Electrician's Mate Third Class	Glouster, Ohio
Thurkettle, William C.	Seaman Second Class	Muskegon, Mich.
Torretta, John M.	Fireman First Class	St. Louis, Mo.
Turner, Charles M.	Seaman Second Class	LaGrange, Ill.
Twible, Harlan M.	Ensign	Michigan City, Ind.
Uffelman, Paul R.	Private First Class, USMC	Fort Wayne, Ind.
Umenhoffer, Lyle E.	Seaman First Class	Rosemead, Calif.
Underwood, Ralph E.	Seaman First Class (Radarman)	Louisville, Ky.
Van Meter, Joseph W.	Watertender Third Class	Bowling Green, Ky.
Walker, V. B.	Fireman Second Class	Tucumcari, N.M.
Wells, Charles O.	Seaman First Class (Radarman)	Camanche, Iowa
Whiting, George A.	Fireman Second Class	Salmon, Idaho
Wilcox, Lindsey Z.	Watertender Second Class	Houston, Tex.
Wisniewski, Stanley	Fireman Second Class	Detroit, Mich.
Witzig, Robert M.	Firecontrolman Third Class	Stitzer, Wis.
Woolston, John	Ensign	Portsmouth, N.H.
Zink, Charles W.	Electrician's Mate Third Class	S. Zanesville, Ohio

INDEX

A

abandon ship: ordered, 61–62, 190–91, 212, 219; charge of failure to order, 174–75; bugle call for, 185

Alamogordo, N.M., 26, 30, 38

Albuquerque, N.M., 27

Alcorn, Army Lt. Richard C.: lands plane on water, 138–139; takes off, 142–43

Allard, Vincent J., QM 3/c: 52, 81–82, 101, 107; testifies on visibility, 196–97

Allen, Capt. Archer M. R., 158

Altschuler, Allen M., S 1/c, 80

Alvey, Edward W., AerM 2/c, 83

Alvin C. Cockrell, 148

Anderson, H. E., MaM, 145

Anderson, Cdr. Marshall A., 131

Anderson, Capt. Paul R., 158

Anunti, John, M 2/c: 53, light showing, 54

Aragi, 3

Archerfish, 51–52

Arkansas, 97

Army 4th Emergency Rescue Squadron, 138

Army & Navy *Bulletin,* 211

Ashworth, Cdr. Frederick L.: arms Nagasaki bomb, 39

atom bomb: convoy from Los Alamos, 27; loading on *Indianapolis,* 29–30; trip out, 33–34; unloaded at Tinian, 38; arming of, 38–39

Atteberry, Lt. Cdr. George C.: rescue effort, 128–29, 131–33, 135–36, 137–38, 140, 153

Aylwin, 149

B

Babelthaup, 45, 133, 136

Backus, Lt. (j.g.) T. H., 70

Baker, R.Adm. Wilder Du-Puy, 175–77, 203

Ban, Lieutenant (j.g.), 12

Barracuda, 214

Barrett, Lt. Michael J., 178–79

Base Hospital, 18, 153

Base Hospital, 20, 150

Base Hopsital, 114, 147

Bassett: rescue record, 134, 146; arrives on scene, 140, 143; cues, 143–44; departs scene, 146; arrives Guiuan, 147

Benton, Clarence U., CFC: 84–85, 105; testifies, 198

Birmingham, 70

265

Blackman, Lt. J. L., 136

Blum, Ens. Donald J.: 147, 158; testifies, 192

Boston *Herald*, 168–69, 220

Bragg, Lt. (j.g.) Kenneth N., 134

Bromley, Cdr. John R., 203

Brooks, Ulysses Ray, CWT, 56

Brophy, Mr. Thomas D'Arcy: 161; Mrs., 20, 161

Brophy, Ens. Thomas D'Arcy, Jr., 20, 161

Broser, Ens. Jack, 143–44

Brown, Ed J., S 1/c, 38, 153–154

Brown, Lt. James Donaldson, 156

Brown, Cdr. Winston S., 135, 144, 148

Buckett, Victor R., Y 2/c, 83, 118, 166

Buckmaster, R.Adm. Elliott, 131, 137, 152

Bullhead, 210

Bunai, Robert, P., SM 1/c, 79

Bungo Strait, 10, 17

C

Cady, Capt. John P.: heads McVay defense, 173; objects to Hashimoto testimony, 200; opens defense, 212; summation, 223–24

Callaghan, 210

Candalino, Lt. (j.g.) P. I., 58

Carter, Commo. James B., 41, 158

Cecil J. Doyle: turns to rescue, 133; informs Guam *Indianapolis* lost, 137–38, 141; first vessel on scene, 139; sinks PBY, 143; leaves for Peleliu, 148; arrives, 150

Centazzo, Frank J. SM 3/c, 79

Chenango, 134

Chicago *Sun*, 206, 226

Chop Line: 48; definition, 93; 146

CIC, 77, 80

CINCPAC: 39–41; orders to McVay, 39, 95. *See also* Nimitz

Claytor, Lt. Cdr. W. Graham, Jr.: 133; orders lights on, 140; informs Guam *Indianapolis* lost, 141

Clemence, Gerald, 178

Clinton, Lt. (j.g.) L. J., 59

Colwell, Lt. (j.g.) Warren, 129–30

combatant vessels, routing of: 94–96, 233, 245–46; new orders issued, 159, 163, 165, 246

Commander Battleship Division 4, 97

Commander Fifth Fleet. *See* Spruance

Commander Marinas. *See* V.Adm. Murray

Commander (acting) Philippine Sea Frontier. *See* Gillette

Commander Seventh Fleet. *See* Kinkaid

Commander Task Force 95. *See* Oldendorf

Commander Task Group 95.7. *See* McCormick

Commander Western Carolines. *See* Buckmaster

Communique 622: announcing *Indianapolis* loss, 160

Condition Yoke Modified: 55–56, 187–88, 209–210; McVay on, 222

Coney, Capt. Charles E., 170, 230–31

Connelly, Ens. D. F., 168, 237

Connelly, Edward: demands Navy explain, 168, 237

Conway, Lt. T. M.: 48, 102; death of, 119

Colorado, 97

Cooper, 58

Correa, Capt. George, USMC, 206

Corry, Cdr. John, 158

Course Peddie, 44–45, 48

court of inquiry: ordered, 155; convenes, 156; testimony secret, 157–58; conclusions, 163–66

court-martial: preparations for, 172; convenes, 173–75; charges, 174–75; bars testimony on water ordeal, 183; prosecution rests, 210; summations, 223–24; findings, 224–25; adjourns, 225

Crary, Gerald C., 167

crossroads, the, 12, 135

Crouch, Capt. Edwin, 42–43, 50, 56, 62, 85

Cullinane, Leo, 227

Cunningham, Bill, 168–69

D

Dale, Elwood E., F 1/c, 20

damage control: 54. manual, 87, 218–19; conditions on ship, 187–88

Davis, Thomas E., SM 2/c, 78

DeBernardi, Louie, BM 1/c: 29, 38; testifies, 212

DeGrave, Cdr. Glen F.: 20, 32, 33, 35; testifies, 196

Denfeld, V.Adm. Louis E., 236

departure dispatch: 47–48, 95; recalled, 137, 152, 233, 243–44

Diamond Head, 35

distress message: 60–61, 74–75; transmission of, 74–76

Donaho, Capt. Glynn R.: testifies on value of zigzagging, 214–18

Doolittle Raid, 7

Doughton, Rep. Robert L., 195

Doyle. See Cecil J. Doyle

"dress rehearsal," 234–35

Driscoll, Lt. (j.g.) Dave, 74–75

Dronet, Joseph E. J., S 2/c, 46, 119

Dufilho: 133–34; depth charge attack, 140–41, 148

E

Eastlake, Francis Royal, 202–203

Effingham, 206

Emery, William F., S 1/c, 59

Enola Gay, 38

escort, question of: 43–44, 177, 213–14; McVay on, 219–20

F

Farallon Islands, 32, 35

Ferguson, Albert E., CMM: 84; in water, 105–6

fire raids, 10–11, 16–17

Fite, Lt. James A., Jr., 141

Flannery, Cdr. Moss W., 159

Flying Fish, 214

Flynn, Cdr. Joseph A., 19, 22, 61, 62, 72, 78–79, 185

Forrestal, James: signs charges against McVay, 175; remits McVay sentence, 228; presides at dress rehearsal, 234–35; cancels all reprimands, 250

Franklin, loss of, 160

French, 148

French, Jimmy, QM 3/c, 59, 81

Fuchs, Machinist H. F., 80

Furman, Lt. Cdr. John R., 134

Furman, Maj. Robert R., 25–38

G

Galante, Angelo, S 2/c, 101

Gambler Leader. *See* Atteberry

Gibson, Lt. Stuart B.: 95; summoned to Guam, 157; reprimanded, 163–64; disclaims blame, 164–66; summoned to "dress rehearsal," 234–35; publicly branded, 238; privately exonerated, 250–51

Gilbert Island, 134

Gillette, Commo. Norman C.:
48; takes command PSF, 93;
orders rescue aid, 134, 139;
learns *Indianapolis* lost,
144; summoned to Guam,
156; reprimanded, 235;
publicly branded, 238; fights
charges, 239–40, 247–50;
privately exonerated, 251

Glenn, Jay R., AMM 2/c,
101

Goss, Seaman, 77, 80

Granum, Capt. Alfred N.: 98;
summoned to Guam, 156;
testifies at court-martial,
214; reprimanded, 235;
publicly branded, 238; fights
charges, 247–50; privately
exonerated, 250–51

Green, Lt. William A., 156

Grosskopf, Capt. Homer
Louis, 176

Groves, Maj. Gen. Leslie R.,
24–25

Guam: build-up, 9; Nimitz'
headquarters, 39–40; *In-
dianapolis* arrives, 41; departs, 47–48; no communi-
cation with *Indianapolis*,
62; doubts born, 137; learns
of sinking, 141; court of inquiry, 155; survivors treated, 166

Guiuan, 146–48

Gwinn, Lt. (j.g.) Wilbur C.:
128; sights survivors, 129–
130; gives alarm, 130–31;
assists rescue, 131–35, 153

H

Hamman, Lt. Louis, Jr., 134,
145

Hanabusa, Cdr. Hiroshi, 3

Hanson, Machinist Harley C.,
212

Harrison, Gunner Cecil M.:
testifies, 191

Harrison, Fred Elliott, S 2/c:
150; funeral, 150

Hart, Fred J., RT 2/c, 75

Hartman, Chief Radioman,
129–30

Hashimoto, Lt. Cdr. Mochitsura: early years, 1–2; war
duty, 2–5; takes command
I-58, 5; first patrol, 9; final
patrol, 11; sights *Indianapolis,* 13; sinks her, 14; war
ends, 17; unemployed, 17;
arrives in Washington, 193–
195; interrogated, 198–200;
testifies, 203–6; returns to
Japan, 206

Hatfield, Willie, S 2/c, 105–6

Havins, Otha A., Y 2/c, 101,
120

Haynes, Lt. Cmdr. Lewis L.:
34–35; burned, escapes, 65–
66; heroism in water, 102–4,
111, 113, 119–24; rescued,
141; consoles kin of lost
men, 168; testifies, 182–84

Helm, 149

Hensch, Lt. Erwin F.: 168.
testifies, 212

Henslee, Lt. Edward B., Jr.,
156

Hensley, Ens. Morgan F.,
137

Hickman, H., Ordnanceman,
129–30

Hilbert, Capt. William E.,
155, 158–159, 199–200

Hill, Lt. N. P., 74–75

Hirao, kaiten base, 7, 17

Hiroshima, 10, 16–17, 23, 39,
153, 155, 183

Hogan, Capt. Bartholomew,
152

Hollandia, 167

Hollingsworth, Cdr. A. F.,
149

Homonhon Island, 43, 146–
147, 152

Horner, Gunner Durward R.:
80–81, 147, 158; testifies,
192

Hosio, Lt. (s.g.) Tameo, 7

Howison, Ens. John D.: 147;
testifies, 212

human torpedoes: *see* kaitens

Hunt, Capt. Charles Boardman, 176
Hunters Point Navy Yard, 23, 28, 182
Hurst, Lt. R. H., 55

I

I-24, 3, 4
I-26: sinks *Juneau*, 160
I-58: description, 5–6; early patrols, 7–10; final patrol, 10–12; sinks *Indianapolis*, 13–15; voyage home, 16–17; sinking of, 17
I-158, 5
I-75: sinks *Liscombe Bay*, 160
Idaho, 13, 16, 97, 242–44
Inagaki, Kyoji, S 1/c, 3
Indianapolis: 17; secret mission ordered, 19–20; explained, 23; loads bombs, 29–31; record trip, 31–35; ship history, 36–37; discharges bomb at Tinian, 37–39; new orders, 39–40; final briefing, 41–45; sails for Leyte, 47–48; departure dispatch, 47–48; last friendly sighting, 49; last day afloat, 49–59; torpedoed, 59–60; bow torn off, 72; damage to ship, 85–86; sinks, 87–89; absence unnoted, 94–98; "still afloat," 117–18; survivors sighted, 122–27; 130; rescue, 130–149; mop-up, 149–50; cause of tragedy, 158–60; loss announced, 160
Itsuno, Lt. (j.g.) Shozo, 7

J

Jacobs, V.Adm. Randall, 161
Jacobson, Commo. Jacob H., 93–95, 156, 232
Jacquemot, Joseph A., S 2/c: 72–73; testifies, 191
Janney, Cdr. John Hopkins: 19, 32, 35; routing instructions, 44–46; "Janney's joke," 50, 184; submarine report, 52, 181–82
Johnson, J. K., Mechanic, 130
Johnson, Malcolm, 229
Johnson, Robert E., Jr., PhM 2/c, 145–46
Juneau, loss of, 160
Jurkiewicz, Raymond S., S 1/c: 77–78; testifies, 191

K

kaitens: 8; description, 6; first attacks, 9–10; 11–12; final patrol, 11–17
kaiten pilots, 7–8, 13–15
kamikaze, 6, 37, 60, 135
Kauffmann, V.Adm. J. F.: 93, 232, 238; commends Gillette, 247; appeals to Forrestal, 250
Kelly, Adm. Monroe, 20
Keyes, Edward H., Cox, 60, 64, 81, 84, 190
King, A. C., S 1/c: 60, 190; testifies, 212
Kinkaid, V.Admiral. Thomas C., 93, 243, 248
Kirchoff, Warren A., S 1/c, 139
Klappa, Ralph D., S 2/c, 100–01
Komori, Pilot 1/c, 12
Kure, 2–4, 7–11, 16
Kurlick, George R., FC 3/c, 101, 107
Kuroda, Lt. (j.g.) Jungi, 7
Kuwahata Lt. (s.g.) Hiroshi, 7, 13

L

Lane, Ralph, CMM, 84
Langen, Cdr. Thomas D. F., 157
Langford, Lt. Malcolm S., 128–130, 153
Lanter, Kenley M., SM 3/c, 79

Larcade, Rep. Henry D., Jr., 207–08

Lefkovits, Ens. Irving D., 137

LeMay, Lt. Gen. Curtis, 38

Letter of Admonition: 164, 240; withdrawn, 251

Letters of Reprimand: 163–166, 239–241; withdrawn, 251

Leyte: advised *Indianapolis* coming, 47–48; description, 92–93; doubts, 137; learns *Indianapolis* lost, 144; orders rescue efforts, 146; witnesses summoned to Guam, 156–57

Leyte Gulf: 43–44; battle for, 92; command of, 93–98

life jackets, supply of: 21–22, 186, 188–89, 191–92, 212

light showing, on *Indianapolis:* 53

Lindley, Ernest, 227

Lipski, Cdr. Stanley W.: 33, 52–53, 56–57, 80–81, 83; death of, 104, 113, 181, 196

Liscombe Bay, loss of, 160

Lockwood, V.Adm. Charles A., Jr., 155–56, 158

Los Alamos, 25–27

MAC AND MC

MacArthur, Gen. Douglas: return to Philippines, 7, 92–93

"MacArthur's Navy," 93–94, 196, 243. *See* Kinkaid

McCarthy, Col. Frank, 25

McCormick, R.Adm. Lynde D., 40–41, 48, 96–98, 157, 233, 244

McCoy, Giles G., PFC, USMC, 68–69

McFarland, Lt. Cdr. Alan R., 177–78

MacFarland, Lt. (j.g.) K. L., 52–53, 181, 196

McGee, Paul B., 226

McKissick, Lt. (j.g.) Charles B.: 49–51, 76–77; in water, 117–18; flies home, 166; testifies, 180–81

McLean, Mrs. Evalyn Walsh, 194

McMorris, Adm. Charles H., 232–233, 245

McVay, Charles B., 18

McVay, Adm. Charles B., Jr., 18, 171–72, 226

McVay, Capt. Charles B., 3rd: background, 18–19; secret mission, 23–24; loads bomb, 29–30; sails, 30–31; trip out, 32–38; mission accomplished, 38–39; new orders, 39–40; meets Spruance and final briefing, 41–46; sails from Guam, 47–48; command philosophy, 50–51; turns in, 56–57; aroused, 60–61; orders abandon ship, 62; leaves ship, 62–63; to whom reporting? 96; in water, 100–101, 105–09, 119–20, 124–125, 127, 135, 138, 141; rescued, 145; arrives Peleliu, 150–52; receives press, 151–52; named "interested party," 157; reprimanded, 164; reaches Washington, 167–68; court-martial ordered, 169–70; charges against, 174–75; pleads, 176; letter to Forrestal, 179, 200; objects to Hashimoto, 202; questions Hashimoto, 203–04; testifies, 219–24; convicted, 224; sentence, 226; clemency recommended, 226; sentence remitted, 228; retires, 229

McVay, Charles B., 4th, 226

McVay, James Wilder, 226

M

Mack, Donald F., B 1/c: 59, 63–65; testifies, 185, 190

Madison: 135, 136; arrives on scene, 144, 148

Makowski, Robert T., CWT, 56

Malone, Ensign, 53

Manhattan Engineer District, 25

Mare Island Navy Yard, 19–21, 23–24, 70

Marianas: 7; base development, 9, 11

Marine Corps League, 195

Marine Detachment, on *Indianapolis,* 20, 29, 69, 85–86

Marks, Lt. R. Adrian: 131–33, 135–36; lands on water, 137–38; picks up survivors, 138–39, 142; orders his PBY sunk, 142–43

Marple, Ens. Paul T., 58, 78

Massier, George, S 1/c, 77

Mayama, Lt. (s.g.) Koya, 7

Merrill, R.Adm. A. S., 228–229

Meyer, Lt.Cdr. William C.: 134; rescues McVay, 145

Miki, Miss Nobuko, 2, 4

Miller, R.Adm. Harold B., 233–234

Miner, Herbert J., RT 2/c, 75–76

Mississippi, 97

Modisher, Lt. (j.g.) Melvin W.: 35, 49, 86, 87, 102, 158; testifies, 212

Moore, Ensign, 78

Moore, Lt. Cdr. Kyle C., 30, 57–61, 64, 87, 196

Moran, Joseph John, RM 1/c: 73–75; testifies, 189–90, 209; electrocuted, 189

Morgan, Glenn, BgM 3/c, 82

Moyles, Murray F., CPhM, 145

Muldoon, John James, MM 1/c, 101, 121

Murray, V.Adm. George Dominic, 43–44, 48, 141, 155, 213

N

Nagasaki, 10, 17, 39, 156

Nagoya, 10

Naguno, Adm. Chiuchi, 3

NANA, 229

Naquin, Capt. Oliver F.: 159; testifies, 212–213

"Narrative," 234, 238, 240–47

Nelson, Commo. Roger E., 176

Neupert, Cdr. K. F., 149

New Mexico, 97, 161

Newsweek, 240

New York *Herald Tribune,* 227

New York *Times,* 162, 170, 193, 238

New York *World-Telegram,* 227, 228

Nienau, Lt. Cdr. Albert H., 133, 140, 148

Nimitz, Fleet Adm. Chester: Guam headquarters, 9; orders to McVay, 39–40; combatant ship control, 94; orders court of inquiry, 155; issues reprimands, 164; presides at final press conference, 236–37; opposed McVay court-martial, 236–237

"Nimitz Navy", 94

Nolan, Army Capt. James F., 25–38

Northover, Lt. R. C., 43

O

Oates, Capt. Eugene T., 131, 151

O'Donnell, Lt. William J., 173

Oklahoma City, 176

Oldendorf, V.Adm. Jesse B., 40–41, 48, 96, 245

Oppenheimer, Dr. J. Robert, 26

Orr, Lt. John I., 58–64, 74, 185, 196

Osmeña, Sergio, 92

P

Park, Ens. D. A., 53
Parke, Capt. Edward L.,
    USMC, 20, 29, 72, 119
Parsons, Capt. William Ster-
    ling: 18, 23, 30, 38; arms
    Hiroshima bomb, 38–39
PBM (serial K9244), 131
Pearl Harbor Striking Force,
    3
Peleliu: duty, 128–29; first
    word of disaster, 130; sec-
    ond message, 131, 133; res-
    cue coordinated, 136; sur-
    vivors arrive, 149–51;
    McVay meets press, 151–
    152; survivors meet saviors,
    153; leave for Guam, 153
Peterson, F. W., MaM 3/c, 46
Philippine Sea Frontier: 92;
    limits of and duties, 93–98;
    "loose organization," 247
Piercy, Lt. Clayton T., 210
Popham, Commo. William
    Sherbrooke, 176
Port Director, Leyte, 94–95
Port Director, Tacloban. See
    Port Director, Leyte
Portland, 36
Potter, John M., MaM 1/c,
    46
Princeton, 70
Providence, 173
Pruett, Lt. (j.g.) Royce, 144
Purnell, Adm. William R., 18,
    23–24
Purple Beach Chapel, 150

Q

Quealy, William G., PR 2/c,
    72

R

Radio I, 73, 75, 86, 190
Radio II, 74, 75, 80
Ralph Talbot, 135, 136, 144,
    148

Ramsey, R.Adm. DeWitt C.,
    153, 235
Redd, Robert Frank, PFC,
    USMC, 78, 79
Redfield, Capt. Heman Judd,
    Jr., 174, 176
Redmayne, Lt. (j.g.) Richard
    Banks: 35, 52, 53, 67, 68;
    in water, 104–105, 121–22;
    hospital, 147; leads sur-
    vivor parade, 167; testifies,
    181–82
Reeves, Chester O. B., S 1/c,
    219
Register: 134, 144; makes res-
    cue, 145, 148–49; arrives
    Peleliu, 149
Reid, James Edgar, BM 2/c,
    200
Reid, Lt. John: 70, 71; in
    water, 111, 118, 119; testi-
    fies, 190
Renoe, Ens. William J., 43
Rhind, 135
Rhodes, Mr. and Mrs. Philip,
    161
Rhodes, Vernon Lee, WT 3/c,
    161
Ricketts, Lt. Cdr. Max V., 136
Rider, Francis, RdM 3/c, 80
Rineay, Francis N., Jr., S 2/c,
    140–41
Ringness: 134; rescues Mc-
    Vay, 135, 144–45; com-
    pletes rescue, 148–49
RO-31, 5
RO-44, 5
Robbins, Lt.Cdr. Reginald
    Chauncey, Jr., 148
Roenke, Lt. Gardner J., 158
Rogers, Rep. Edith Nourse,
    206–7
Rogers, Ens. Ross., Jr.: 20;
    in water, 105–6; testifies,
    191
Romberg, Cdr. Albert K., 209
Route Peddie. See Course
    Peddie
Ruark, Robert, 195
Russell, R.Adm. George L.,
    170

Ryan, Capt. Thomas J., Jr.: assigned to prosecute McVay, 173; court opens, 174; interrogates Hashimoto, 198; defends calling Hashimoto, 200–2; questions Hashimoto on stand, 203–5; summation, 223–24; records verdict, 224–26; consoles McVay, 225

S

Sakamaki, Sub. Lt. Kazuo, 3
Samar, 139, 146–47, 156–57, 179
Sancho, Lt. Cdr. Jules C.: 94–95, 157, 163; admonished, 164, 232–33; publicly branded, 238; privately exonerated, 250
Sanford, Cdr. M. M., 148
Santa Fe, N.M., 26, 27
Sasebo, 5, 6
Schecterle, Harold J., RdM 3/c, 34, 35, 104, 111, 166
Schmueck, John A., CPhM, 49, 66
SCOMA, 47, 158. See Allen
Seabert, Clarke W., S 1/c: 71; testifies, 198
Sebastian, C. H., RM 2/c, 75
Seattle Star, 133
sharks, attacks by, 107, 111–112, 120, 166
Sheperd, Roland A., ARM 3/c, 139
Sherman, V.Adm. Forrest P., 236
Shimonoseki Strait, 7, 10
Shinano, 51
Shipman, Robert Lee, GM 3/c, funeral, 150
Sikes, Ens. T. A., 53–54
Sinclair, J. Ray, S 1/c, 71, 190–91
Singerman, David, SM 3/c, 79–80
Site Y, See Los Alamos
Smith, Lt. (j.g.) Allan, 193–194

Smith, Cozell L., Cox., 166
Snyder, Adm. Charles P.: 170; final report, 231
SOS. See distress message
Spencer, Boatswain S. A., 55
Spinelli, John, SC 2/c, 101
Spruance, Adm. Raymond A.: 19, 39; meets McVay, 42, 48, 153, 219; commends McVay, 226
Squalus, 213
Stauffer, 1st. Lt. Edward H., USMC, 69
Stevenson, Alan, 195
Stiles, Lt. (j.g.) H. A., 144
Stout, Lt. Cdr. Kenneth I., 49
Sturtevant, Elwyn L., RM 2/c: 74–75; testifies, 192
submarine contacts, 45–46, 52, 73, 213–15
Sullivan, John L., 174
Sullivan, Capt. John Raymond, 176
Swayback Maru. See Indianapolis

T

Tacloban: 48; description, 92, 93, 94, 95, 164
Talbot. See Ralph Talbot
Tanaka, Lt. (s.g.) Hiromu, 7, 13
Tanaka, Lt. (s.g.) Toshio, 6, 13
Task Force 95, 40
Task Group 95.7: 40; composition of, 97
Taylor, Capt. E. B., 147
Texas, 97
Theiss, Commo. Paul Seymour, 176
Theriault, Lt. Cdr. Harold J.: 134, 140, 143; informs PSF Indianapolis lost, 144; delivers casualties to Samar, 146–47
Tibbets, Col. Paul W., Jr., 24, 38

Tinian: first runway opened, 9; atom bombers arrive, 24; airfields, 37; bomb arives, 38–39

Todd, Cdr. Donald W., 135, 144, 148

Tokyo, fire raid on, 10

Tolosa, 48, 93, 97, 156

torpedoes, Japanese, 5

Tranquility, 152–53, 156

Trinity shot, 30

Truman, President Harry S., announces war's end, 160–161

Twible, Ens. Harlan M.: 59, 88, 147, 158; testifies, 212

Type 95, torpedo. *See* torpedoes, Japanese

U

ulcers, salt-water, 115, 166

Ulithi, 37, 133–35, 149

Uranium 235, 24–25, 38

V

Van Metre, Commo. Thomas E., 170, 230–31

Van Wilpe, William E., S 1/c, 143

visibility, question of: 52–53; clearing, 55, 56, 77, 178–79, 181, 191, 196–99, 204–6; McVay on, 220–22

Volberg, Lt. Ernest, 173

VPB-23, 131, 136

VPB-152, 128, 153

W

Waldron, Lt. Joseph J.: 43–45, 157; testifies, 176–77, 230

Washington *Post*, 195

Watts, Lloyd A., CPhM, 49

Wendover, Utah, 23

West Virginia, 97

White, Capt. D. C., 203

Whiting, R.Adm. Francis E. M., 155

Whitman, Lt. R. T., 73

Wie, Capt. Anton, 50

Wilcox, Lindsey Z., WT 2/c, 20, 55–56, 118

Wild Hunter, messages of, 50, 210

Willicutts, Commo. H. D., 153

Winter, Lt. Arch R., 134

Woods, L. T., CRE, 74–76

Woolston, Ens. John: 54–55, 66–67, 105, 150, 158; testifies, 185–89, 208

Y

Yagi antenna, 6

Yagi, Dr. Hidetsugu, 6

Yokosuka, 5

Yorktown, 219

Z

zigzagging: instructions for, 45; *Indianapolis* ceases, 51; value of, 51–52, 215–18; not ordered, 56–57; court-martial charge on, 174–75; Hashimoto on, 204–205; McVay on, 220–23

ABOUT THE AUTHOR

RICHARD F. NEWCOMB is a veteran of more than forty years of journalism including five years with daily newspapers, twenty-five years with the Associated Press and ten years in magazine and book editing and publishing. During World War II, he served as an enlisted naval correspondent in the Pacific, winning the Purple Heart at Okinawa. Other books by Mr. Newcomb include *Savo* and *Iwo Jima*. He is currently a literary agent and editorial consultant from his home on Cape Cod.

BANTAM WAR BOOKS

These action-packed books recount the most important events of World War II. They take you into battle and present portraits of brave men and true stories of gallantry in action. All books have special maps, diagrams, and illustrations.

☐	12657	**AS EAGLES SCREAMED** Burgett	$2.25
☐	12658	**THE BIG SHOW** Clostermann	$2.25
☐	13014	**BRAZEN CHARIOTS** Crisp	$2.25
☐	12666	**THE COASTWATCHERS** Feldt	$2.25
☐	*12664	**COCKLESHELL HEROES** Lucas-Phillips	$2.25
☐	12916	**COMPANY COMMANDER** MacDonald	$2.25
☐	12578	**THE DIVINE WIND** Pineau & Inoguchi	$2.25
☐	*12669	**ENEMY COAST AHEAD** Gibson	$2.25
☐	*12667	**ESCORT COMMANDER** Robertson	$2.25
☐	12927	**THE FIRST AND THE LAST** Galland	$2.25
☐	*11642	**FLY FOR YOUR LIFE** Forrester	$1.95
☐	12665	**HELMET FOR MY PILLOW** Leckie	$2.25
☐	12663	**HORRIDO!** Toliver & Constable	$2.25
☐	12670	**THE HUNDRED DAYS OF LT. MACHORTON** Machorton	$2.25
☐	*12668	**I FLEW FOR THE FUHRER** Knoke	$2.25
☐	12290	**IRON COFFINS** Werner	$2.25
☐	12671	**QUEEN OF THE FLAT-TOPS** Johnston	$2.25
☐	*11822	**REACH FOR THE SKY** Brickhill	$1.95
☐	12662	**THE ROAD PAST MANDALAY** Masters	$2.25
☐	12523	**SAMURAI** Sakai with Caidin & Saito	$2.25
☐	12659	**U-BOAT KILLER** Macintyre	$2.25
☐	12660	**V-2** Dornberger	$2.25
☐	*12661	**THE WHITE RABBIT** Marshall	$2.25
☐	*12150	**WE DIE ALONE** Howarth	$1.95

*Cannot be sold to Canadian Residents.

Buy them at your local bookstore or use this handy coupon:

Bantam Books, Inc., Dept. WW2, 414 East Golf Road, Des Plaines, Ill. 60016

Please send me the books I have checked above. I am enclosing $_____
(please add 75¢ to cover postage and handling). Send check or money order
—no cash or C.O.D.'s please.

Mr/Mrs/Miss _____

Address _____

City _____ State/Zip _____

WW2—10/79

Please allow four weeks for delivery. This offer expires 4/80.

Bantam Book Catalog

Here's your up-to-the-minute listing of ove
1,400 titles by your favorite authors.

This illustrated, large format catalog gives
description of each title. For your convenience
it is divided into categories in fiction and non
fiction—gothics, science fiction, westerns, mys
teries, cookbooks, mysticism and occult, biogra
phies, history, family living, health, psychology
art.

So don't delay—take advantage of this specia
opportunity to increase your reading pleasure

Just send us your name and address and 50¢
(to help defray postage and handling costs).